The Cyborg Caribbean

Critical Caribbean Studies

Series Editors
Yolanda Martínez-San Miguel, Carter Mathes, and Kathleen López

Editorial Board: Carlos U. Decena, Rutgers University; Alex Dupuy, Wesleyan University; Aisha Khan, New York University; April J. Mayes, Pomona College; Patricia Mohammed, University of West Indies; Martin Munro, Florida State University; F. Nick Nesbitt, Princeton University; Michelle Stephens, Rutgers University; Deborah Thomas, University of Pennsylvania; and Lanny Thompson, University of Puerto Rico

Focused particularly in the twentieth and twenty-first centuries, although attentive to the context of earlier eras, this series encourages interdisciplinary approaches and methods and is open to scholarship in a variety of areas, including anthropology, cultural studies, diaspora and transnational studies, environmental studies, gender and sexuality studies, history, and sociology. The series pays particular attention to the four main research clusters of Critical Caribbean Studies at Rutgers University, where the coeditors serve as members of the executive board: Caribbean Critical Studies Theory and the Disciplines; Archipelagic Studies and Creolization; Caribbean Aesthetics, Poetics, and Politics; and Caribbean Colonialities.

For a list of all the titles in the series, please see the last page of the book.

The Cyborg Caribbean

*Techno-Dominance in
Twenty-First-Century Cuban, Dominican,
and Puerto Rican Science Fiction*

Samuel Ginsburg

RUTGERS UNIVERSITY PRESS
NEW BRUNSWICK, CAMDEN, AND NEWARK, NEW JERSEY
LONDON AND OXFORD

Rutgers University Press is a department of Rutgers, The State University of New Jersey, one of the leading public research universities in the nation. By publishing worldwide, it furthers the University's mission of dedication to excellence in teaching, scholarship, research, and clinical care.

Library of Congress Cataloging-in-Publication Data
Names: Ginsburg, Samuel, author.
Title: The cyborg Caribbean : techno-dominance in 21st century Cuban, Dominican, and Puerto Rican science fiction / Samuel Ginsburg.
Description: New Brunswick, New Jersey : Rutgers University Press, [2023] | Includes bibliographical references and index.
Identifiers: LCCN 2022052761 | ISBN 9781978836259 (hardcover ; alk. paper) | ISBN 9781978836228 (paperback ; alk. paper) | ISBN 9781978836235 (epub) | ISBN 9781978836242 (pdf)
Subjects: LCSH: Science fiction, Caribbean (Spanish)—History and criticism. | Caribbean fiction—21st century—History and criticism. | Science fiction—Political aspects. | Technology in literature. | LCGFT: Literary criticism.
Classification: LCC PQ7361 .G56 2023 | DDC 863/.08762099729—dc23/eng/20230314
LC record available at https://lccn.loc.gov/2022052761

A British Cataloging-in-Publication record for this book is available from the British Library.

Copyright © 2023 by Samuel Ginsburg

All rights reserved

No part of this book may be reproduced or utilized in any form or by any means, electronic or mechanical, or by any information storage and retrieval system, without written permission from the publisher. Please contact Rutgers University Press, 106 Somerset Street, New Brunswick, NJ 08901. The only exception to this prohibition is "fair use" as defined by U.S. copyright law.

References to internet websites (URLs) were accurate at the time of writing. Neither the author nor Rutgers University Press is responsible for URLs that may have expired or changed since the manuscript was prepared.

♾ The paper used in this publication meets the requirements of the American National Standard for Information Sciences—Permanence of Paper for Printed Library Materials, ANSI Z39.48-1992.

rutgersuniversitypress.org

For Rae, Lucy June, and Grandma Jane

Contents

Introduction: Broadcasting Resistance 1

1 Electroconvulsive Therapy: Treatment, Torture, and Electrified Bodies 16

2 Nuclear Weapons: Missiles, Radiation, and Archives 43

3 Space Exploration and Colonial Alienation 68

4 Disruptive Avatars and the Decoding of Caribbean Cyberspace 98

Conclusion: New Caribbean Futures 125

Acknowledgments 129
Notes 131
Works Cited 135
Index 147

The Cyborg Caribbean

Introduction

BROADCASTING RESISTANCE

The 1972 Miss Universe pageant was filmed in the newly opened Cerromar Beach Hotel in Dorado, Puerto Rico, marking the first time that the event was held outside the continental United States. As an advertisement of U.S. imperialism, the television broadcast represented Puerto Rico as an island-sized beach resort replete with flashing images of the contestants playing golf, posing poolside in their swimwear, and wearing straw *pava* hats. What stands out beyond these touristic visions of Puerto Rico is the eerie emptiness of the landscape, as if the beaches were constructed on a movie set, in which all Puerto Ricans were removed and replaced by an international team of beauty queens. The pageant, claiming to judge feminine beauty on an intergalactic level, offered the simultaneous objectification and infantilization of the female body; contestants were evaluated based on an abstract model of womanhood while host Bob Barker addressed them all as "girls."

Just as Barker called Miss Brazil and Miss Australia to the center of the stage to announce the winner, the visual feed from the live broadcast went dark, though the audio remained intact. Pro-independence protestors had attacked the network's antenna at the moment of the crowning in an attempt to bring attention to the U.S. colonial occupation of Puerto Rico. Barker, who was unaware of the technical malfunction, continued explaining the winner's responsibilities to the contestants and the audience. The video feed remained down as Miss Australia's name was called, though technicians eventually replaced the black screen with the event's logo: a silhouette of a woman in an evening gown, surrounded by orbiting planets and stars, with her feet planted in the main island of Puerto Rico. This cosmic woman can be seen as either powerfully towering over the island or emerging up from it. This science fiction–like image remained on the screens of home audiences for ninety seconds. Just under two minutes after the initial loss of the visual feed, the full broadcast was restored, just as the newly crowned Miss Universe had finished her victory lap. Between the anticolonial protest, the women on stage, the antenna attack, and the cosmic figure, this moment highlights the intersections between colonialism, bodies, technology, and speculation. The event's relationship to technology is complicated further by the fact that this moment is now rewatchable on YouTube, both immortalizing it and drowning the clip in an anonymous sea of digital media. Most of the comments on the clip's YouTube page complain that Miss Brazil was robbed of her crown, with very few even acknowledging the blackout.[1]

Pro-independence protestors, later labeled as "terrorists," had reappropriated the pageant and its international audience to broadcast their anti-imperialist agenda. The manifestation of this struggle focused on the network antenna, a mechanical object that gave material form to the economic, cultural, and political occupation of Puerto Rico by the United States. This was not the only time that antennae were attacked as part of an anti-U.S. protest. In 1978, activists Carlos Soto Arriví and Arnaldo Darío Rosado allegedly attempted to burn down two communications towers in Cerro Maravilla but were killed by an undercover police officer who had infiltrated their group. The murders and subsequent official cover-up turned the event into an international symbol of Puerto Rican corruption and U.S. imperialism (Nelson, 1986). Scholar Manuel Avilés Santiago (2015) argues that attacking the communication towers had both tactical and symbolic implications for the *Movimiento Armado Revolucionario* (Armed Revolutionary Movement), as the group claimed in a public letter to target the antennae for its role in the "penetration and colonialism" of Puerto Rico by state and federal officials (9–10). Avilés also notes that the two communications towers remain standing, "functioning as a disciplinary techno-power in the service of the U.S.," but that resistance has changed as technology has evolved: "The new disciplinary society is not necessarily one with a single and always visible technology. The new disciplinary society is one where the state controls many methods of coercion and operates them throughout many networks" (11). While there may be fewer antennae to target, power is still mediated through technology, and hacking, targeted computer viruses, leaks, or social media campaigns have found their way alongside marches, sit-ins, and other methods of in-person civil disobedience. As the tools for political repression have changed, the methods of resistance must attempt to combat the technologies that help maintain colonizing and authoritarian structures.

This book, *The Cyborg Caribbean: Techno-Dominance in Twenty-First-Century Cuban, Dominican, and Puerto Rican Science Fiction*, argues that recent Caribbean science fictions participate in this struggle to combat techno-colonialism and techno-authoritarianism through narratives that highlight technology's role in oppressive power structures. In order to analyze these literary and popular culture interventions, one must first investigate the historical moments of techno-dominance and resistance that authors like Pedro Cabiya, Yoss, and Rita

Indiana cite and contest. Techno-dominance, which will be further explained later in this introduction, is a term for the ways technologies and technology-based rhetoric or imagery interact with, maintain, and facilitate colonization and authoritarianism. In the case of 1972 Miss Universe pageant, the image of an extraterrestrial figure towering over an empty island transmitted during a broadcast blackout perpetuated an idealized yet impossible image of the female form, an alienation of Caribbean bodies, and the roll of technology in both colonizing and decolonizing projects. The archive of speculative Caribbean texts that highlight the antenna as a symbol of techno-dominance includes comic book creator Edgardo Miranda-Rodríguez's *La Borinqueña #1* (2016), which tells the story of a Brooklyn-raised, Afro–Puerto Rican marine biology student named Marisol who acquires superpowers after finding the ancient crystals of the Taíno goddess Atabex.[2] Unlike the silhouette shown on television screens in 1972, La Borinqueña actively flies over Puerto Rico with her face uncovered and a star shining brightly over her heart. That star, made out of Atabex's crystals, functions as an intergenerational broadcast antenna, linking Marisol to other Puerto Rican fighters throughout history, including Taíno warriors, Pedro Albizu Campos, the Young Lords, and the victims of the 2016 Pulse nightclub shooting in Orlando, Florida. Frederick Luis Aldama (2017) notes that "Latino superheroes tend to accessorize in ways that root them in pre-Colombian histories and the Latino community," citing La Borinqueña's Puerto Rican flag-colored costume and connection to Taíno ancestry. Like the celestial figures orbiting around the Miss Universe logo, La Borinqueña is depicted controlling the natural elements around her and using those powers to rescue victims from floodwaters, an image that takes on added significance in the aftermath of Hurricanes Irma and María in 2017.

The story of La Borinqueña is especially useful for an examination of technology's role in colonizing and decolonizing struggles. While *The Cyborg Caribbean* focuses primarily on the political and rhetorical implications of electroconvulsive therapy (ECT), nuclear weapons, space exploration, and digital avatars, La Borinqueña and her fight for ecological justice rely on the reappropriation of an equally persuasive and colonizing technology—the television. When the superhero uncovers a plot by a U.S.-based corporation to dump radioactive waste in Peñuelas, Puerto Rico, she enlists the help of a local New York City television station and its Afro-Latina reporter to publicize the crime. The dumping story line references the real-life disposal of carcinogenic ash in Peñuelas by U.S.-based Applied Energy Systems, a target of protest since 2015. By going to a television station instead of the police, La Borinqueña recognizes the power of the medium and its ability to disseminate (de)colonizing messages, similar to those who used the Miss Universe pageant in 1972. The power of television to maintain and resist colonizing structures has been depicted before in Ana Lydia Vega's apocalyptic short story "Puerto Rican Syndrome" (1982), which recounts the pandemonium after the Virgin Mary appears on Puerto Rican TVs and vows to return on an even bigger screen (Rodríguez Marín, 2004–2005). However, *La Borinqueña* stands apart for its modernization of this critique, showing the heroine streaming the news story on her laptop and implying that these messages are now easily sharable among Puerto Ricans on and off the island. This approach is similar to the actual Peñuelas protests, which spread their message over social media with the hashtags #ToxicAshesKill and #PeñuelasSinCenizas (#PeñuelasWithoutAshes), using digital media to make visible the communities being affected by the dumping. By redefining the channels that had previously been used to control and spread colonizing or authoritarian narratives, *La Borinqueña* speculates on the future of decolonizing struggles and challenges readers to question how the technologies around them can be repurposed by and for the resistance.

Representing these struggles through science fiction texts offers its own set of issues and advantages. While communicating anti-colonial politics through a medium like science fiction may expand readership and help diversify popular culture, texts like *La Borinqueña*, a superhero comic with science fiction elements, must also be read within the problematic tendencies of the genre. According to Jeffrey A. Brown's *Dangerous Curves: Action Heroines, Gender, Fetishism, and Popular Culture* (2011), progressive superheroines are often still fetishized and hypersexualized to assuage male fears of female sexuality (65). Despite La Borinqueña's skintight uniform, Miranda-Rodríguez has been credited with giving his protagonist a more realistic body type and filling the comic with strong women, including Marisol's Chinese-Dominican best friend Lauren "La La" Liu. According to Mauricio Espinoza (2016), while some argue that Latinx superheroes are unavoidably connected to forms of Othering and alienation throughout science fiction, these characters also offer transgressive reappropriations through "resistance against the forces of cultural assimilation and superheroic activism aimed at cultural empowerment and self-determination" (184). Texts like *La Borinqueña* have the opportunity to articulate real-world political struggles and push back against histories of racism and misogyny in mainstream speculative and genre fictions.

Like the example above, this book analyzes twenty-first-century Cuban, Dominican, and Puerto Rican science fictions to better understand the cultural, political, and rhetorical legacies of techno-dominance and resistance. These texts opt for a posthumanist understanding of technology that sees the blurred line between body and machine as an opportunity for destabilizing normative binaries while also recognizing how increased technology may amplify the marginalization of bodies based on race, gender, sexuality, ability, or other factors. The argument that science fiction writers are using the genre to combat historical legacies of techno-dominance begs two important questions: "Why science fiction?" and "Why now?" To answer the first question, science fiction has long felt the responsibility of questioning the relationship between technology and power. In Samuel Delany's "The Necessity of Tomorrow(s)," a talk given in 1978 at the Studio Museum in Harlem and later published in the anthology *Starboard Wine: More Notes on the Language of Science Fiction* (2012), the author said, "If science fiction has any use at all, it is that among all its various and variegated future landscapes it gives us images *for* our futures.... [Its] secondary use ... is to provide a tool for questioning those images, exploring their distinctions, their articulations, their play of differences" (10). The connection between imagining the future and social justice has only grown in recent years. In her introduction to the 2015 anthology *Octavia's Brood: Science Fiction Stories from Social Justice Movements*, the activist and critic Walidah Imarisha connects social action to science fiction, saying, "Whenever we try to envision a world without war, without violence, without prisons, without capitalism, we are engaging in speculative fiction. All organizing is science fiction" (3). She continues, noting that "'visionary fiction' is a term we developed to distinguish science fiction that has relevance toward building new, freer worlds from the mainstream strain of science fiction, which most often reinforces dominant narratives of power" (4). While Imarisha's concept of visionary fiction opens spaces to imagine the destruction of capitalist imperialism, it also highlights the immense powers of these systems. The Caribbean science fiction texts studied in this project similarly provide potential visions of the future while also challenging the supposed inevitability of those dystopic possibilities. The objective here is not to overstate the political impact of science fiction but to show how these texts can articulate political struggles and assist them by challenging the rhetorical and cultural structures that support techno-dominance. The ultimate goal of this book is to show how Caribbean science fiction can be used to highlight historical and present techno-domination, such as the ways in which repressive technologies feed off rhetorical power, while mapping out a possible means of resistance for the future.

As for the second question—"Why now?—this project was born out of an observation that the line between real life and science fiction in the Caribbean continues to be blurred. The last decade has seen numerous examples of real-life narratives of technological attacks and resistance from the Caribbean and its diasporas. In 2013, a team of Dominican hackers from Yonkers, New York, was caught participating in an international ATM heist that stole $45 million worldwide (Santora, 2013). In 2017, the possibility of covert attacks on diplomats using weaponized supersonic devices starting the previous year caused the U.S. Embassy in Havana to recall all nonessential personnel, though a Central Intelligence Agency (CIA) assessment in 2022 has ruled out the theory that the mysterious "Havana syndrome" was the result of a coordinated, hostile attack (Harris, 2017; Dilanian and Lederman, 2022). Since 2018, the aftermath of devastating hurricanes have opened the door for digital currency investors to flock to Puerto Rico with the hopes of creating a "crypto utopia" on the island (Bowles 2018). The genre of science fiction allows Caribbean writers and artists to negotiate the past, navigate the present, and speculate on the future of techno-domination. As Dominican science fiction writer Odilius Vlak (2017) writes:

> Son los géneros de la ciencia ficción y la fantasía los que cuentan con los recursos para lidiar con la realidad.... Es imposible que los escritores caribeños nos quedemos impasibles frente a una realidad que nos avasalla: hay que combatir el fuego con el fuego. No basta con imitar, sino que hay que tomar los principios fundamentales de la literatura de género... y extrapolarlos a nuestra historia, mitos, folklore, leyendas urbanas y, obviamente, a nuestro futuro. (125, It is the genres of science fiction and fantasy that have the resources to contend with our reality.... It is impossible that we as Caribbean writers remain apathetic in front of a reality that dominates us: one must fight fire with fire. It is not enough to imitate, but instead one must take the fundamental principles of genre literature... and extrapolate them to our history, myths, folklore, urban legends, and, obviously, our future.)[3]

Science fiction narratives are not merely a method of escaping current realities; they are also a tool for articulating their lasting social, political, and rhetorical effects. That so many authors have chosen to use science fiction in their attempts to navigate complicated legacies of techno-dominance speaks to the political potential of the genre and its ability to cite and contest oppressive rhetoric. Even more, the fact that many of the texts analyzed in this book come from authors—including Rita Indiana, Rey Emmanuel Andújar, and Vagabond Beaumont—who do not identify primarily as science fiction writers highlights the utility of this mode of writing for citing and contesting structures of repression and resistance.

By engaging with Puerto Rican, Dominican, and Cuban history and literature, this book is centered around an idea of shared Caribbean history and cultural traditions. In *Le Discours Antillais* (1981, translated into English in 1989 as *Caribbean Discourse*), Édouard Glissant writes, "The notion of Caribbean unity is a form of cultural self-discovery. It fixes us in the truth of our existence, it forms part of the struggle for self-liberation. It is a concept that cannot be managed for us by others: Caribbean unity cannot be guided by remote control" (1999, 10). Glissant highlights the decolonizing potential of Caribbean, especially Afro-Caribbean, solidarity. The texts studied in this project lend themselves to a similar pan-Caribbean politics and, like Glissant's reference to the "remote control," can be read as particularly in tune with technology's role within colonizing and decolonizing efforts. The Caribbean referenced in this book also defies any sort of geographic limitations or violent implementation of political borders. As Antonio Benítez Rojo writes in *La isla que se repite: El Caribe y la perspectiva posmoderna* (1989, *The Repeating Island: The Caribbean and the Postmodern*

Perspective), "Perservar en el intento de remitir la cultura del Caribe a la geografía... es un proyecto extenuante y apenas productivo (xxxii, "The preserved effort to bind the Caribbean's culture to the geography... is an exhausting and hardly productive project"). He continues, "El Caribe no es un archipiélago común, sino un meta-archipiélago... y como tal tiene la virtud de carecer de límites y de centro." (Benítez Rojo v, "The Caribbean is not a common archipelago, but instead a meta-archipelago... and as such it has the virtue of lacking limits and a center.") The cartographic ambiguity of the Caribbean becomes compounded in science fiction by the fact that the genre often challenges dominant borders or territories by imagining stories on a planetary or intergalactic level. While some of the texts studied in this book are set in semi-recognizable versions of Havana, New York City, or Santo Domingo, others appear in outer space, cyberspace, or on unnamed islands or continents that both allude to the Caribbean and reject conventional mappings. The decision to expand the scope of this book beyond national borders reflects the political projects of the studied science fiction texts. Similarly, the journeys and movements of the authors and texts studied in this book highlight the fluidity and mobility within and beyond the islands of the Hispanic Caribbean. The authors studied in this project include a Puerto Rican writer living in Santo Domingo, a Dominican writer living in San Juan, and several Caribbean writers either from or currently living in the United States. These movements highlight the impossibility and impracticality delineating the region geographically.

Though *The Cyborg Caribbean* is greatly indebted to thinkers and theorists like Glissant, Sylvia Wynter, and Frantz Fanon, *The Cyborg Caribbean* does not analyze in depth any of the many speculative works from the Anglophone and Francophone sectors of the region. This book would look very different, though it would be equally productive, if it included texts from beyond the Hispanophone Caribbean and its diasporas. This alternate-dimension project would by necessity include discussions of the broadcast antenna in Nalo Hopkinson's *Brown Girl in the Ring* (1998), genetic engineering in Stephanie Saulter's *Gemsigns* (2013), and speculative worldbuilding in Marlon James's *Black Leopard, Red Wolf* (2019). The conversation about alternative visions space exploration would be greatly enhanced by the inclusions of Karen Lord's *The Best of All Possible Worlds* (2013) or Tobias Buckell's *Hurricane Fever* (2014), which references Project HARP and the installation of a satellite-launching cannon in Barbados in the 1960s. In her foreword for *New Worlds, Old Ways: Speculative Tales from the Caribbean* (2016), Lord writes of the grander stakes involved in the reading, writing, and anthologizing of Caribbean speculative fiction:

> Unmitigated dystopia in fiction may be enjoyed by those who live securely, but this region suffers under crises of economy and climate and a history shadowed with genocide. I am wary and weary of literature that depicts the utter

extinction, physical or cultural, of a people who still fight to survive.... The voice of our literature declares that in spite of disasters, this people and this place shall not be wholly destroyed. (9)

The urgency described by Lord is one that travels throughout the varied and intersecting Caribbean literary traditions.

The choice to focus on works from Cuban, Dominican, and Puerto Rican authors began with the recognition of the historical connections between the three islands. Beside their shared (though still unique) histories of colonialism, slavery, and authoritarianism in the region, these islands have been similarly affected by the specific technologies studied in this project. For example, ECT abuse was used to dehumanize dissidents under both the Trujillo and Castro regimes; the presence of nuclear weapons has disrupted sovereignty and the promise of space exploration has highlighted colonizing power imbalances in both Puerto Rico and Cuba; the internet and space exploration continue to reshape understandings of relations on global or planetary scales. However, Juan C. Toledano Redondo (2021) notes that just because the same hurricanes hit Cuba, Puerto Rico, and the Dominican Republic does not mean that every experience is equal or that their science fiction production comes out the same (55). He continues, "Without a doubt, the Hispanic Caribbean is not a homogeneous region, and although some themes are repeated in its production, it would be daring to say that there is a clearly defined regional sf with identifiable parameters.... It is true, however, that many of the authors of the three islands know each other and are in contact more than ever before" (Toledano Redondo 65). These international connections are apparent in the texts themselves, as many of the studied authors do not limit their explorations of the legacies of technodominance to their own national histories; for example, Dominican writer Rey Emmanuel Andújar reimagines the Cuban Missile Crisis, Cuban writer Yasmín Silvia Portales cites the United States' continued colonial occupation of Puerto Rico, and Puerto Rican filmmaker Vagabond Beaumont alludes to the torture carried out at Guantanamo Bay. These references to a shared (Hispanophone) Caribbean history and culture contribute to shaping a collective radical politics.

More than a study of representations of the future, this book highlights Caribbean science fiction's ability to articulate conceptual shifts in corporeality and humanness throughout history. The texts analyzed in this project feature representations of people that are electrocuted and dismembered, exploded and poisoned, alienated and infected, digitized and erased. Through science fiction, authors can offer unique views of alternative lifeforms and personhood. In *Ariel's Ecology: Plantations, Personhood, and Colonialism in the American Tropics* (2013), Monique Allewaert introduces the concept of parahumanity to articulate the state of personhood when the body is broken down into parts by colonialism and slavery and writes that "it is not the hybridity that offers a response to the brutal fragmentations of colonialism but the negotiation of intimacies that can endure for certain times and can also be contracted and dissolved" (99). Similarly, this project highlights how Caribbean science fiction reenvisions humanity not just in terms of how bodies, people, and communities are dismantled but also by focusing on the new connections and solidarities that can be created in the aftermath. In this way, electrified, radioactive, extraterrestrial, and virtual Caribbeans can be used to show the lasting effects of techno-dominance, along with how dehumanization can be reimagined and reappropriated into a strategic advantage.

Technology, Posthumanism, Techno-Dominance, and Cyborgs

Science fiction is a useful tool in combating the rhetorical consequences of techno-dominance because the genre allows authors and readers to question the role of technology in our conceptualizations of humanity. In response to a review that claimed her fiction avoided technology, science fiction writer Ursula K. Le Guin wrote in "A Rant about 'Technology'" (2004) that the term is often misused to describe "complex and specialized" systems. However, Le Guin argues for a broader definition: "Technology is how society copes with physical reality.... Technology is the active human interface with the material world." In this way, technology can be understood as anything used that organizes or orders the world around us. Afro-Caribbean philosopher Sylvia Wynter (2015), in conversation with Katherine McKittrick, understands humanity in a similar way. Our current conceptualization of humanity, *homo economicus*, a model based on efficiency, rationality, and self-interest, "provides our present order of knowledge—an order of knowledge that is indispensable to the continued reproduction of our present neoliberal/neo-imperial, secularly biocentric, global order of words and things" (30). Wynter cites global warming as a contemporary crisis that cannot be solved without a change in perspective, as proposed solutions are devastating for the global poor and based in the same structures that caused the problem (24). While not specifically mentioning science fiction, Wynter suggests that we can "'give humanity a different future' by giving it a new and species-inclusive account" of our origins, questioning our current and oppressive models for understanding humanness (72–73). Putting Le Guin's and Wynter's words together and understanding both concepts as organizing systems underscores how shifts in technology can influence who is granted humanity, how narratives of social progress inform technological development, and how speculation can illuminate these connections.

The social histories of ECT, nuclear weapons, space exploration, and avatars can be examined and questioned through science fiction because their classification as technologies means that they all have greater political and cultural implications that reach past their originally intended uses. In "Technology: The

Emergence of a Hazardous Concept" (2010), Leo Marx argues that the conceptual shift from machinery to technology was based on the creation of socio-technological systems, blurring the boundaries between material and cultural aspects of technologies. He argues that focusing on the mechanical object may actually obfuscate our understandings of the consequences for humans of the development and deployment of these complex systems: "By consigning technologies to the realm of things, this well-established iconography distracts attention from the human—socio-economic and political—relations which largely determine who uses them and for what purposes" (576). These hidden socio-technological networks include popular narratives and conceptualizations, what Burnett, Senker, and Walker (2009) refer to as the "mythic structures" that are generated around technologies (1). The myths created around and in support of particular technologies may be used to promote colonizing and oppressive systems by underestimating the human factors that create and maintain inequality: "These myths are based on technological determinism which envisages technology as an autonomous force that drives social and economic change in directions which humankind is powerless to affect, and often embody the promise that new technology will reduce inequality" (Burnett et al. 18). By looking at the intersections between literary representations and popular understandings of different technologies, we gain better insight into the influence of socio-technological networks and cultural narratives on material structures of techno-dominance.

Through respective representations of specific technologies in recent science fiction texts, this book studies how the abuse of certain technologies and their surrounding socio-technological networks contribute to colonizing and authoritarian structures in the Caribbean. In the case of techno-colonialism and techno-authoritarianism, technologies and narratives are manipulated by oppressive regimes to facilitate violent processes of racialization, gendering, and other forms of marginalization. For the purposes of this study, the concepts of techno-colonialism and techno-authoritarianism are grouped under the umbrella term of techno-dominance, appropriated and remixed from Michel Foucault's *Technologies of the Self* (1988). In this lecture, Foucault offers his definition of the four major types of technology, the third of which is "technologies of power, which determine the conduct of individuals and submit them to certain ends or *domination*, an objectivizing of the subject" (18, emphasis added). While Foucault was theorizing technology in a much broader sense, techno-domination will be used in this book to describe the use of technology in the establishment and reinforcement of unequal power dynamics within state, social, or colonizing systems. However, studying the ways in which science fiction authors push back against these oppressive regimes highlights the fact that structures of techno-dominance are not impenetrable. In *Technology and Social Power* (2008), Graeme Kirkpatrick argues that people intrinsically question the systems behind the tools they use: "Part of what makes technology technological is precisely the notion that there is a concealed structure and the inclination to reflect on it" (37). In *Technoculture: The Key Concepts* (2008), Debra Benita Shaw argues that "the boundaries that technoscience is invested in maintaining for the sake of its continuing dominance are paradoxically threatened by the very technologies they produce," since said tools can also be manipulated and redeployed as part of a resistance (171). Juxtaposing these ideas, the Caribbean science fiction authors' reflections on the role of technology within larger systems of techno-dominance may allow these technologies of power to be rethought and repurposed.

When theorizing the intersections of technologies and bodies, the cyborg is a central theoretical model that has evolved over time. Though popularized by Donna Haraway's *Simians, Cyborgs, and Women: The Reinvention of Nature* (1991), the concept has been examined and updated in important ways. For example, Jasbir K. Puar (2012) questions the cyborg/goddess binary that Haraway proposes at the end of her essay, while Hil Malatino (2017) argues that reparative readings of Haraway have obfuscated the violence involved in cyborg embodiment. For this book, the most foundational iteration has been Joy James's "'Concerning Violence': Frantz Fanon's Rebel Intellectual in Search of a Black Cyborg" (2013), which argues that Fanon's decolonizing methods prove ineffective at a time in which military and financial technologies are so dominant. One possible solution is to reject the concept of humanity altogether by recognizing it as a product in a repressive system and its most devastating weapon. For James, black cyborg rebels, or "biological-mechanical-divine entities in service of freedom," have the ability to "refuse blackness-as-victimization and reconstitute blackness-as-resistance," enacting a new order that transcends power relationships instead of merely reorganizing them (68). Part of this rebellion involves reframing understandings of technology and socio-technological systems against the "scientist who reduces the divine to superstition or colonialist propaganda, the biological to the colonizer's war against nature embodied in the native, and the mechanical to technologies of warfare and finance that enabled the colonialist to triumph" (68). James's cyborg serves as an update to the "Cyborg Manifesto" in which Haraway seeks to take advantage of technology's increasingly ubiquitous and invasive presence to challenge corporeal and gender norms. As the boundaries between human and machine disappear, so should other repressive binaries (Haraway 177). Like James, Haraway suggests a rebellion that appropriates aspects of repressive technological systems, such as the concept of network connections, that could help form feminist solidarity.

One important difference between Haraway's and James's cyborgs is that the former connects the hypertechnological shift to more recent innovations while the latter roots the issue in long histories of colonization and slavery, a perspective that offers important context for any conversation of the history of technology in the Caribbean. The cyborg model has proved to be particularly useful for studies on Caribbean and Latin American science fiction, possibly because of its ability to emphasize the everyday interaction between bodies, technology, and the structures that regulate their respective borders. As M. Elizabeth Ginway (2020) writes, "Cyborg bodies, queer bodies, and zombified or vampiric bodies offer resistance to the positivist ethos and provide and alternative perspective on rapid growth and modernity in the twentieth and twenty-first centuries and the political and economic challenges they have brought" (167). Antonio Córdoba (2021) similarly compares the cyborg in Latin American science fiction to other posthuman beings like aliens and mutants, writing that "cyborgs offer a way of inscribing a past that invades the present with a traumatic loop of repetition. . . . Cyborgs are thus avatars of overflowing, overwhelming time; of a past that refuses to become such and stays irreducibly present" (255). J. Andrew Brown (2010) explains that Latin American narratives featuring "scarred cyborgs, the confused posthumans, the ungendered and regendered motherless bodies" demonstrate "the power of these figures to enunciate contemporary realities, be they those traumatized realities of the postdictatorship, be they the everyday lives of individuals surrounded by effects of neoliberal policy" (178). Cyborgs and the rest of these models are used to attempt to narrate the history and ever-shifting state of Latin American and Caribbean humanity, which has been reshaped through colonizing and authoritarian projects.

As previously mentioned, each chapter in this book focuses on the histories, legacies, and science fiction representations of specific technologies. Chapter 1, "Electroconvulsive Therapy: Treatment, Torture, and Electrified Bodies," focuses on the abuse of ECT technology and the manipulation of narratives of health and science to subdue entire populations, along with the ways "excessive" bodies can reassert themselves within these socio-technological networks. The analysis begins with a historical look at the misuse of the technology on political enemies under the regimes of the Dominican Republic's Rafael Trujillo and Cuba's Fidel Castro. Special attention will be paid to how this ECT abuse conceptualizes the body as a mechanical object that can be rewired to remove unwanted characteristics, including political dissidence and homosexuality. The literary texts studied in chapter 1 all feature ECT and discussions on the narratives that support its abuse. First, in Puerto Rican author Pedro Cabiya's *La cabeza* (2007), a mad scientist and his brother conduct medical experiments on the women in their lives; one woman survives as only a head in a capsule, her emotions modulated through electrical pulses to her brain, while another victim lives with her upper body connected to a stationary life-support machine. The rhetoric of science and experimentation used by the brothers to justify their actions highlights the problematic narratives that attempt to legitimize ECT abuse. Next, in Puerto Rican author Alexandra Pagán Vélez's science fiction/

horror short story collection *Horror-REAL* (2016), suicide has been declared illegal and those that attempt it are tortured with ECT. At the same time, a filicide epidemic reaches a critical point and parents are replaced by cyborg caregivers that program more obedient offspring. These stories discuss the rhetoric behind state-sponsored violence and efforts to create robot-like homogeneity in humans. Finally, in Puerto Rican artist, filmmaker, and writer Vagabond Beaumont's "Kafka's Last Laugh" (2015), a woman is arrested at a protest on Wall Street and sentenced to working in retail, to reprogram her respect for capitalism. A special nanotechnology is used to monitor her location and give her electrical shocks whenever she misbehaves. This story imagines the economic and political factors that contribute to human rights violations. All the texts studied propose the excessive body as part of a resistance that can push back against the supposed mechanical efficiency of the dehumanized, docile, electrified subject.

Chapter 2, "Nuclear Weapons: Missiles, Radiation, and Archives," examines the rhetorical power of nuclear weapons and how challenging popular narratives concerning the use of this technology can loosen the colonizing aspects of nuclear archive. The primary historical instance of techno-dominance studied in this chapter is the Cuban Missile Crisis, which both put the Caribbean on the edge of nuclear destruction and highlighted Cuba's secondary place within global hierarchies. This crisis, in addition to protests over radiation from weapons testing in Vieques, Puerto Rico, consolidated the place of nuclear rhetoric in anti-imperial resistance. The three science fiction texts studied attempt to rewrite the nuclear archive, providing a place for affected bodies and proper mourning. In Dominican author Rey Emmanuel Andújar's short story "Gameon" (2014), Cuba launches a nuclear weapon at the United States and causes an ecological disaster that reshapes the definition of humanity. The struggle of a cyborg soldier attempting to recapture human imperfection is juxtaposed with a hungry adjunct professor trying to survive until the next semester begins. Next, Cuban author and activist Yasmín Silvia Portales's short story "Las extrañas decisiones de Vladimir Denísovich Jiménez" (2016) imagines an alternate dimension in which the Soviet Union does not back down during the Cuban Missile Crisis and takes complete control over the island. The protagonist considers his loyalty to a Soviet colonial government that wants to mine him for information and then kill him, along with the realization that there is no place for his queer body within a power structure based on nuclear weapons. Finally, Cuban author Erick Mota's novella *Trabajo Extra* (2014) imagines a group of exploited cadets tasked with disposing dangerous nuclear materials. When a crew member's radiation exposure brings to light her survival of a Chernobyl-like disaster, the pilot is responsible for the lives of his crew and a hidden dissident community that he accidentally rediscovers. All of these texts challenge popular understandings of nuclear weapons by exposing the ongoing and overlooked dangers of nuclear rhetoric and radiation.

Chapter 3, "Space Exploration and Colonial Alienation," digs deeper into the complicated history of space exploration in the Caribbean. The circumstances surrounding the construction and ultimate collapse of Puerto Rico's Arecibo Observatory, along with the rhetoric used to describe Cuban cosmonaut Arnaldo Tamayo Méndez's historic participation in the *Soyuz 38* mission, highlight the colonizing and nationalist rhetoric that is often used to celebrate space exploration. The science fictions studied in chapter 3 explore understandings of discovery, contact, and how feelings of alienation can both maintain violent structures or be reappropriated into tools of resistance. Dominican-Pakistani-American author Haris Durrani's novella *Champollion's Foot* (2017) follows the rogue crew of the *Mariposa Negra* spaceship as they search for an intelligent species that the corporate overlords have disavowed. Reframing space travel as acts of diaspora and decolonization, the crew must also come to terms with their exploitation and mistreatment of the jinn that power and direct their ship. In Cuban author Yoss's novel *Condonautas* (2013), contact specialists initiate commercial agreements through sex with alien species. Demythologizing the nationalist and colonizing reasons behind space exploration, the novel questions the liberatory potential of non-normative sexualities in service of empire. Lastly, Puerto Rican author Luis Othoniel Rosa's novel *Caja de fractales* (2017) shows a group of intoxicated wanderers imagining new futures amid environmental and social crisis. When news arrives that extraterrestrials have made contact, the novel asks how an alien invasion could break down dominant capitalist and colonizing structures, along with human-centric understandings of Earth's place in the greater universe. All of these texts speculate on the ways space exploration and the creation of new borders bring up questions about discovery and belonging in the Caribbean.

Chapter 4, "Disruptive Avatars and the Decoding of Caribbean Cyberspace," argues that representations of future internet technologies and disruptive avatars attempt to decode the power structures that operate online. It traces the history of how artists and video game programmers have been using avatars to define digital culture while also showing how even new digital constructions are affected by histories of violence. The science fiction texts analyzed mix globalized internet cultures and concerns specific to the Caribbean. First, in Cuban author Maielis González Fernández's short story "Slow Motion" (2016), avatars organize a revolt against their human users, questioning the relationship between digital and physical bodies. The story looks deeper into fears of technology, shedding light on the ways powerful institutions can manipulate cyberspace and disrupt political solidarities. Next, in Cuban author Jorge Enrique Lage's novel *Carbono 14: Una novela del culto* (2010), a young girl is transformed into an avatar for public consumption and fears losing her real-world identity, blurring the line between physical and virtual realms. Her juxtaposition with a man who spends his time enjoying touristic and disembodied experiences online highlights the inequalities coded into cyberspaces. Finally, Dominican author and musician Rita Indiana's *La mucama de Omicunlé* (2015) features a trans protagonist who uses internet technologies and Afro-Caribbean religious connections to project avatars into different historical periods. As they are charged with saving the island from ecological disaster, the novel questions the roles of spirituality and queer bodies within hyper-connected digital futures. All of these texts show the importance of challenging not only how digital technology is coded but who is responsible for the coding, along with how avatars can be used to interrupt repressive structures online.

With each of these readings, *The Cyborg Caribbean* offers new ways of discussing the cultural and rhetorical legacies of colonial and authoritarian control in the Caribbean through the lens of science fiction. They underline the continued relevance of historical moments of techno-dominance and resistance. Revisiting technologies and their rhetorical consequences is the first step in counteracting their roles within oppressive systems. In doing so, these texts demonstrate the political potential of science fiction and its ability to imagine and participate in the fight for more liberated futures.

CHAPTER 1

Electroconvulsive Therapy

TREATMENT, TORTURE, AND ELECTRIFIED BODIES

In sociologist Lloyd Rogler's 2008 ethnographic memoir, *Barrio Professors: Tales of Naturalistic Research*, he recounts a scene in the late 1950s in which a woman named Juana enters a state-run psychiatric institution in Río Piedras, Puerto Rico, under pressure from her husband and mother-in-law. According to Juana, she had recently developed *facultades*, or connections with the spiritual world, and was currently undergoing challenging *pruebas* or tests that honed her supernatural skills but also caused fits of sadness, insomnia, and decreased appetite. Dr. Federico Badillo, the New York–trained psychiatrist who attended to her, quickly dismissed her claim to spiritual powers, diagnosing her with schizophrenia and prescribing electroconvulsive therapy (ECT). When Juana argued against this prognosis, Badillo reminded her that he was the only medical doctor in the room. Juana responded, "I know you are a scientist and you know material things. *Pero*, but my difficulties aren't material. I have *una causa espiritual*, a spiritual problem" (Rogler 72). To her, his credentials and training fell well short of being able to comprehend her otherworldly situation; these newfound powers were a great gift to be controlled and explored, not a problem to be fixed. The doctor then attempted to explain his prescribed treatment in an objective, scientific manner. "The procedure is simple: A mild electrical current is passed through the patient's brain and it produces convulsions, and then temporary amnesia. It appears to relieve symptoms of depression" (Rogler 72). Not only did this response minimize the position of the patient receiving these "mild" shocks, but it also assumed that Juana was depressed, reducing Juana's *facultades* to a symptom. In the end, the doctor and patient could not reconcile their perspectives of Juana's situation or whether the proposed ECT represented a legitimate treatment or a violent punishment.

While the presence of Rogler, a U.S.-based ethnographer, may have compounded Juana's sense of institutional marginalization, the account offers insight into the rhetoric surrounding ECT and the gendered and colonizing nature of its deployment. For example, Juana seemed to have been prepared for Badillo's prescription of ECT, having already talked to a man named Julian in the waiting room about the therapy. Pushing back on the idea that such a procedure could be "simple," she said:

> Julian told me from his own experience that they take you into a room with six or eight persons and trap you down on a board of wood about the size of a door. The board has a thin padding. They put something in your mouth to keep you from biting off your tongue. The doctor walks behind each patient, from one to the next, with a machine that looks like those battery chargers used in gasoline stations. He wheels the machine in back of you as another person holds the wires on your temples. The lightning explodes inside of your head. You see a darkness swirling around. Then you see nothing and there is silence. You wake up and your body hurts all over and you feel weak and nauseous and cannot remember anything. (73)

Rogler later confirmed Juana's description of the treatment, adding that the patients in question did not receive anesthesia and often broke bones from the convulsions. Juana's verbalization of the pain and fear involved in receiving ECT highlights how much was hidden within Badillo's reductive explanation. She also compared the therapy to "being put on the electric chair the way Americans do criminals" (Rogler 73). Connecting ECT to capital punishment and U.S. colonialism, Juana recognized the technology's potential for abuse, along with alluding to the historical mistreatment of Puerto Ricans and other marginalized people within American medical and criminal justice institutions. The idea that Juana's *facultades* could be cured by electricity also underlines the ways in which technologies like ECT help redefine popular understandings of the human body. As Timothy Kneeland and Carol Warren (2002) have argued, "Treatments practiced upon the body reflect current theories of the 'nature' of body (or soul).... Electricity healed the electric body" (xxv). Through the lens of the medical institution tasked with treating her, Juana's divergence from a more traditional, scientifically explained path was merely a case of faulty wiring or a malfunctioning power source, an electrical problem that could be fixed with more electricity.

Electroconvulsive therapy has a long history in the Caribbean as both a cure and punishment, blurring the line between treatment and torture. Though seizure induction had been used as far back as the sixteenth century, Hungarian Ladislas Meduna and Italians Ugo Cerletti and Lucio Bini developed in the 1930s the practice that most closely resembles the current iteration of ECT. By the 1940s and 1950s, ECT was already a common practice in the Caribbean. The act of electrifying bodies underlines the way in which humans are already conceptualized as electrical and the idea that dissenting or nonconforming subjects can be rewired or reprogramed. In this chapter, I connect the history of ECT abuse in the Caribbean to the twenty-first-century science fiction narratives that speculate on the future of electrified and electrocuted bodies. These science fiction texts look back at the historical manipulation of medical and scientific language as they question the rhetorical legacies of these electrified instances of technodominance in the Caribbean. First, in Pedro Cabiya's *La cabeza* (2007), a cyborg named Gloria searches for physical pleasure in a world where women are treated like domestic appliances. Next, in Alexandra Pagán Vélez's *Horror-REAL* (2016), a government attempts to maintain control by torturing citizens and centralizing reproduction. Finally, Vagabond Beaumont's "Kafka's Last Laugh" (2015) outlines a future in which the prison system colludes with the globalized marketplace and nanotechnology to further marginalize political dissidents. In all of these texts, excessive bodies are deployed as resistance to repressive electrocution, enacting a posthuman rebelliousness that questions dominant narratives of efficiency and productivity. By highlighting the horrors of ECT abuse, these texts engage with and challenge rhetoric that blurs the line between legitimate therapy and state torture.

The convergence of mental health institutions and prisons has long set the stage for ECT abuse. As Michel Foucault claims in *Discipline and Punish: The Birth of the Prison* (originally published in French in 1975), the hospital has become yet another disciplinary institution, helping shape the "the present scientifico-legal complex from which the power to punish derives its bases, justifications and rules" (1979, 23). Foucault includes doctors, psychiatrists, and psychologists, tasked with creating a scientific or medical reasoning for cruelty, in his list of technicians that have taken over for the classic executioner (11). In Caribbean history, one of the best recorded examples of this convergence between treatment and torture is Rafael Trujillo's manipulation of the Dominican Republic's health system, allowing for the widespread mistreatment of political prisoners and dissidents. Trujillo was given the perfect opportunity to reshape mental healthcare and rhetoric in the country in 1930, just eighteen days into his presidency, when the country's largest mental health institution was destroyed by a hurricane. The Padre Billini Psychiatric Hospital was eventually moved in 1940 to a prison in Nigua, outside of Ciudad Trujillo, as the city of Santo Domingo was called from 1936 until Trujillo's death in 1961. The site in Nigua also had long roots in U.S colonialism on the island, as the United States originally built the prison during its occupation of the Dominican Republic from 1916 to 1924. The psychiatric hospital became a key site in Trujillo's project to control political dissent, both as a place to stow political rivals and as a refuge for those enemies that feared even worse conditions in prison. Military prison guards, not medical personnel, were said to attend to these patients (Romero 55). The blurring of the line between patient and prisoner, between treatment and punishment, reinforced biopolitical narratives of health and nation in the Dominican Republic. The regime's political ties to the United States and the history of the Nigua site itself also show that the regime's approach to mental health and ECT abuse must be understood within contexts of both Trujillo's authoritarianism and U.S. imperialism.

According to Lino A. Romero's *Historia de la psiquiatría dominicana* (2005, *History of Dominican Psychiatry*), when Trujillo was first approached about improving conditions for the country's psychiatric patients, he responded, "Aquí no tenemos suficiente para los cuerdos, y mucho menos para los locos" (Romero 41, "Here we don't have enough for the sane ones, much less the crazy ones"). This rhetoric alienated those patients from the rest of the country and questioned how they would fit into Trujillo's conceptualization of a healthy and strong Dominican Republic, especially given his emphasis on public health through the *Campaña Sanitaria*.[1] Dr. Antonio Zaglul, who ran the Padre Billini Psychiatric Hospital from 1955 until he was forced into exile by Trujillo in 1960, reiterated the idea that his patients did not fit into Trujillo's vision of a healthy republic: "De todas las personas a las que despreciaba más profundamente, eran los locos, a quienes no podía ver" (35, "Of all the people he most deeply despised, the worst were the crazy ones, whom he could not look at"). Trujillo's rhetoric separated mental health patients from the rest of the nation, enacting something similar to what Italian philosopher Roberto Esposito (published in original Italian in 2004; translated by Timothy Campbell in 2008) refers to as biopolitical immunization in which individual bodies are quarantined or destroyed in the name of protecting an abstract definition of life. ECT abuse became a tool through which Trujillo attempted to immunize the Dominican Republic, treating both mental health patients and political enemies as pathogens that threatened the greater political body. To Esposito, biopolitical immunization is inherently violent because it destroys subjects that are not seen to naturally belong to the greater political entity: "Immunity continues to speak the language of the negative, which it would like to annul: in order to avoid a potential evil, it produces a real one; it substitutes an excess with a defect, a fullness with an emptiness, a plus with a minus" (92). This process of destroying bodies in order to protect a greater good also feeds into the rhetoric used to justify experimentation on or inhumane treatment of marginalized subjects. In Esposito's explanation of biopolitical immunity, "excess" is understood as a danger to the system, something to be destroyed; in the science fiction texts analyzed later in this chapter, excessive bodies are called on to contest the rhetorical and political systems that seek to create docile, productive subjects.

Zaglul, who recounted his time at Padre Bellini in the 1956 memoir *Mis 500 locos* (*My 500 Crazies*), mentions treating several political prisoners, including patients from Venezuela and Cuba who had traveled to the Dominican Republic to aid the anti-Trujillo cause. He admitted to using ECT on many of his patients without fully understanding the reasoning behind its supposed effectiveness, highlighting how marginalized bodies are often used as experimental subjects in the support scientific discovery. When describing the hospital's therapeutic arsenal, he mentions "un aparato para electrochoques que agonizaba de puro usado" (126, "A device for electroshocks that was fading from heavy use"). This depiction of a worn-down machine supports the idea that Zaglul overprescribed ECT, an accusation that Romero insinuates in his book but does not openly claim (Romero 51). Zaglul also recounted one scene in which many patients refused to undergo ECT because the convulsions were too reminiscent of the epileptic seizures that they watched others suffer. Zaglul said that he was able to convince most of the patients of the benefits of ECT, but then added, "Huelga decir que tratamos deshacernos de los *no convencidos*" (28, "It goes without saying that we tried to break down the *unconvinced*"). In a text that mostly attempts to show the doctor's compassion for his patients, this line stands out as particularly ominous. The doctor, even after admitting that the reasons behind ECT's effectiveness remained a mystery, paid no mind to the legitimate fears of his patients. Recent scholarly studies on ECT, such as Ottoson and Fink (2004) and Shorter and Healy (2007), seek to lessen the impact of these popular fears of the therapy, arguing that exaggerated concerns get in the way of legitimate medical advancements. However, by studying ECT as a technology, one must consider the popular stigma against the practice as part of its socio-technological network.

While the social and political projects of Trujillo and of Cuba's Fidel Castro were vastly different, especially in terms of their respective relationships to socialism and to the United States, it is noteworthy that Castro similarly abused ECT during his authoritarian reign. In 1991, Charles Brown and Armando Lago published *The Politics of Psychiatry in Revolutionary Cuba*, responding to allegations of psychiatric abuses by Fidel Castro. The initial assumptions concerning these practices most likely stemmed from the regime's longtime political connections to the Soviet Union, which had been publicly accused of such abuses in the 1970s and 1980s.[2] In his prologue to Brown and Lago's report, Vladimir Bukovsky notes the irony of Castro's refusal to end the misuse of psychiatry at a time in which former Soviet doctors were working with the international community to eliminate these practices (7). In 1992, the British Medical Association also called on Castro to allow for an independent human rights inspection of the country's mental health institutions (76). Brown and Lago's report focuses on twenty-seven cases of abuse, among them instances of political dissidents being confined to hospitals after forced interrogations labeled them as criminally insane and of patients with mental health issues being denied treatment based on their political beliefs. The report also includes dissidents with no history of mental illness being administered ECT and psychotropic drugs, or patients with low-level mental illnesses who were given ECT dosages much higher than normal practice would recommend (Brown and Lago 13–14). According to Brown and Lago, the treatment was used to "terrorize the dissident into cooperating with his captors; at times it serves to punish the dissident for specific behavior" (13). Among those dissidents listed in the report is filmmaker Nicolás Guillén Landrián, who was accused of ideological deviation and conspiring to assassinate Fidel Castro. Guillén Landrián came into conflict with the government after his 1968 documentary *Coffea Arábiga* showed Castro climbing a mountain with the Beatles' "Fool on the Hill" playing in the background, along with the filmmaker's refusal to direct a film that would sully the reputation of the controversially imprisoned poet Heberto Padilla. (Brown and Lago 68–69).

Of the twenty-seven political prisoners included in *The Politics of Psychiatry in Revolutionary Cuba*, eleven were administered ECT, while the treatment of seven other patients could not be confirmed. ECT was often applied with the patient strapped to vomit- or urine-soaked floors, with electrodes attached to the victim's head or testicles, without the customary use of anesthesia, muscle relaxants, or a rubber mouth guard (Brown and Lago 23). One of the victims listed, businessman Eugenio de Sosa Chabau, was brought to the Havana Psychiatric Hospital after being arrested for conspiring to overthrow Castro and rejecting the Cuban prison system's reeducation program. He says:

> Six patients were grabbed and rubber pieces were stuffed in their mouths. They were thrown to the floor in a row side by side. Right there, on the floor, the electrodes were applied to both sides of their heads and shocks [were] applied. Six bodies started to contort one by one.... The shocks were applied to the temples of the patients, but to me they applied most of the shocks to the testicles instead. (Brown and Lago 60)

Forcing patients to receive treatment on the floor and covered in bodily fluids (either their own or someone else's) highlights ECT abuse's goal of humiliation and dehumanization, as the bodies cease to function as more electricity is introduced. Another victim, former civil servant Gualdo Hidalgo Portilla, was one of many to claim that the ECT caused short-term memory loss. This side effect coincides with Naomi Klein's characterization of electricity-based torture as a metaphor for disaster capitalism, as stated in *The Shock Doctrine: The Rise of Disaster Capitalism* (2007): "We are told it's about getting information, but I think it's more than that—I think it may also have to do with trying to build a model country, about erasing people and then trying to remake them from scratch" (26). The electrified body becomes the conceptual site on which the model country and model citizen is produced. Hidalgo also claimed that those administering the shocks were often prison guards instead of medical personnel and that ECT was applied "sometimes as entertainment, sometimes as punishment" (Brown and Lago 76). Hidalgo emphasizes the spectacular aspect of conducting ECT simultaneously on multiple patients, with the visual display of a convulsing human body serving as either a diversion or a warning for other prisoners in the room.

ECT abuse in the Caribbean has been deployed as a particularly gendered form of punishment. In the case of Doña Juana, the patient believed she was being punished for stepping outside her prescribed role as a wife and daughter-in-law. For other victims, masculinity was at the center of ECT abuse. Multiple accounts have shown that it was common practice to torture male prisoners by connecting electrodes to their testicles, a symbolic attack that could be interpreted as either emasculation or an attempt to revive one's masculinity. One must consider the ways in which the treatment was deployed in support of heteronormative social structures and how political dissidence was connected to a failure to achieve a hypermasculine ideal. For example, the intersection of official Cuban homophobia and mental healthcare is clear in the case of psychiatrist Eduardo Gutiérrez Agramonte's experiments with ECT as a cure for homosexuality in the late 1960s. As Jennifer Lambe shows in *Madhouse: Psychiatry and Politics in Cuban History* (2017), Gutiérrez Agramonte moved to separate homosexuality from psychosis or criminality, instead understanding it as an abnormal, learned behavior (159). Gutiérrez Agramonte turned to aversion therapy, a practice both pioneered and later rejected by Czech scientist Kurt Freund. In Gutiérrez Agramonte's variation, Freund's injections were replaced by electroshocks, which were applied to patients' hands and forearms while they were forced to look at different examples of erotic imagery. The doctor's state-funded research into conversion therapy through ECT linked sexual nonconformity to political dissidence. ECT was a tool used in shaping the New (Heterosexual) Man deemed acceptable by the Cuban Revolution. Gutiérrez Agramonte's individual treatment of homosexuality was soon after replaced by widescale "social hygiene" projects through the infamous *Unidades Militares de Ayuda a la Producción* (UMAP, or Military Units to Aid Production) forced labor camps.[3] As the next section will show, ECT abuse and its cultural representations in the Caribbean cannot be understood without an intersectional look at the ways scientific or medical rhetoric is distorted to support the oppressive treatment of marginalized bodies.

Images and rhetoric surrounding historical ECT abuse in the region have shaped the deployment of electrified and electrocuted figures in Caribbean science fiction. The science fiction texts studied in this chapter represent electrified and electrocuted bodies to discuss legacies of techno-dominance and the socio-technological network surrounding ECT abuse in the Caribbean.[4] While forced electrocution is a common occurrence throughout the works, these particular works were chosen for how their respective authors use speculative fiction to arrive at different aspects of ECT's socio-technological network and legacy. Cabiya's *La cabeza* (2007) considers the patriarchal and colonial influences within medical procedures, affecting which bodies are chosen as disposable test subjects for scientific experimentation. Pagán Vélez's *Horror-REAL* (2016) connects the desire to control one's own body to political dissidence and highlights the blurring of the line between mental healthcare and state torture. Beaumont's "Kafka's Last Laugh" (2015) links the incarceration of and technological intervention into marginalized bodies to a global capitalist network and consumerism's ability to defuse moral and political objections. All of these texts suggest maintaining humanity in the form of excessive corporeality as a strategy to survive hypertechnological futures.

LA CABEZA: EXPERIMENTATION AND SEXUAL AUTONOMY

Just as the socio-technological network surrounding ECT includes popular fears and reactions to the practice, it must also consider texts and images about robotic or electrified bodies to shed light on the physical and social effects of forced electrocution. In *Anatomy of a Robot: Literature, Cinema, and the Cultural Work of Artificial People* (2014), Despina Kakoudaki argues that "narratives of mechanical embodiment thus debate the limits of the body not just by presenting the body in terms of frailty and enhancement but most importantly by questioning the meanings of what is inherent in the body and what is exterior to it" (83–84). The relative inhumanity of these electrified or robotic characters calls for a deeper questioning on how humanity is constructed. The conjunction of electricity and bodies into these narratives adds a mystery or intrigue that reconnects the artificial body to qualities of humanness that avoid mechanical or empirical explanation: "As forces, electricity and electromagnetism join other invisible, ineffable, and permeating forces such as faith, sexual attraction, inspiration, the imagination, and the will" (Kakoudaki 108). In this way, electrified bodies serve as narrative devices to contemplate both material and intangible aspects of the human. The electrified bodies analyzed in this chapter force readers to consider the physical and psychological effects of torture, treatment, and experimentation.

Texts that deploy robotic, electrified, or cyborg women, such as the three texts to be discussed in this chapter, must additionally contend with science fiction's historically engrained misogyny. Teresa López-Pellisa outlines the complexities of traditional accounts of artificial women in *Patologías de la realidad virtual: Cibercultura y ciencia ficción* (2015, *Pathologies of Virtual Reality: Cyber-culture and Science Fiction*). López-Pellisa connects these woman-machine narratives to fears over hypertechnological dehumanization, though they often fail to take into account the repression of women. Electrified women have often been used in popular science fiction to show traditional masculinity's inability to adapt to hypertechnological futures, while simultaneously reinforcing heteronormative structures that dehumanize and objectify women (243–244). In particular, in many romantic or sexual situations between organic men and inorganic women, the latter's experience of either pain or pleasure is rarely discussed. In her book *Cyberpunk Women, Feminism and Science Fiction* (2013), Carlen Lavigne highlights texts that contest the literary tradition of misogyny within science fiction.

Lavigne notes that while early cyberpunk was notorious for hypersexual machine-woman hybrids, feminist cyberpunk "emphasizes the importance of physical contact and the relation between body image and a unified sense of self... [with] a tendency to portray body images more realistically than in work concentrating on the travails of cyberspace junkies" (78). Narratives of electrified women thus tend to either reinforce or contest the genre's historical objectification of women's bodies.

Pedro Cabiya's novel *La cabeza* uses electrified women and ECT to examine patriarchal techno-dominance and scientific rhetoric that converts marginalized bodies into test subjects. Cabiya, who was born in Puerto Rico but has resided in Santo Domingo since the early 2000s, is a writer of experimental, fantastical, and science fiction, including *Trance* (2008), *Malas hierbas* (2010), *Reinbou* (2017), and *Tercer mundo* (2019), and the 2015 film *Uqbar*. In particular, *Malas hierbas* represents an attempt to decolonize speculative fiction, investigating the cooptation of Haitian zombie narratives by U.S. popular culture. A similar project is also apparent in Cabiya's comic book *Anima Sola* (2012), created in collaboration with artists Israel González and Yovanni Ramírez, which combines superhero and zombie narratives with Afro-Caribbean deities and discussions of hunger and poor social services. In his review of *Tercer mundo*, Luis Othoniel Rosa (2019) points out that while Cabiya's work appears innovative and inventive, it is actually deeply set in a reverence for a Caribbean narrative tradition:

> Vemos cómo el *Tercer Mundo* homenajea el grotesco de Virgilio Piñera en *La carne de René,* la polifonía radial de Luis Rafael Sánchez en *La guaracha del macho Camacho,* el dominó santero y cósmico de Manuel Ramos Otero en *La novelabingo,* la libertad estrafalaria y alucinante de las novelas de Reynaldo Arenas, también el diálogo con algunos de sus contemporáneos, como con la poética y metafísica malhablada y políticamente incorrecta de Juan Carlos Quiñones o el punk santero cínico de Rita Indiana Hernández en su *La mucama de Omicunlé.* (Othoniel Rosa, 2019, We see how *Tercer Mundo* pays homage to the grotesque of Virgilio Piñera in *La carne de René,* the radial polyphony of Luis Rafael Sánchez in *La guaracha del macho Camacho,* the *santera* and cosmic domino of Manuel Ramos Otero in *La novelabingo,* the extravagant and hallucinatory freedom of the novels of Reynaldo Arenas, along with a dialogue with some of his contemporaries, like the foulmouthed and politically incorrect poetics and metaphysics of Juan Carlos Quiñones or the cynical, *santero* punk of Rita Indiana Hernández in their *La mucama de Omicunlé.*)

Cabiya's short novel *La cabeza* focuses on Daniel and Gloria, a newly married couple who suffered a horrific car accident on their wedding night. Gloria was standing up through the sunroof at the time of the crash, and her body was severed in half. Daniel quickly called Ezequiel, his mad scientist brother, who built a life support system to keep alive Gloria's upper half while restraining her to the bed. The novel chronicles the sexual and romantic exploits between multiple characters—Daniel and Gloria, Daniel and his secretary Marta, Daniel and Gloria's nurse Raquel, and Gloria and Raquel. Marta eventually donates her body to Gloria, who then runs off with Raquel, leaving Daniel alone to question his hubris and his relationships. The novel touches on questions of cruelty committed in the name of science and how much technological intervention one can receive before they can no longer be considered alive. Cabiya's text relies on schlock or B-movie horror tropes, raising questions about why the public is attracted to such gruesome images and whether the consumption of such materials should be considered voyeuristic. The reader of Cabiya's novel is put in the uncomfortable position of feeling both appalled by and complicit in Gloria's situation. Still, while the particulars of the situation—mad scientists and severed heads—are outlandish, the structural repressions felt by the women in the story are meant to be familiar. As Lola Aponte (2017) writes, "En *La cabeza* de Cabiya, la heteronormatividad representada por el esposo con su buena dosis de racismo, acoso laboral y misoginia se sostiene aun en un mundo tecno. Perviven estructuras jerarquizantes y de poder" (74, "In Pedro Cabiya's *La cabeza*, the heteronormativity represented by the husband with a dose of racism, workplace harassment, and misogyny, is sustained even in the high-tech world. Hierarchizing and power structures pervade").

While the figure of Gloria blurs the line between human and machine, the character that actually confronts ECT abuse in the novel is Marta, Daniel's secretary and mistress. Marta, who throughout the story is the character most concerned over Gloria's quality of life, agrees to donate her body to Gloria and live as just a head in a capsule that sits on Daniel's desk. For Daniel, this decision represents a double victory: Gloria will no longer be half-machine, and he had begun preferring Marta's body even to his wife's original form. Daniel does initially worry about the pain that Marta experiences, but Ezequiel explains that the process will actually make her happier, even without the use of drugs. He says, "Si nos deshacemos del cuerpo podemos controlar las emociones directamente por medio de estímulos eléctricos. Con este dial tú decides cuán feliz se siente la cabeza, o cuán triste o grave, lo que tú quieras. Tienes hasta diez emociones para elegir" (74, "If we get rid of the body, we can control the emotions directly via electric stimuli. With this dial, you decide how happy the head feels, or how sad or serious, whatever you want. You have up to ten emotions to choose from"). Ezequiel goes as far as to compare the process to adjusting the thermostat on an air-conditioning system, effectively turning Marta into a domestic appliance. At a different point in the novel, Daniel cannot help but treat Gloria as a machine, as he asks the nurse Raquel to turn off the digestion system between meals to save energy, as one would with a fan or lamp. This link between efficiency and electrified bodies can also be connected back to the history of ECT.

In the 1940s, ECT was promoted as being cleaner and more efficient than other therapies, and the portability of the device evoked future possibilities of home-based self-treatment (Kneeland and Warren xxi). The idea that ECT should be as simple to operate as any other domestic appliance informs popular conceptualizations of mental health, reducing the complex causes and consequences linked to emotional and psychological distress to glitches that can be easily fixed by flipping a switch. In the case of Ezequiel and Daniel's treatment of Marta, narratives of efficiency and convenience are used to obfuscate any issues of physical pain or long-term effects from undergoing ECT outside of legitimate psychiatric institutions. Ignoring the electric stimuli controlling Marta's brain and emotions, the experiment is justified by how it will benefit everyone but the test subject.

Ezequiel's explanations of the experiment focus on Daniel's comfort around his new bodiless companion, adding that he can adjust the device according to the type of conversation that he wants to have with Marta. This technology and the rhetoric surrounding it serve Daniel's desires more than Marta's needs, ignoring her pain and immobility. The scientist also reasons that Marta's life will be better without having to worry about her body, and that she will be much happier living a contemplative life. This patronizing justification of his actions disavows the possibility of a women being both embodied and cerebral and highlights how scientific rhetoric has historically been used to disregard women's bodies, minds, pain, and labor. To underline Ezequiel's lack of concern for his test subject, the reader later learns that Ezequiel hopes that this successful experiment will serve as revenge to the scientific community that rejected him, showing how personal pride and aggressive masculinity can be mixed with scientific curiosity in ways that ignore the effects on human subjects. Daniel also connects his offering up of Gloria as a lab subject to the times in his childhood when he used to provide his brother with animals for diabolic experiments. The treatment of Gloria not only brings into question the human-machine binary but also that of human-animal.

Gloria, an immobile, electrified body, does not receive ECT directly, though she is implicated in a narrative that such technology creates: that human health issues can have "simple" electrical or mechanical solutions. Her immobility sets her situation apart from other biomedical innovations such as prosthetics and pacemakers, which attempt to mimic or restore certain functions. Gloria's inability to leave her bed highlights the fact that Daniel and Ezequiel's version of saving her life includes little more than the recreation of a heteronormative fantasy of helplessness and sexual availability. Her mechanical form before receiving Marta's body is described as both a technological marvel and a source of terror:

> El horror comenzaba justo debajo de las formidables mamas, donde el cuerpo de Gloria llegaba a su fin con un corte abrupto y desgarrado que más o menos

seguía la curvatura del costillar: ajustado al diafragma había un estómago artificial construido a base de polímeros orgánicos de cual surgía un ramillete de tubos que bifurcaban. El conjunto se asemejaba como una gaita escocesa. (23–24, The horror began just below her formidable breasts, where Gloria's body ended with an abrupt and torn cut that more or less followed the curve of her ribcage: attached to the diaphragm there was an artificial stomach made of organic polymers from which emerged a bouquet of bifurcating tubes. The assemblage resembled a Scottish bagpipe.)

Daniel is offended when Marta refers to Gloria as a monster, since admitting such a thing would go against his beliefs that his wife is alive and doing well. More importantly, references to monstrosity contradict the scientific and medical rhetoric the brothers use to justify their actions. While Daniel claims to be working in Gloria's best interests, the reader later learns that she is most likely too heavily medicated to make real decisions about her own situation. Cabiya's inclusion of this voyeuristic peek into Gloria's undercarriage speaks to a wider fascination with humanizing machines and mechanical corporalities. As Kakoudaki mentions in her analysis of the curiosity and fetishization involved in these moments of peering inside the robot anatomy, "Looking inside the mechanical body projects the desire for meaning onto a space designed to hold little insight" (2). By humanizing Gloria's mechanical functions, Daniel and Ezequiel can more easily tell themselves that their cruel experimentations are actually restoring life to their patient/victim/test subject (depending on one's perception).

The complicated nature of Gloria's life support system forces readers to question whether or not she should be considered alive. While her upper torso appears human, elaborate machines carry out the majority of her bodily functions, such as digestion and blood flow. Even Gloria's breathing must be mediated by electricity:

> El diafragma se relajaba y se contraía, llenando y vaciando los pulmones con un ritmo preciso, estimulando a propósito por una serie de electrodos injertados directamente en la médula espinal; esto quiere decir que la respiración estaba todavía a cargo del cerebro de Gloria, y que podía responder perfectamente a su estado de ánimo. (24, The diaphragm relaxed and contracted, filling and emptying the lungs with a precise rhythm, stimulated by a series of electrodes inserted directly into the spinal cord; that is to say that respiration was still controlled by Gloria's brain, and that it could respond perfectly to her mood.)

This technological intervention into the most basic human functions signals how dependent Gloria is on the machines. The mornings are dangerous times for Gloria, as she runs the risk of looking down at her disfigured body before her painkillers and antidepressant drugs are administered. Daniel's instructions to the nurse Raquel are more practical than humane: "¿Cuántas veces tengo que repetírtelo? ... Nunca, nunca, bajo ningún concepto, apartes la frazada" (25, "How many times do I have to repeat this to you? ... Never, never, under any circumstance, remove the blanket"). Daniel is more worried about having to deal with Gloria's morning panic attacks than with the cause of his wife's distress. This episode highlights the lack of consideration of the psychological effects on those whose bodies are appropriated by techno-science. Cynthia Morales Boscio (2009) writes that *La cabeza* shows how techno-scientific advances tend to view the body "como una masa orgánica sujeta a las manipulaciones tecnológicas sin tomar en consideración los efectos psíquicos. ... La humanidad así tratada se convierte en un producto más de la industria capaz de ser reciclable e intercambiable por las demandas de la tecnociencia" (214, "as an organic mass subject to technological manipulations without considering the psychic affects. ... Humanity treated in this way is converted into one more product of industry fit to be recyclable and interchangeable by the demands of techno-science"). *La cabeza* shows the power of scientific rhetoric to minimize the damages and psychological distresses of those labeled as disposable test subjects, all in the name of a greater good or decontextualized social advancement.

When Gloria accidentally sees her mechanical body before receiving her morning antidepressants and painkillers, she goes into shock: "Gloria se tapó los ojos con las manos y parecía al borde de un grave ataque de nervios. Quería gritar, pero estaba demasiado aterrorizada" (Cabiya 25, "Gloria covered her eyes with her hands and seemed to be on the verge of a panic attack. She wanted to scream, but she was too terrified"). The term "ataque de nervios" has a particular history that illustrates the oftentimes colonizing biases within psychiatric treatment. As Patricia Gherovici (2003) argues, "ataque de nervios" is the repackaged version of what has been known since the 1950s as the "Puerto Rican syndrome," an explanation, accepted by the American Psychiatric Association, for nervous breakdowns experienced by many Puerto Rican soldiers at that time (71). "Ataque de nervios" is officially listed in the appendix to the *Diagnostic and Statistical Manual of Mental Disorders, Fifth Edition* (2013) as a culturally specific disorder. As an example of ethnocentrism infecting scientific discovery, the illness was studied and analyzed as if the soldiers' psychological issues arose from their regional and racial origins and not from their military service. Gherovici adds that the set of symptoms grouped under the "Puerto Rican syndrome" remains undefined and fluid (70). Psychological rhetoric and institutions thus pathologized Puerto Rican-ness, as the ambiguous nature of the "illness" allowed the diagnosis to be applied widely and based on cultural assumptions. This subtle reference in *La cabeza* offers another example of the potential for colonizing and racist structures within medical research, along with the ability of science fiction to illuminate and challenge the rhetorical legacies of such moments.

Gloria resists her imposed immobilization by continuing to engage in activities that bring her sexual pleasure. This could seem complicit in her imprisonment, as her captors purposefully saved her breasts from destruction and attached her to a bed. However, Gloria does not seek out her husband for that pleasure but instead goes to her nurse Raquel, who in turn is also having an affair with Daniel. While Daniel has lost his sexual attraction to his wife—he absently kisses her on the forehead before heading off to work—Raquel voluntarily explores Gloria's electrical body. Serving as a sort of anti-ECT, Raquel and Gloria's sexual adventures manipulate electrical wires and currents to provoke pleasure, not pain or confusion. For example, "[Raquel] se inclinó sobre Gloria para alcanzar uno entre los muchos filamentos conectados a su cuerpo a través de un cable matriz injertado directamente en la medula espinal. Estaba marcado con cinta adhesiva roja. Raquel lo tomó entre las manos y lo dobló.... Inmediatamente Gloria se arqueó y lanzó un gemido de intenso placer. Raquel seguía frotando y Gloria se iba calentando, gimiendo con voz cada vez más febril y entrecortada" (38, "[Raquel] leaned against Gloria to reach one among the many filaments connected to her body through a cable matrix inserted directly into the spinal cord. It was marked with red tape. Raquel took in in her hands and bent it.... Immediately Gloria arched herself and moaned with intense pleasure. Raquel kept rubbing and Gloria was getting more and more excited, moaning with an increasingly feverish and breathy voice"). As Raquel continues to manipulate the filament, she begins to experience pleasure as well. Even in this moment, Gloria cannot escape her electrified state; her moans are accompanied by rapid beeping from her life-support system and the loud hum of a dilation machine on overdrive trying to keep up. Still, even though her pleasure is mediated by technology, satisfying the human desire to both give and receive sexual pleasure is an important part of her resistance to patriarchal techno-dominance. Because of this, it is no surprise that in the end Gloria (with Marta's body) leaves Daniel for Raquel, writing to her husband that only the nurse knows exactly how and where to touch her. The erotic scene between Gloria and Raquel is a literal interpretation of Haraway's (1991) cyborg in that embracing one's cyborg-ness leads to the deconstruction of heteronormative binaries and repressions. In this instance, queerness and the posthuman converge in a way that offers an alternative path for two women who feel unfulfilled in a hypermasculine, techno-patriarchal system.

Cabiya's novel shows an extreme example of patriarchal techno-dominance and its ability to manipulate scientific and medical rhetoric. It also attempts to break down the totalizing nature of technology in visions of the future. While the driving force of the story is the construction of docile, electrified women, it ends with a moment that questions the primacy of technology. Months after the operation, Daniel arrives at the office where Marta's head coyly jokes that she knows he did not get much sleep the night before. When Daniel gives her a confused look, the disembodied secretary reminds him that she can still feel any orgasms experienced by her old body. Daniel is later alarmed when Marta's head begins to giggle and moan next to him on the desk. By the time he realizes what is happening, Gloria has already run off with Raquel. Daniel is left alone, despite spending much of the novel attempting to construct an ideal sexual partner. Though he still can turn to Marta's disembodied head for company, he is ironically left as the only character not experiencing sexual pleasure. As Lola Aponte asks, "¿Es entonces este texto una mirada sonreída sobre el poder inefectivo de la masculinidad, sobre su pobre entendimiento del deseo femenino?" (71, "Is this text then a smiling look at the ineffective power of masculinity, at its poor understanding of feminine desire?"). Aside from being a sign of Gloria's rebellious act of choosing to break the social structure of normative monogamy in search of physical pleasure, the scene of Marta's head giggling also suggests that not everything can be rationalized through science and technology. There is no scientific explanation for Marta's head feeling a connection with her old body, despite Ezequiel and Daniel's belief that they can control and intervene in all of the bodies around them. This invisible link leaves open the possibility of a spiritual or nonempirical force that goes beyond the capacities of modern electronics, putting into question narratives that idolize technological development and decontextualized narratives of progress.

Horror-REAL: State Torture and Reproduction

As Cabiya focuses on the abuse of ECT and scientific rhetoric on a personal level, Alexandra Pagán Vélez's short story collection *Horror-REAL* (2016) shows how these same methods are applicable in a large-scale project of state torture. Puerto Rican author Pagán Vélez is an essayist, poet, editor, and professor. Her extensive literary production includes the short story collections *Amargo* (2014) and *Relatos de domingo* (2014), the poetry collections *Del Alzheimer y otros demonios* (2014) and *Cuando era niña hablaba como niña* (2014), and the children's books *El diccionario y el capitán* (2010) and *Eneida y Martín: dos coquíes muy distintos* (2017), while her academic work focuses on Puerto Rican narrative and poetry. *Horror-REAL* deals with both the creation of mechanical subjects and the use of ECT against political dissidents. *Horror-REAL* is a collection of interrelated stories set in a future dystopia where the concept of humanity has been degraded. The collection's title refers to a live horror/reality show that was created to entertain and scare citizens, filming them committing horrible acts against their loved ones. For example, Río is offered financial security for him and his family and a way out of his dangerous job at the electromagnetic plant in exchange for killing his mother on live television. The show is marketed as part of a fight for freedom of information and entertainment, highlighting the ways that media technology and cultural narratives can work together to break down social and moral structures. Pagán Vélez also connects this horrifying future vision to the current political situation in the United States: "Bienvenidos a horror-REAL, su primer programa de horror transmitido en vivo a todo el globo terráqueo y a las estaciones espaciales de Monsato, McDonald's, Trump Embassies y Walmart, a quienes saludamos y agradecemos su patrocino" (43, "Welcome to *horror-REAL*, your first horror show transmitted live to all of the terrestrial globe and to the Monsato, McDonald's, Trump Embassies and Walmart space stations, to whom we welcome and thank for their patronage"). Thus, the spectacle of real-time psychological and physical torture is connected to environmental crimes, the public health crisis, exploitative capitalism, and White nationalism.

One of the darkest stories in *Horror-REAL*, "El Surgimiento de las Clínicas Tanásicas" ("The Emergence of the Suicide Clinics"), features detailed scenes of a man named Rodrigo Díaz being tortured by electric shock. The story centers on a political debate about the right to commit suicide. While clinics are being set up for those that want to end their lives—the story is careful to point out that these people are not the same as those terminally-ill citizens seeking euthanasia—the opposition forms a movement focused on keeping these people alive. After sedating people who claim interest in suicide and instituting mandatory meditation in public schools, *los provida* (pro-lifers) decide that the only way to curtail the suicide epidemic is through detention and torture. As Rodrigo's case shows, citizens of this future dystopia lose the right to decide what to do with their bodies and are ironically punished through physical torment. This paradox is similar to what Esposito refers to as "humanitarian bombardment": "The most acute oxymoron of humanitarian bombardment lies rather in the superimposition that is manifested in it between the declared intention to defend life and to produce actual death" (4). By referring to the anti-suicide movement as pro-life, the story also connects this horrifying future to the current issues of reproductive rights and the fight for corporeal autonomy still going on in the United States and throughout Latin America. As Iris López (2008) has argued, the particular history of reproductive freedom among Puerto Rican women cannot be reduced to binaries of choice and victimhood but instead must take into account the social, political, historical, and personal conditions and restraints that make it nearly impossible for any choices concerning fertility and reproduction to be truly free (142–143). Labeling the group responsible for kidnapping and torturing citizens as "provida," and thus implying that those fighting for corporeal autonomy must be "anti-vida," serves as an example of the ways reductive language can manipulate political struggles and camouflage abuses of power. While Pagán Vélez does not explicitly discuss women's reproductive rights in this story (though she does in others), there is a clear illustration of the struggle between repressive sociopolitical forces and the right to control one's own body.

The scene of Rodrigo's torture with electric shocks is detailed and strikingly similar to the previously mentioned accounts of ECT abuses in the Caribbean. Pagán Vélez writes:

> Le tapaban la boca con cinta adhesiva de tuberías electromagnéticas. Lo rodean con cordones eléctricos que lo paralizan al menor movimiento. A pesar de esto, el hombre resiste y embiste. Los impulsos y cargas eléctricas lo hacen babearse.... Ahora esa cinta platinada electrificante le pilla su bigote y lo quema poco a poco; el hedor a vellos chamuscados lo aterroriza.... Solloza, le duelen los pómulos, la cabeza, las costillas, sabe que lo matarán, huele su muerte en el pelo quemado. Un puño certero en el estómago lo hace doblarse hacia el frente mientras los voltios lo aguijonean y lo emboban. (34–55, They cover his mouth with adhesive tape made of electromagnetic piping. They surround him with electric cords that paralyze him at the smallest movement. In spite of this, the man resists and pushes forward. The pulses and charges make him drool.... Now that electrified silver tape catches his mustache and burns it bit by bit; the stench of singed hair horrifies him.... He sobs, his lungs, head and ribs hurt, he knows that they will kill him, he smells his death in his burnt hair. A direct fist to the stomach makes him bend forward as the volts sting and put him into a trance.)

Many details in this scene could allude back to historical abuses of ECT. Rodrigo loses all control over his body, including his lungs and head. The multiple mentions of the stench of burning hair reflect how abusers of electroshock technology attempt to dehumanize and disgust the victim. Just as in Brown and Lago's accounts of ECT abuses, here smells and bodily fluids play a large role in situating the victims of this treatment as nonfunctioning and nonhuman. The appearance and odor of biological waste represents a drastic departure from the conceptualization of the body as a series of electrical systems that can be shocked back into compliance. The popular rhetoric surrounding ECT and its medical effectiveness center on its efficiency and tidiness, especially compared to lobotomies and other surgical measures. However, when converted into a means of torture, ECT abuse highlights the messiness and visceral nature of the human body. Both real-life accounts of these abuses and recreations like those in Pagán Vélez's work push back against the narratives of simplicity and efficiency that can be manipulated into justifying electrical torture.

Rodrigo is labeled as a political prisoner for attempting to control his own body. During Rodrigo's torture, "Uno de los brutos lo inclina y ríe a carcajadas porque la electricidad le hace cosquillas.... La taquicardia le produce síncopes y los pequeños sollozos lo hacen objeto de burla de sus captores" (35, "One of the brutes leans him back and roars with laughter because the electricity tickles him.... The tachycardia makes him faint and his small sobs make him the butt of his captors' jokes"). The brute laughing at Rodrigo's pain and the jokes from the other guards signal a complete breakdown of human compassion. The prisoner is no longer viewed as a person who feels pain but as an object to be poked and prodded. Toward the end of "El Surgimiento de las Clínicas Tanásicas," a doctor appears as part of the team overseeing the torture. At this moment, the reader is reminded that all of this is supposedly being done to save Rodrigo's life and that cultural narratives of health and medicine are contributing to this abuse of power. As Colin Dayan notes in *The Story of Cruel and Unusual* (2007), legal jargon and shifting definitions of cruelty are used to justify the dehumanization of prisoners or political dissidents. Through seemingly enlightened rhetoric, the violent regime rationalizes its use of torture or physical harm as a means to reach an idealized level of humanity that would not need such violent measures: "They returned to the cruelties of old in order to testify to the continuation of these cruelties in more 'humane' forms in a politer time" (92). Just like the legal rhetoric used to protect the rights of torturers, narratives of healthcare and public wellbeing can also be manipulated to obfuscate the harm done to individual subjects. "El Surgimiento de las Clínicas Tanásicas" shows the collaboration of state, punitive, and medical institutions in the policing of dissident bodies.

Just as in Cabiya's *La cabeza*, Pagán Vélez's collection shows how ECT abuse can reframe popular understandings of humanity by transforming the body into a mechanical object that can be rewired and controlled. The first story in *Horror-REAL*, "Apocalipsis," shows a possible repercussion of future redefinitions of human worth and hypertechnology, as a government attempts to program model citizens. "Apocalipsis" recounts the spread of a deadly virus that causes parents to kill their children. While superficially the state wants to save the lives of its citizens, in reality they are worried about what their mortality rate would look like compared to the rest of the international community. After a few other ill-conceived solutions, the state eventually turns over child-rearing to a group of cyborgs who promise to convert the process into something both efficient and heavily regulated. One child does manage to escape, offering a quick glimpse at the developmental effects of this dehumanizing program. The story's connections to Caribbean history begin when the government declares a state of emergency and closes the borders, not letting anyone in or out of the country other than doctors or members of the United Nations. Within the context of recent Caribbean history, this point recalls the controversy surrounding UN "peacekeeping" missions in Haiti, started in 2004, that included military raids, accusations of sexual assault, and possible human rights violations. These instances are key examples of both state corruption in the Caribbean and the region's place within international aid organizations. In Pagán Vélez's story, the fact that the only doctors allowed into the country are "representantes médicos solicitados por el propio gobierno" (16, "medical representatives solicited by the government itself") reflects how the state can co-opt medical care, deciding who gets treatment and who doesn't. Apart from involving the United Nations and foreign doctors, the government decides to provide financial incentives and relieve debts for those parents who do not kill their children, but these measures have little effect on the problem. Part of the problem is that the state is fighting to save itself, not the children: "El país necesitaba gente que lo poblara, que produjera, que consumiera, que permitiera el curso natural de la sociedad" (17, "The country needed people to populate it, to produce, to consume, to allow for the natural course of society"). These murders unintentionally reinforce the collective power of the people; without its citizens, the state has no one to govern.

The government's solution is to remove all children, including the president's daughter, from their parents' homes. The first attempt to create a protected community ends in a disaster, as the people meant to guard them incite a massacre that kills all but 144 of the country's children. After the government appeals to the international community for help, an unlikely benefactor emerges:

> Después de largas sesiones con ministros y representantes de los estados y países extranjeros, una delegación de ciborgs hizo aparición en los Asilos Nacionales, Orfanatos de Distrito y Hospitales. Ante tal barbarie, solo unos entes desligados de lo corpóreo y lo emocional del ser humano podrían solucionar esta crisis macabra. (18, After long sessions with state and foreign ministers and representatives, a delegation of cyborgs appeared in the National Asylums, District Orphanages and Hospitals. Facing such barbarity, only entities disconnected from human beings' corporality and emotions could solve this macabre crisis.)

According to this cyborg delegation, the only solution for such a brazen lack of humanity is to allow human-machine hybrids to raise the children. The Orphanage is created, and the childcare model is reconfigured: Pregnant women are brought to the top floor of a tall building, where they give birth with the help of a cyborg doula and a cyborg nurse. As the children develop, they are sent further down the building; each level appears more and more like human reality, slowly conditioning them for outside life. In this way, childcare is compartmentalized and made more efficient; human subjects are constructed in a type of developmental assembly line, merging capitalist modes of production with human reproduction. This foreign takeover of reproduction also cites a history of U.S.-colonial rhetoric and action against Puerto Rico that connected issues of fertility to economic developmental policies. As Laura Briggs (2003) argues, narratives of overpopulation and victimized mothers converted Puerto Rico into a laboratory for contraception and sterilization measures that would then be exported globally (110). Often lost in these discussions, as Pagán Vélez's story shows, is the health and autonomy of the women in question.

The cyborgs, immune to the virus that is turning biological parents into murderers, are engineered to be human enough to not scare the children but still mechanical enough to keep up with manufacturing quotas. For example, the cyborg wet nurse is described as "una máquina hermosamente confeccionada que hacía el simulacro de una reina de belleza, a no ser por el espanto de estar compuesta solo de un torso tendido sobre cables que servían para mantener lactados los infantes" (19, "a beautifully constructed machine that simulated a beauty queen, if it weren't for the fright of being composed of only a torso hanging by cables that served to keep the infants fed with milk"). This same cyborg can also carry out blood, urine, and stool tests while feeding the children. Multitasking and efficiency are connected to a normative concept of beauty and womanhood, and the reference to beauty queens reflects Puerto Rico's long pageant history that both subjects the island to a global colonial gaze and allows it to compete independently of the United States.[5] The cyborgs offer a level of care that is unattainable for humans, and establishing them as the standard indirectly marks biological parents (even before the murderous turn) as unfit. Kathryn Woodward (2000) argues that representations of such reproductive technologies provoke debates on traditional gender roles, the division of labor, and parenthood's connection to progress and development; these interventions into the parent–child relationship "inform our understanding of motherhood: of good and bad mothers, of who is allowed to be a mother and who is not, who is allowed to speak and who has the power to make decisions" (162). In "Apocalipsis," the state-sanctioned removal of the biological mother from the reproduction process highlights the lack of control that people who give birth have over their own bodies and those of their offspring.

This childcare process that conforms to capitalist modes of production creates docile, efficient subjects. The children emerging from this program are described as disciplined, calm, considerate, and healthy. They are said to have "una fría cortesía que permita que no desarrollaran siquiera los roces ni las discusiones típicas de la adolescencia" (20, "a cold courtesy that made it so they didn't develop the typical adolescent frictions or arguments"). In short, while they look and act like model human beings, these children lack the rebelliousness and creativity often apparent in the most formative years. This moment also serves as an allegorical critique of a public education system that has been co-opted more and more by neoliberal forces and a desire to foster uniformity instead of creativity. Despite protests from dissident groups, the government publicly supports the program and encourages parents to continue sending their children, saying, "El proyecto había funcionado a unas escalas inimaginables, había una socialización sana, cívica y homogénea, y en cada generación el Estado contaba con ciudadanos dedicados al servicio y a la paz" (21, "The project had functioned at unimaginable scales, there was a healthy, civic and homogeneous socialization, and in each generation the State can count on citizens dedicated to service and peace"). The program is thus incorporated into a decontextualized narrative of the greater good, marking all dissent as a dangerous and inhumane.

While the system is made as airtight as possible, there are moments in which the children naturally develop these undesired qualities: "El carácter espontáneo y curioso, natural del ser humano, fue subestimado por mandatarios y ciborgs, y numerosos niños tuvieron que ser asesinados al intentar escapar del Orfanato" (19, "The spontaneous and curious character, natural for human beings, was underestimated by officials and cyborgs, and many children had to be killed upon trying to escape the Orphanage"). Electric fences and mechanical dogs are also employed to keep the children inside. Connecting this scene to the ECT abuse in the previous story, just like how Rodrigo's torture was meant to save his life, these children are being detained or killed *for their own good*. One child who managed to escape was LZ34, with a level of perseverance and desire for freedom that the cyborgs could neither understand nor predict. After escaping the compound, LZ34 is picked up by someone named Suix, who initially had trouble believing the stories about the Orphanage. Suix perceives the government's role in LZ34's personality (or lack thereof): "El monótono expresivo y las palabras de LZ34 eran la reminiscencia de los anuncios de los hologramas y altoparlantes del Estado" (23, "LZ34's expressive monotone and words were reminiscent of the announcements from the State's holograms and loudspeakers"). Not only is the former prisoner a product of this system, but the child has also been engineered in a way that perpetuates authoritarian reach. The state has so infiltrated modes of production and reproduction that original thought can only come out as official propaganda. Suix smiles at LZ34 and later that night catches the child practicing this same smile in the mirror. While this only provides a small glimmer of hope at the end of a dark, twisted story, the fact that LZ34 escapes because of human characteristics that could not be engineered out of them suggests that maintaining humanity could be a key to resisting techno-dominance.

Kafka's Last Laugh: Crimes against Capitalism

While Vagabond Beaumont's "Kafka's Last Laugh" also features an electrified woman narrative that deals with colonial repression, this story separates itself in that it highlights the role of the global marketplace and consumerism in the exploitation and extraction of marginalized bodies. Beaumont is a New York–born activist, artist, and filmmaker. He has participated in and organized for the Puerto Rican independence movement since the late 1990s, and his creative work, including the artist collective Ricanstruction Netwerk and the 2008 feature film *Machetero*, reflects these politics. He produced the 1999 punk rock documentary *Ricanstructing Vieques*, which highlights U.S. military occupation of the island. His cinematic work that centers New York includes the shorts *Coney Island Dreaming* (2016), *Coney Island Siren* (2017), *Coney Island Sunrise* (2018), *Baron Saturday of Coney Island* (2019), *Papa Legba of Coney Island* (2020), *The*

Blind Seer of Coney Island (2021), *The Demise of Coney Island* (2022), and the feature-length documentary *All Roads Lead to the Fire Escape* (2017), about Nuyorican poet Jesús Papoleto Meléndez. Vagabond's story "Kafka's Last Laugh" appeared in the 2015 anthology *Octavia's Brood: Science Fiction Stories from Social Justice Movements*, edited by Walidah Imarisha and adrienne maree brown.

"Kafka's Last Laugh" follows Resister Fernandez, a Puerto Rican woman who is arrested in the year 2024 for participating in a protest on Wall Street, the "very epicenter of the capitalist technocracy" (Beaumont 178). Setting the beginning of the story on Wall Street has gained significance in the years after the story's publication, as the role of U.S. banks and hedge funds in the Puerto Rican debt crisis has become clearer; in 2016, the Puerto Rico Oversight, Management, and Economic Stability Act (PROMESA) created the *Junta de Supervisión Fiscal para Puerto Rico* (Financial Oversight and Management Board for Puerto Rico), formally putting the island's financial situation under even more direct U.S. control. PROMESA and its drastic austerity measures represent the latest reinforcement of Puerto Rico's colonial status, fueling both economic distress and state-violence on the island. As Marisol Lebrón (2019) has argued, the inability or disinterest of U.S. and Puerto Rican authorities in renegotiating Puerto Rico's colonial status has pushed both state repression and popular resistance into the realm of biopolitics (4). The rest of the story follows Resister through her wrongful detainment, her shoddy legal defense, and her placement in a prison slavery program in which incarcerated people are drugged with nanotechnology and forced to work retail jobs. Beaumont's story illustrates how global economic and political struggles can be inscribed on the bodies of individual marginalized subjects.

At the Wall Street rally, Resister attempts to cross the barriers that are caging in the protestors, euphemistically labeled as "free speech assembly zones" (Beaumont 178). She is not satisfied with the limited freedom granted to the protestors, which is more a symbol of what the state could take away. She pushes over a police officer in riot gear, and another one grabs her as two fellow protestors break through to help her out. The ensuing tug-of-war marks the first time in the story that Resister's recognizes the loss of control of her body: "For a moment, she felt like a ragdoll being fought over by siblings" (Beaumont 178). Though she finds the strength to wrestle herself away, she trips over another protestor sprawled out on the ground. The cop pounces on her and hits her in the head with a club, knocking her unconscious. The violent way in which these protestors are treated shows how their ideological contestations are counteracted with physical repression, putting the focus back on the dissenting body. Resister later wakes up briefly while being waterboarded. Her treatment alludes to the torture of political prisoners in the Guantanamo Bay detention camp, a focal point in the history of the U.S. military and its colonial presence in the Caribbean.

While the military prison was established in 2002 during President George W. Bush's War on Terror, the naval base was inaugurated in 1903. The base is technically leased by the United States from the Cuban government. However, the checks have not been deposited since the start of the Cuban Revolution, except once in 1969, which Fidel Castro called a mistake. Despite campaign promises, President Barack Obama also failed to close the Guantanamo Bay detention center during his two terms in office. While there has been much international debate over the continued use of Guantanamo Bay, Vagabond's story imagines a world in which state torture is openly conducted in or around New York City. Resister tries not to submit to the interrogation, though it is unclear what information they are trying to get out of her or if the goal is to simply break her down. The state-sanctioned violence causes her to lose control and possession of her body. Vagabond writes, "In her mind, she had it all figured out. Instead of using the adrenaline kick to breath, she would use it to break her bonds and then bash their brains in. But her body would not cooperate with her thoughts. It was locked in an instinctual survival mode" (179). Her "locked" body, torn down by the repressive forces that she resists, is transformed into an object or machine to which she does not have access. Colonial and authoritarian control has taken away her ability to define and control her own body in an attempt to both destroy and rebuild it as part of an ideal subject.

When Resister finally wakes up three days later in a hospital bed, her court-appointed public defender informs her that she has taken a plea deal instead of going to trial. Resister was not involved in these decisions, since the doctors had ordered that she remain sedated for a few days. It is unclear if the doctors were saving her life or purposefully colluding with a justice system that offers punishment instead of rehabilitation. Resister's lawyer defends his actions by saying, "I tried to move the trial to a date when you could be present, but the judge felt pressure, both politically and from the media, to wrap up as many of these Wall Street Riot trials as soon as he could" (Beaumont 179). Resister is too beaten down, both physically and emotionally, to protest her lack of a fair trial, possibly because she doubts that the treatment would have been any different even if she had been conscious. The lawyer goes on, explaining the charges: "You were charged with 680 counts of seditious conspiracy to overthrow legitimate business interests; terrorism; and assault of six police officers. I pleaded you down to a mandatory three-year sentence for aggravated organized protest" (Beaumont 180). By the lawyer's list, the most serious charge against Resister is not terrorism but threatening business interests. The public defender exits after fifteen minutes, leaving Resister to contemplate the ridiculousness of her situation. Unable to do anything else, Resister begins to laugh hysterically. Her deliriousness passes to the other patients in the room, until a doctor enters with a syringe and sedates them all back into unconsciousness. Her lack of control in the situation, obfuscated by a network of secrecy and lawyers, is reminiscent of Josef K's issues in

Franz Kafka's 1925 novel *The Trial*, illuminating a possible reason for the title of Beaumont's story.

Resister is then taken to Sunny Day Prison, Incorporated, and finds out that a psychological evaluation has shown her to be an ideal candidate for a special program called CROC: Corrective Retail Operation Confinement. This conflation of psychological treatment and incarceration is reminiscent of the previously mentioned abuses of these systems by Trujillo and Castro, as well as the ways that the justice system in the United States disproportionately targets people of color. However, "Kafka's Last Laugh" takes this issue a step further, connecting unfair treatment of political prisoners to a global neoliberal market. The CROC program forces incarcerated people to work in large chain retail stores, known popularly as Prison Malls. The program is seen as doubly beneficial, as the store receives cheap labor—workers receive "fifty percent reduction of one-tenth of the federally set minimum wage, minus 360 percent of taxes paid by the median household," which comes out to 0.7 cents/hour—while the prisoners are "rehabilitated" though a reorientation with capitalism (Beaumont 182). As the intake officer explains to Resister, "The best way to rehabilitate you and others like you is to develop a healthy respect for capitalism. In doing so, you'll channel all your desires and energies through capitalism. If you can learn to place proper value on your desires through capitalism and use it as a moral compass, you could be cured of your criminal tendencies" (181–182). Not only does this rhetoric represent a horrifying magnification of our current obsession with consumerism, but it also extrapolates on the role of shopping centers in the reshaping of public space and mobility. Arlene Dávila (2016) argues that "as shopping malls continue to dominate the physical landscape of so many Latin American cities, they are becoming the space where equity and citizenship rights are consistently contested" (161). Though "Kafka's Last Laugh" takes place in and around New York, the appropriation of commercial spaces by punitive institutions suggests a similar move in which consumerism and buying power continue to inform legitimacy within a larger understanding of who makes up the public and who can inhabit public space.

The CROC program involves a daily dose of a medicine-like nanotechnology called Contentina, which monitors the prisoner's vital signs, tracks them via GPS (Global Positioning System), and transmits "corrective electroshock signals to the nervous system if it's deemed that your behavior is working against your rehabilitation" (Beaumont 183). These punitive electroshocks are the detail that connects this story to the historical and rhetorical legacies of ECT abuse. By using the language of "rehabilitation," the prisoner's crimes are converted into illnesses or ailments that can be overcome. In this case, the social illness that the institutions want to cure is a criminal disrespect for capitalism. The nanotechnological version of ECT abuse presented in "Kafka's Last Laugh" represents a particularly ominous deployment of the practice that already blurs a line between treatment and torture. In the other accounts and fictional representations of ECT abuse, the machine itself is bulky and intimidating, but it is at least visible. Advocates have written about how fear-inducing science fiction narratives on nanotechnology that predict the worst-case scenarios reduce society's complex relationship to techno-science and even inhibit important scientific research and development. For example, sociologist José López (2006) writes, "Discourses that extrapolate technoscientific development into the future, through SF narrative elements, contain assumptions about, amongst other things, the nature of being, the dynamics of historical change, the aspirations of citizens, and the relationship between society, culture and technoscience" (331). While meant to highlight the irresponsibility of many nanotech science fiction narratives, I would argue that it is precisely by understanding technology not as an isolated entity but as part of a socio-technological network made up of past and present human actions that these representations and warnings become more useful and necessary. Just as with traditional ECT, it is not the technology itself that makes nanotech dangerous but the ways in which people misuse it in order to reinforce historically oppressive structures.

While the punitive aspect of the Contentina nano-drug represents an alarming speculation into the future of state violence, the technology's ability to monitor the prisoner with GPS capabilities highlights another aspect of Beaumont's vision of the future of political dissidence. This detail alludes to how the increased surveillance of those labeled as terrorists or potential terrorists—labels that are doled out under racist assumptions of who represents a threat and who should be protected—has put marginalized populations in the United States at higher risk of state violence and imprisonment long before but especially since 2001. The story also mentions how Contentina tracks vital signs by attaching to the prisoner's nervous system to "monitor and transmit information such as body temperature, eye dilation, adrenaline, oxygen intake, and heart rate," (183). This inclusion of biological surveillance represents a seemingly dystopian lack of personal privacy and *Minority Report*-like practices of predictive policing, while also referencing the intrusive surveillance techniques already being developed and deployed, such as the use of facial recognition software and artificial intelligence. Resister is surveilled as both a prisoner and low-wage worker, highlighting how policing and retail institutions have colluded and converged. Madison Van Oort (2019) has studied the increased surveillance of retail employees and notes that those workers are often women, people of color, and queer, "members of populations that have been tracked and policed by both the state and capital for many years" (212). Van Oort continues, "Technoscience, capital, and the state work together to normalize surveillance, exacerbate inequality, and increase points of contact between marginalized workers and police" (220). By combining these violent surveillance practices with ECT abuse, the Contentina drug represents the present and future of state violence via techno-dominance.

With so many forces working against her, Resister feels as if there is nothing she can do. The invasive technology inside her, with its ability to both track and shock her, symbolizes her complete loss of control. Her body becomes the center of dissidence and punishment, reminiscent of another Kafka text from 1919, "The Penal Colony," in which prisoners' crimes are violently inscribed into their flesh. When Resister asks why nobody speaks out against this obviously abusive program, she is told that the short-lived protests ended when people saw how the "new 'Prison-hire' initiative" made retail prices so much cheaper (Beaumont 182). This repressive machine runs because its nonfunctioning parts—that is, political disobedience—are rooted out of the system. While the prisoners in the story are the only ones directly controlled by invasive nanotechnology, it is clear that the complicit supporters of this program have also been converted into docile subjects, giving up their political agency. Resister spends some time navigating through the bureaucracy of the CROC program, highlighting the inefficiencies of this social machine. Eventually, she feels so defeated that once again all she can do is laugh. The guards try to shock her into submission, but nothing happens. In that moment, Resister realizes that Contentina can neither track nor punish her as long as she is laughing. Resister takes back control of her body and begins to plan the resistance. She thinks to herself: "This laughter at the absurdity of it all brought the mad reckless optimism every revolution needs. This wasn't just a threat to the prison. It was a threat to everything. Laughter was the means by which everything could change" (Beaumont 186). The story ends as the laughter spreads throughout the prison, with doctors and guards scrambling to regain control.

For Resister, laughter was a natural response to how absurd her world had become; it was also a very human one. She realizes in this moment that the way to dismantle the repressive structures that want to dehumanize her is to reassert the part of her that remains human—to laugh at the technologies that wish to control her. In *Humoring Resistance: Laughter and the Excessive Body in Latin American Women's Fiction* (2004), Dianna C. Niebylski argues that laughter can be a rebellious act because of its incomprehensibility, untranslatability, and strangeness (72). In the context of Latin American literature, laughter "opens up a space for indecorous excess and illicit pleasure ... to counter the rarefied images and purified sounds of victimized femininity" (Niebylski 2). Resister's laugh is not only a rebellion to the socio-technological system that attempts to enslave her but also to the social construction of gender that restricts and defines her body. The excessive body that comes out of laughter becomes a site of contestation, offering "unsuspected and unexpected powers of dissolution, disruption and dislocation" that are "often aimed at dissolving fixed limits and borders or poking holes in the pretentions or reductive solemnity of social institutions and cultural grammars" while encouraging "ex-centricity and civil disobedience" (Niebylski 4). Despite the forces trying to control and objectify her, Resister's laughter at the end of the story re-centers her corporeality and pleasure—a grave threat to the repressive machine that runs on docile, electrified subjects.

LZ34's attempted smile at the end of Pagán Vélez's "Apocalipsis" has a similar affect. Smiling is a human display of humanity and a physical act that transcends verbal language. LZ34 was engineered in a way that removed all other traces of emotion or curiosity, a subject created to fit neatly and obediently into a larger mechanism. In a system in which efficiency is valued above everything else, in which conveyor-belt-style child-rearing replaces affective parenthood, any corporeal gesture that veers away from conformity is unnecessary and unwanted. By applying emotionless economic practices and modes of production to human development, the state in *Horror-REAL* marks the personal pleasure normally associated with childhood as a threat to the fragile nation. The image of LZ34 smiling in the mirror after such a mechanized upbringing suggests that humanity could be an innate quality that is not easily programmed out. This sort of embodied resistance is also clear in the sexual defiance of Gloria in Cabiya's *La cabeza*. Gloria, despite being drugged and used in a scientific experiment without her consent, refuses to play the role of the docile body. Instead, she escapes a system of patriarchal power in search of her own sexual pleasure. While her husband loses interest in her mechanical body, Gloria never stops understanding herself as a sexual being with desires and needs, even when she is mostly a collection of wires and tubes. Gloria goes beyond the prescribed purpose of her cyborg body; the electrification of sexual pleasure returns the act to its most simple and corporeal level, allowing Gloria to make the practical decision of staying with whoever best pleases her physically. While the technological repression enacted by the abuse of ECT attempts to disregard the body and elevate the mind as the container of the true self, the manifestation of a rebellious, excessive body in a physical gesture highlights the body's power to assert itself and its own agency.

The excessive bodies described in the texts of Cabiya, Pagán Vélez, and Beaumont show the discursive and political potentials of rebellious electrified bodies through the re-centering of their excessive corporeality. While these characters do not expect that these gestures alone will topple structures of techno-dominance, they do use their bodies to reflect the importance of maintaining essential human characteristics—happiness, empathy, a desire for equality and justice—even as hypertechnology alters our understandings of humanity. Instead of blindly embracing or rejecting new technologies, these science fiction texts question them and delve deeper into their histories and potentials, illuminating the socio-technological rhetorical networks that sustain the official repression of vulnerable subjects. While there is little in the way of hope at the end of these stories, they do provide possible strategies for embodied resistance in the face of uncertain hypertechnological futures.

CHAPTER 2

Nuclear Weapons

MISSILES, RADIATION, AND ARCHIVES

On April 14, 1948, Rafael Trujillo held a groundbreaking ceremony for the *Faro a Colón*, or Columbus Lighthouse, a monument, museum, and mausoleum commemorating Christopher Columbus's arrival in the Americas. While the planning of this monument, including an international architecture competition, had started before he came to power, Rafael Trujillo saw the massive project as a symbol of the Dominican Republic's European, Christian, and capitalist ideals and as a way to publicly display this historical link to Columbus on an international stage. As Edgardo Rodríguez Juliá writes in his 1992 crónica "La isla al revés" ("The Upside-Down Island"), Trujillo contracted Puerto Rican physicist Amador Cobas to design a nuclear detonator for the inauguration of the building site (108). Less than three years after the United States detonated devastating bombs over Hiroshima and Nagasaki, the Dominican president saw the use of nuclear weapons for construction as a symbol of Western progress: "Por impulso de la fuerza nuclear desgarramos la superficie de la tierra para la construcción de este monumento, utilizando por primera vez en la historia ese fin destructor en un propósito de paz y fraternidad" (108, "Powered by nuclear force we will tear open the earth's surface for the construction of this monument, utilizing for the first time in history this destructive end for a purpose of peace and fraternity"). Trujillo's rhetoric at this event showed a desire to dominate nature, redefine the destructive weapon, and forge international solidarity using nuclear technology. Such larger-than-life technologies often lend themselves to grandiose rhetoric and narratives, often ignoring the concrete implications of their physical use. In a sign that the regime was more prepared for the symbolism of a nuclear detonator than its actual repercussions, Trujillo then watched as the enormous rocks that shot into the air from the explosion came crashing down on the hood of Vice President Manuel Troncoso's car (108). According to Rodríguez Juliá, the embarrassment from this episode dissuaded the notoriously superstitious

Trujillo from pursuing the project any further (107). Whether it was because of that explosion, World War II, or Trujillo's desire to commemorate his own successes over anything else, the construction of the lighthouse did not resume until 1986, during Joaquín Balaguer's regime.

Trujillo's call for harmony and goodwill at the ceremony went against the dictator's violent actions and policies. The elevation of this historical connection to Christopher Columbus reflected Trujillo's reliance on promoting the Dominican Republic's Whiteness in nationalist discourse, complemented by a racist and violent anti-Haitianism. This monument to Columbus fit well with Trujillo's educational policies at the time, which emphasized Christian civilization and Hispanic tradition while minimizing and justifying the massacre of thousands of Haitians in 1937 (Sagás 61–62). The use of nuclear technology can also be connected to this desire to promote Whiteness on a national stage. In *Race, Ethnicity and Nuclear War: Representations of Nuclear Weapons and Post-Apocalyptic Worlds* (2011), Paul Williams critiques the racially coded language of nationhood, civilization, modernity, and terrorism both in official discourse on nuclear war and in many mainstream literary or cinematic representations. Williams argues that nuclear weapons are popularly understood as sources of White power "because the weapons themselves symbolize the achievements, atrocities and attitudes of European and American modernity" and "because the post-nuclear-war future that such weapons could make possible is deemed to reproduce a (European) colonial or (American) frontier dynamic" (15–16). The result is a popular mindset that deems certain superpowers as legitimate peacekeepers that can be responsible for dangerous weapons, protecting the developed world from smaller nations or non-White Others that cannot be trusted with such power. Wittingly or not, Trujillo's desire to exhibit control over nuclear weapons aligns with his goals of promoting Whiteness and placing the Dominican Republic in a lineage of European civilization.

Nuclear technology is weaponized in many ways: larger-than-life explosions, silent radiation, or even the mere hypothetical threat of its use. Fear of unforeseeable future devastation or ongoing repercussions from past exposures contribute to the power of nuclear weapons within structures of technodominance. The socio-technological network of popular narratives makes up a nuclear archive that informs the public's relationship to the technology; this collective archive affects how nuclear events are remembered, how victims are mourned, and how survivors are understood. This chapter examines the ways in which science fiction can reshape and contest the colonizing rhetoric and narratives surrounding the historical deployment of nuclear weapons in the Caribbean. The three texts studied in this chapter—Rey Emmanuel Andújar's short story "Gameon" (2014), Yasmín Silvia Portales's "Las extrañas decisiones de Vladimir Denísovich Jiménez" (2016), and Erick Mota's novella *Trabajo Extra* (2014)—insert themselves into the socio-technological networks surrounding nuclear weapons, pushing past sublime explosions and mushroom clouds to create a more honest nuclear archive. These texts recognize and combat the rhetorical legacies of nuclear weapons in the Caribbean, creating spaces for proper mourning, recovery, and survival.

The most notable single event in Caribbean nuclear history is the Cuban Missile Crisis, known in Cuba as the *Crisis de octubre* ("October Crisis"). From October 16–28, 1962, the United States and Soviet Union veered dangerously close to nuclear war because of a delivery of Soviet missiles to Cuba in response to the U.S. missiles already stationed in Turkey. Six years later, in his 1968 plenary session of the central committee of the Communist Party of Cuba, Fidel Castro's reflections on the missile crisis suggest that the regime was more prepared for the talking points concerning nuclear weapons than the missiles themselves. At this meeting, Castro admitted that he was shocked by how large the weapons were: "Nosotros no sabíamos ni cómo era un cohete de esos, ni que tamaño tenía, ni dónde había que instalarlo, ni por dónde se disparaba, porque si nosotros hubiésemos sabido cómo eran los cohetes esos ... qué fácil habría sido tomar una decisión" (84, "We didn't even know what one of those rockets was like, nor what size it was, nor where to install it, nor from where to shoot it, because if we had known what those rockets were like, it would have been easy to make a decision"). This break between the rhetorical power of nuclear weapons and the danger of the actual weapons highlights the fact that much of the technology's power is based in language and performance. As Jacques Derrida (1984) argued, "Just as all language, all writing, every poetico-performative or theoretico-informative text dispatches, sends itself, allows itself to be sent, so today's missiles ... allow themselves to be described more readily than ever as dispatches in writing (code, inscription, trace, and so on)" (29). This conceptualization of nuclear war as textual also recognizes the power of the socio-technological narratives that surround nuclear technology: "Nuclear war has not taken place, it is a speculation, an invention in the sense of a fable or an invention to be invented in order to make a place for it or to prevent it from taking place (as much invention is needed for the one as for the other), and for the moment all this is only literature" (Derrida 28). These speculations are invented to create a space for nuclear war (such as the invention of an enemy that can only be defeated through nuclear intervention) or to prevent it from happening (such as public fears over the long-term health and environmental effects of radiation). Recognizing the role of text in the deployment or deterrence of nuclear war highlights the importance of studying how popular narratives and rhetoric surrounding nuclear weapons contribute to the technology's power.

Tomás Diez Acosta's *Octubre de 1962: un paso del holocausto* (2008, *October 1962: One Step Away from Holocaust*) offers one account of the official conversations between the Soviet Union and Cuba leading up to the international crisis. According to Diez Acosta, Soviet leader Nikita Khrushchev understood the implications of placing such powerful technology so close to the United States, saying: "Tenemos que pagarles con la misma moneda, darles a probar su propio remedio, y obligarlos a sentir en su propio cuerpo lo que significa vivir colmados por armas nucleares" (90, "We have to pay them with the same currency, give them a taste of their own medicine, and make them feel in their own body what it means [to] live surrounded by nuclear weapons"). This quote stands out because while the nuclear missiles were to be pointed at the United States, it was the Cubans who were actually surrounded by this volatile technology. Cuba was ultimately left out of the negotiations that put an end to the thirteen-day nuclear showdown; this quote suggests a disregard for the political and physical dangers put on the Cuban people. At the same time, the idea that one could "feel in their own body" the threat of nuclear war highlights the technology's effect on corporality even before any missiles are launched. As Arundhati Roy (2003) writes, "That's what nuclear bombs do. Whether they're used or not, they violate everything that is humane. They alter the meaning of life itself" (7). While the science fiction texts studied in this chapter primarily focus on the postnuclear-event effects on conceptualizations of bodies and humanity, they also highlight the damage that nuclear rhetoric and threats can have beyond explosions and radiation.

In another notable moment, Diez Acosta quotes Khrushchev as reassuring skeptical Cuban officials by saying, "No te preocupes, yo voy a coger a Kennedy por los testículos" (98–99, "Don't worry, I am going to grab Kennedy by the testicles"). Khrushchev frames this potentially devastating conflict as a challenge of masculinity, emphasizing the role of hypermasculine rhetoric and anxieties within military actions. This quote reshapes the potential nuclear war as a battle of virility between two men, making invisible all possible victims that would lose their lives or be affected by the aftermath. Carol Cohn (1993), who has analyzed the role of gender in the rhetoric surrounding the development and deployment of nuclear weapons, argues that hypermasculine perspectives and an aversion to all seemingly feminine language among defense intellectuals makes it difficult to discuss or deliberate outcomes other than massive destruction and death. Cohn writes, "What gets left out, then, is the emotional, the concrete, the particular, the human bodies and their vulnerability, human lives and their subjectivity—all of which are marked as feminine in the binary dichotomies of gender discourse" (232). The hypermasculine rhetoric and symbolism that increases the chances of nuclear disaster has also been deployed in official memory projects around the Cuban Missile Crisis. In the essay "What the Russians Left Behind" (2012), Cuban science fiction writer Yoss writes that in 1992, the Cuban government attempted to celebrate this historic moment as a challenge to U.S. imperialism, most notably with the construction of what he calls the "vertical, phallic" monument on El Chivo beach. Yoss writes, "Although we proved to be a mere chess piece to the superpowers, we came out of the mess with an inflated sense of our own importance in the world stage" (213). This mix of triumphant rhetoric and embarrassment toward Cuba's secondary role in the negotiations makes this moment a key point of departure for nuclear fiction, especially in the texts by Andújar and Portales to be analyzed later in this chapter.

The historical framing of this moment by the Cuban government speaks to the role of nuclear weapons in shaping nationalist imaginaries. In Diez Acosta's account of Che Guevara's postcrisis words, the missile worked better as a rhetorical, nationalist device than as a military strategy: "Hemos sido dignos del [espíritu de Maceo] en estos momentos difíciles que acaban de pasar, en esta confrontación donde hemos estado a milímetros quizás de la catástrofe atómica" (214, "We have dignified [the spirit of Maceo] in these difficult moments that have just passed, in this confrontation where we have been maybe millimeters from atomic catastrophe"). Even though there is a tone of regret in Guevara's statement, and an admission that a political move could have ended in nuclear disaster, the weapons fit a revolutionary and anti-colonial narrative, as illustrated by the reference to Antonio Maceo, the leader of the Cuban War of Independence and a national hero. During the crisis, Castro framed his rejection of the international community's call for independent weapons inspections on the island as an issue of Cuban sovereignty. However, he would later admit that he risked Cuba's autonomy by accepting the missiles, rightly fearing the political consequences of entering an uneven military relationship with the Soviet Union. Castro said, "A nosotros no nos gustaban los cohetes ... por la forma en que eso dañaría la imagen de la Revolución ... y que la presencia de los proyectiles, de hecho, nos convertía en una base militar soviética y eso tenía un costo político alto" (Diez Acosta 96, "We didn't like the rockets ... because of the way in which they could harm the image of the Revolution ... and that the presence of the missiles, in fact, converted us into a Soviet military base and that had a high political cost"). Nuclear rhetoric can seemingly fortify nationalism, while the dangers associated with the actual weapons can threaten notions of sovereignty. This paradox highlights both the rhetorical power of this technology within structures of techno-dominance and the difficulties of ever really being in control of something so inherently volatile.

While the Cuban Missile Crisis remains the center of Caribbean nuclear history, it is not the only case of nuclear rhetoric working its way into national and anti-colonial politics. For example, popular opinion and narratives surrounding nuclear weapons have also fueled the debate over techno-colonialism in Vieques, the Puerto Rican island that was home to a U.S. Navy base from 1941 to 2003. Decades of narratives featuring the mistreatment of *viequenses*, including Carmelo Rodríguez Torres's *Veinte siglos después del homicidio* (1971) and Pedro Juan Soto's *Usmaíl* (1959), intertwined with real anxieties over radiation and poisoning, have fueled a credibility gap between residents and the military.

High levels of cancer on the island and the dangers of radiation became primary talking points in the protests to shut down the base, and debates over radiation intensified in the mid-1990s when the U.S. Navy announced the construction of a massive radar installation as part of the "war on drugs" (Baver 105). This focus on physical health, led by women activists on the island, was an essential step toward pushing out the U.S. Navy, as demonstrators could no longer be accused of anti-patriotism (Kadalie 107).[1] However, the dismissal of the military has not completely calmed fears of U.S. colonial interference and coverup. Since closing the base, the U.S. Fish and Wildlife Service designated most of that land as a wildlife refuge. Many residents of Vieques mistrust the fact that the land remains under federal control and believe that its status blocks nongovernmental researchers from learning more about the continued environmental effects (Davis et al. 177). The globalizing forces of the tourism industry have also colluded in obstructing the situation, as U.S. publications have lauded this colonial occupation and the current protected status for allowing Vieques to maintain its natural beauty (Davis et al. 170). Nuclear techno-colonialism, environmental-scientific rhetoric, and the global market appear to collude against the people of Vieques who seek answers.

Fears over the long-term effects of nuclear radiation have been fueled by government secrecy on the part of the United States. For example, the USS *Killen*, a destroyer used in the 1958 Operation Hardtack I for atomic bomb tests in the Marshall Islands, was moved to Puerto Rico for weapons testing in 1963. The ship was retired and scuttled close to Vieques in 1975. In 1999, a marine research team investigated the site of the sunken USS *Killen* and discovered carcinogens in the water around it, possibly caused by the ship's role in nuclear testing. They also found live bombs and many barrels that may have been storing toxic waste in the wreckage (Levin, 2003). While the Agency for Toxic Substances and Disease Registry, part of the U.S. Department of Health and Human Services, declared the site safe in 2013, many in Vieques doubt the objectivity of the federal study. In 2000, the *Comité Pro Rescate y Desarollo de Vieques* (Committee for the Rescue and Development of Vieques, or CPRDV) issued a press release calling for a full investigation into a practice weapon lost off the coast of Vieques in 1966. This came after journalist Pedro Rosa Nales reported on San Juan's WAPA-TV that recently declassified documents characterized the weapon as a nuclear bomb. The U.S. Navy denied the incident, tried to have the journalist arrested for espionage, and asked the U.S. Federal Communications Commission (FCC) to rescind the channel's license ("Comunicado," 2000). In 2001, the Puerto Rican government asked to be included in the European Union's investigation into the possible carcinogenic effects of depleted uranium, which the U.S. Navy admitted to testing in Vieques (Irizarry, 2001). Whether or not depleted uranium represents a significant health risk, the request for an outside investigation shows a lack of trust in the objectivity of U.S. institutions, based on a history of official obfuscation. The inability to achieve emotional closure and scientific understanding in the aftermath of a nuclear event represents an assault on memory, both in terms of public remembrance and personal mourning. David Kupferman (2015) writes, "The erasure of survivance and prolepsis of victimhood . . . totalizes the experience of the nuclear-affected other, not the least result of which is the denial of the face (and face to face) of survival in its binary dance with that of victimization". This is a doubly violent outcome of the deployment of nuclear technology: dominant power is established through the nuclear event (or the threat of such event), and then that same power is reinforced though the official institutions that control historical records and shape public archives.

This Caribbean nuclear history has inspired an overwhelming number of texts—both in the genre of science fiction and within other narrative styles—that negotiate legacies of nuclear techno-dominance.[2] The three texts chosen for analysis in this chapter all investigate different but important aspects of nuclear technology, from the sublime explosions and radiation fears to the structural and social changes within a techno-colonial system built on the threat of nuclear war. Rey Emmanuel Andújar's "Gameon" focuses on the ecological impact of nuclear weapons and shows how such affronts to nature also harm human bodies. Yasmín Silvia Portales's story "Las extrañas decisiones de Vladimir Denísovich Jiménez" looks at the colonial and social effects of nuclear war, and whether there is a place for queer bodies in a postnuclear society. Erick Mota's novella *Trabajo Extra* delves into the ongoing dangers of radiation and imagines an escape from nuclear techno-colonialism that evokes Afro-modernity and alternative modes of progress. By inserting themselves into the popular nuclear archive that surrounds these weapons, these texts push back against the ongoing legacy of colonizing nuclear narratives and rhetoric.

"Gameon": Eco-Critical Responses to Nuclear Disaster

Popular nuclear archives that obfuscate events, diminish ongoing dangers, and forget survivors maintain colonizing structures of techno-dominance. In such cases, two types of bodies disappear—those lost in the nuclear event and those that survived but were not granted the space to reconcile or negotiate their experiences. By alluding to past near-apocalyptic events and the ongoing dangers of exposure, the fictions analyzed in this chapter create a space for affected bodies and places to be recognized and remembered. Redefining how these events and victims are remembered could help prevent future disasters; as Junot Díaz writes in his 2012 essay on apocalyptic events, "ruin-reading" allows one to challenge the underlying social and geopolitical structures behind large-scale devastation. This type of project often requires perspectives and dramatizations that keep going where the official record stops, filling in the gaps and silences. According to Díaz, ruin-reading "requires nuance, practice, and no small amount of heart.... It could in fact save your life". In this way, challenging and reshaping the popular nuclear archive is a rebellious act against techno-dominance. In *Savage Perils: Racial Frontiers and Nuclear Apocalypse in American Culture* (2007), Patrick Sharp argues that the authors of popular and official nuclear histories have often promoted racist and colonizing narratives that link technological and social progress. However, Sharp argues that politically engaged nuclear fictions can and should highlight and challenge the gendered and racially coded narratives and rhetoric that advance large-scale repression: "They should remind us of the dangers of unchecked racism, militarism, and nationalism and keep us vigilant against the never-ending stream of distortions and outright lies disseminated by our leaders" (223). The power of nuclear science fiction comes from its ability to provide warnings and potential worst-case scenarios while also forcing the reader to reconsider their relationships to technology, technological development, and techno-nationalist rhetoric.

While nuclear fictions may predict future disasters, they can also rewrite histories and reimagine possible outcomes of past threats. One such text is the short story "Gameon" (2014), by Dominican writer and performer Rey Emmanuel Andújar. Andújar was born in Santo Domingo and currently resides in Chicago. He has published *El factor carne* (2005), *El hombre triángulo* (2005), *Candela* (2008), *Saturnario* (2011), and *Los gestos inútiles* (2016), and he has created the performance pieces *Antípoda* and *Ciudadano Cero*. "Gameon" was published as part of a special section on science fiction in *Contratiempos*, a Chicago-based literary magazine that promotes Spanish-language writing in the city. The story's focus on the environmental effects of technology also classifies it as climate fiction (cli-fi), an increasingly popular literary field that delves into climate change and corresponding environmental disasters. Cli-fi has become particularly useful to discussions of techno-dominance in the Caribbean, due to the possibility that smaller islands will be first to suffer from rising water levels caused by the environmental sins of larger economic and political superpowers. As Lizabeth Paravisini-Gebert (2010), who links the destruction of the Caribbean ecosystem all the way back to the arrival of Columbus, writes, "The rapid deterioration of the environment in the Caribbean region, which has taken place within the lifetime of many of its residents, has led to a 'sense of ending,' to the apocalyptic dread of a potential ecological disaster that can erase the islands, their peoples, and cultures" (114). This "sense of ending" has led to several fictional takes on the future of Caribbean environmentalism.[3] Paravisini-Gebert continues:

> In the Caribbean region, where post-colonial politics, foreign controlled development, and the struggle for economic survival has [for] many decades forced environmental concerns out of the mainstream of national discourse,

writers and artists have responded to increasing fears of global warming, food insecurity, habitat losses, mangrove destruction, and the uncontrolled tourism-related development with eloquent defenses of the fragile ecologies of the islands in the name of the nation. (114)

While texts like Andújar's "Gameon" attempt to highlight the dystopic futures that are becoming more and more plausible, there are still questions as to the impact that fiction can have on environmental policy and activism.

"Gameon" is a meta-literary text, first describing the narrator's failed attempt at writing a science fiction story and then recounting a made-up nuclear novel entitled *Gameon*, written by fictional author Lester Dakeng. The narrator at the beginning of the story is uneasy about writing science fiction but ultimately decides to try because he is an adjunct professor and needs money in the middle of the summer. "Gameon" takes the form of a personal essay and book review, making it possible to fit an entire science fiction world into just a single page. The narrator finds Dakeng's *Gameon* in Bucket O'Blood, a popular horror and science fiction bookstore in Chicago, adding to the context of the story by positioning the narrator as a Latinx writer exploring themes of techno-dominance from within the United States. This detail stresses the complex position of many Latinx and Latin American writers, especially in the genre like science fiction, with a long history of colonizing, racist, and misogynistic rhetoric. Dakeng's *Gameon* imagines a world in the aftermath of a nuclear incident in which "la crisis de los misiles en Cuba no fue evitada" (23, "the missile crisis in Cuba was not avoided"). Andújar's story is a uchronia, a subgenre in which alternative worlds are created based on specific historical changes. According to Javier de la Torre Rodríguez (2012), the uchronia is one of the most complex and transgressive science fiction subgenres because of its ability to contest official histories and analyze the consequences of human actions (8). For example, "Gameon" repositions the Cuban Missile Crisis as a conflict between Cuba and the United States instead of a U.S.-Soviet clash that manipulated the Castro regime as a pawn in a much larger global struggle. This reframing emphasizes the possibility that if missiles had been launched, Cuba would have felt the immediate retaliation more than the Soviet Union. Highlighting the dangers that the Cuban people risked as two larger world powers and the Cuban government played political games is a step toward a clearer history of nuclear techno-dominance in the Caribbean.

While the main plot of the fictional novel focuses on a cadet with cyborg appendages named Gameon who attempts to smuggle himself out of what is left of the Caribbean, most of Andújar's story focuses on describing the dystopic world that the missile attack created. While Cuba launched the rockets, the United States deployed an ectoplasmic shield that protected the country from most of the effects of the nuclear weapons. Referencing a history of U.S. technocolonialism in the region, this shield increased the damage done by the missiles to the Caribbean region: "En cuanto al Caribe, el escudo actuó como reflejo, así que las islas recibieron una dosis doble de radiación" (23, "As for the Caribbean, the shield acted like a reflector, so that the islands received a double dose of radiation"). The Caribbean islands and people feel the brunt of the impact from the nuclear strike, showing the risks of ever launching nuclear weapons, especially at such a close target. In the story, nuclear weapons represent an uncontrollable power that is as likely to affect those that deploy them as much as the intended target. In the United States, while the shield mostly did its job, some radiation did manage to seep through: "Aunque el daño fue disminuido por la resistencia del escudo protector, el sur quedó afectado para siempre" (23, "Although the protective shield diminished the damage, the South would be forever affected"). By singling out the Caribbean and the American South as the victims of this nuclear crisis, this story points to the historical, economic, and ecological connections between the two regions. As Deborah Cohn (2007) argues, Latin America, the Caribbean, and the U.S. South are linked through, among other things, "the ongoing experience of colonialism and imperial expansionism, and the continuing hegemony of white subjects, policies, and ideology" (39). By naming casualties on both sides of the conflict, "Gameon" highlights the repressive biopolitics that span borders and regions, while also making visible the affected bodies so often ignored by nuclear narratives that represent these conflicts as ideological or diplomatic clashes.

Not only does the reflection of radiation from the American shield affect the Caribbean people, but it also contaminates the Caribbean Sea and transforms it into "algo comparable a una caldera de ácido" (23, "something comparable to a cauldron of acid"). Soon after the attack, the sea begins to consume the island territories, redrawing the Caribbean map and creating the newly named Archipiélago Vivisector. Like the Caribbean Sea, the Gulf of Mexico was irreversibly destroyed by the nuclear radiation, now occupied by "una suerte de infierno de lava y granizo que flotaba como un hoyo negro" (23, "a sort of inferno made of lava and hailstones that floated like a black hole"). This ecological disaster creates a physical barrier between the Caribbean and the United States that only a small number of specially equipped ships can cross. As in many other texts on nuclear weapons and power, nature itself seems to be revolting against humanity, possibly in response to the human hubris that chose to manipulate its natural elements and laws. This image of a black hole in the middle of the Gulf of Mexico also may recall the 2010 Deepwater Horizon oil spill, also known as the BP oil spill, in which an estimated 5.9 million barrels leaked into the water. Images of ecological damage and the deaths of eleven oil rig workers have turned this disaster into a much-cited example of corporate greed and its deleterious effects on human and animal lives. By alluding to this moment in the sociotechnological history of the region, "Gameon" highlights the extractive, corporate, and geopolitical interests that could predetermine or worsen natural disasters in the Caribbean and emphasizes the gap between those that control nuclear technologies and those left to negotiate its repercussions.

In the novel *Gameon*, nuclear war is the point of no return for the conceptualization of humanity. In the postnuclear aftermath described by Andújar, true humanity is an unachievable concept: "En la era posnuclear, llegar a ser en algún momento de la vida totalmente humano, es un deseo casi poético" (23, "In the postnuclear era, becoming totally human at some point in one's life is an almost-poetic desire"). As the total destruction of nuclear war questions previously held notions about human rights, achieving humanity is more of a literary exercise than a real possibility. In the story, the cadet Gameon is a Humanaiden, a new classification designated for those who are mostly human but have bionic limbs. Despite the doubts surrounding the possibility of humanity in such dystopian times, he conceives of a plan to steal a ship that could navigate through the Gulf of Mexico to the former United States, hoping for a return to humanness. Though his cyborg limbs hold certain mechanical advantages, the cadet and the other Humanaidens dream of feelings that are not mediated by technology, suffering from the "anhelo de experimentar la compleja sensación del impulso imperfecto de los humanos" (23, "yearning to experience the complex sensation of the humans' imperfect stimuli"). In a world full of postnuclear cyborgs, this moment signals a turn back to human imperfection, challenging the transhumanist idea that invasive technologies represent an evolutionary process of perfection or that such perfection should be the singular species-wide goal. Instead, Gameon's bionic appendages remind him of his past, of what his body used to be. As Rita De Maeseneer and Fernanda Bustamonte (2013) argue, Andújar's fiction often features characters with injured or scarred bodies to show how past violences can condition the future (402). Andújar thus contests conceptualizations of technological advancement that ignore human consequences and historical violences. Within the context of the story, this move highlights the connection between nuclear weapons and problematic understandings of technological and social advancement.

Besides the ecological and human fallout from a failed nuclear attack, Andújar also notes how these issues cannot be separated from their political effects. As Arundhati Roy (2003) and others have suggested, nuclear weapons are not just dangerous because of the physical damage they cause but also because of the political repressions that may be carried out under the guise of public security or defense when nuclear war is a possibility. She writes, "The threshold of horror has been ratcheted up so high that nothing short of genocide or the prospect of nuclear war merits mention.... Displacement, dispossession, starvation, poverty, disease—these are now just the funnies, the comic-strip items" (4). This same issue appears in "Gameon," as the United States takes advantage of the postnuclear confusion to expand its territory, taking control of half of Mexico and signing a treaty with Canada to unite the two countries into one national entity. The time-bending nature of science fiction allows authors like Andújar to both reference the Cuban Missile Crisis of the 1960s and allude to the later implementation of NAFTA (the North American Free Trade Agreement) in 1994. In the story, the missile attack gives the United States an excuse to intensify its already-rampant military, economic, and cultural imperialism in the Americas; as the Caribbean islands are devoured by the acidic sea, the United States continues to expand its territory and influence. This new super-nation is renamed Warfar, a land of perpetual war. Andújar's representation of Warfar reflects what John Louis Lucaites and Jon Simons (2017) refer to as the paradox of war's in/visibility in the twenty-first century, creating "a public culture in which war is continuous and altogether present, but largely unseen and/or unacknowledged" (3). While domestic policies and rights are greatly affected by specters of outside threats and calls for national security, the near-constant deployment of fighting abroad is normalized and ignored. By reimagining a postnuclear United States as Warfar, Andújar's text highlights the ways in which the perpetual war paradigm reshapes the nature of citizenship and nationhood.

After a brief look into how Gameon's access to a secret text allows him to prepare for a journey back to Warfar, Andújar ends his story by returning to the narrator's situation as an underpaid adjunct professor, connecting nuclear dehumanization to the exploitation of scholars within an academic system increasingly influenced by economic and political interests: "No terminaré nunca a tiempo el cuento para la revista, me quedaré pegado con la lectura de Gameon y sus quijotadas nucleares. El verano agotará sus posibilidades y yo mitigaré el hambre pensando en el libro perdido de Lester Dakeng" (23, "I will never finish the story for the magazine on time, I will stay stuck to the reading of Gameon and its quixotic nuclear acts. The summer will run out and I will mitigate my hunger thinking of Lester Dakeng's lost book"). More than a glorification of the escapist power of fiction, the narrator's musings on his own hunger follow what Herb Childress (2019) refers to as adjunctification's damage beyond low pay and a lack of opportunities: namely, the "fear, despair, surrender, shame—the messy, hidden human elements that finance and policy always miss" (159). While this reference to contingent faculty and academic precarity may feel out of place in a short story about nuclear war and environmental disaster, it could also be a signal to readers to reconsider the less-sublime ways in which vulnerable subjects are marginalized. In this way, the destruction of higher education can be read alongside nuclear disaster, as hegemonic power can be deployed through university budget allocations as well as missile launches.

"Las extrañas decisiones de Vladimir Denísovich Jiménez": Postnuclear Queerness

Different from Andújar's postnuclear ecological disaster, Yasmín Silvia Portales's reimagining of the Cuban Missile Crisis focuses primarily on the political and colonial implications of the appearance of nuclear weapons on the island. Portales is a Cuban writer, scholar, and activist. Besides "Las extrañas decisiones de Vladimir Denísovich Jiménez" (2016), her other published science fiction texts include the stories "Ajuste de cuentas" (2015) and "Las noches del león y los pájaros del fuego" (2015). In the scholarly essay "En busca de Estraven" (2011) about homophobia and feminism in recent Cuban science fiction, Portales investigates traces of misoginy and heteronormativity in recent Cuban science fiction. The short story "Las extrañas decisiones de Vladimir Denísovich Jiménez" was published in the anthology *Órbita Juracán: Cuentos cubanos de ciencia ficción* (2016), edited by Cuban science fiction writer Leonardo Gala Echemendía.[4]

The story imagines Vladimir, from present-day Cuba, who falls into an alternate version of Havana as a trans woman named Vania, who is a member of the People's Commissariat of Foreign Affairs. In this parallel universe, Cuba is now a Soviet colony and has been since the Soviet Union defeated the United States in the Cold War. While the causes behind this interdimensional travel are never explained, the story finds Vladimir on the day before they are set to travel back to Moscow, presumably to be debriefed and then disposed of. When asked if Moscow would just allow them to return to their original world, Vladimir answers, "No me dejarían, aunque pudieran. Sé demasiado. Quieren mis conocimientos, no ayudarme" (246, "They wouldn't let me go, even if they could. I know too much. They want my knowledge, not to help me"). That knowledge, from living in a different world in which the Soviet Union loses the Cold War and falls, is the only value they hold for officials in Moscow. Vladimir's last night before this final trip is spent with their sister Tamara, brother-in-law Guennadi, and Iván. To Vladimir's surprise, Vladimir and Iván are lovers in this alternate world, even though they are brothers in his original one. Most likely linked to Portales's own social activism, there is a particular focus in the story on the treatment of and spaces for queer bodies under this postnuclear regime.

"Las extrañas decisiones de Vladimir Denísovich Jiménez" could feel out of place in this chapter, since it only includes one reference to nuclear weapons, when Vladimir notes that in this alternative world, the Cuban Missile Crisis marked the "pérdida de la soberanía cubana" ("loss of Cuban sovereignty") and the island's transformation into a Soviet colony (241). However, just as nuclear violence in enacted in ways other than explosions, science fiction that challenges nuclear archives can also take on subtler forms. As Castro had feared in real life, Portales imagines a world in which Cuba's role as weapon holder and ideological pawn cleared the path for the Soviet Union to take full control of the country.

Despite only this fleeting mention of the technology, this text is read here as what scholar of Russian science fiction Anindita Banerjee (2016) has termed "contaminated fiction," which "deploys the nuclear in an intimate set of relations that help make sense of the world after utopia and define what it means to be a subject in a precarious new order of the twenty-first century" (71). By focusing on these intimacies or relationships, as opposed to the techno-political institutions, contaminated fiction allows for a closer look into how nuclear war or disaster may reshape interpersonal connections. Banerjee continues, "Contaminated fiction thus provides a powerful way for bridging the discursive spheres of the real, imagined, lived, and speculative potentials of nuclear power" (71). This contamination or bridging is similar to the way that radiation can silently reconfigure the most basic biological or social building blocks. As a text that travels back and forth between present-day Havana and a postnuclear version, "Las extrañas decisiones de Vladimir Denísovich Jiménez" folds together real and imagined impacts of the Cuban Missile Crisis, highlighting nuclear technology's ability to infiltrate popular language and memory.

Analyzing this story as contaminated fiction means that minor details can take on greater significance as insight into how Portales envisions a nuclear event would affect Cuban social and political systems. For example, Vladimir says that their time in alternate Havana "era como mirar al abismo" (235, "was like looking into the abyss"). This moment achieves new meaning when one considers how close the island came to suffering nuclear apocalypse. There are also clues as to how Cubans are treated by their Soviet colonizers. Vladimir mentions that nobody knew for sure if the imported gasoline they used contained lead, hinting at a lack of Soviet concern for the health and wellbeing of their subjects in Cuba (237). The subtlest detail comes when Vladimir and Tamara debate taking the streetcar to lunch. Historically, the Cuban streetcar system was dismantled in 1952, so it is notable that this modern-day, alternate version of Havana still uses them. What makes this detail a comment on nuclear techno-dominance is the fact that Cold War–era architects designed the Moscow metro system as both a model of Soviet modernity and a fallout shelter for possible future nuclear attacks.[5] That these same projects were not extended to Havana makes clearer the position that Cuba holds in this imagined nuclear empire.

On the surface, this alternate timeline shows a very different version of Cuba. Despite economic advances and the fact that foreign products are readily available to Cuban citizens, Vladimir wonders, "¿Era mejor ser este Puerto Rico soviético que aquel país independiente y hambreado de donde venía él?" (237, "Was it better to be this Soviet Puerto Rico or that independent and hungry country from which he came?"). The question is not rhetorical; Vladimir seems to be honestly torn between the two possibilities. At the same time, this line draws a connection between the colonial history of Cuba and the current colonial occupation of Puerto Rico by the United States. One of the biggest changes for Vladimir is that the restaurant Moscú is now a reservation-only establishment with long lines of people trying to get a table. Vladimir finds this especially odd, having considered the restaurant to be a dilapidated embarrassment in the other, original world: "En su Habana, el edificio estaba hecho una ruina, nada más que se usaba por filmar escenas de ambiente post apocalíptico . . . se había convertido en lugar común de la filmografía que 'demostraba' el fracaso del Revolución Cubana" (237, "In their Havana, the building was in ruins, used for nothing more than to film postapocalyptic background scenes . . . it had been converted into a common location for films that 'showed' the failures of the Cuban Revolution"). Portales offers a different take on the science fiction motif of postapocalyptic futures, proposing that the future of techno-dominance may look more like present-day San Juan and less like recent dystopic imaginings of Cuba's future, such as in the films *Omega-3* (2014) and *Los desastres de la guerra* (2012). This moment also brings up the role of film in creating both dystopic and utopic narratives of Cuba. As Ana María Dopico (2002) argues, internationally distributed apocalyptic or dystopian images of Cuba fulfill an "ethnovoyeuristic fantasy": "The cultural tourist experiences firsthand (and all at once) the fruit of revolution, third-world lifestyle, and a living experiment in disaster, apocalypse, and survival. The allure of Cuba lies precisely in both its suffering and its surviving collapse" (463). The formation of popular culture imagery of what an apocalypse or dystopia should look like helps obscure the dystopian acts being carried out under the guise of shiny, sleek technological progress.

The most noticeable difference in this new Havana is the complete absence of Fidel Castro. Instead, Lenin's name and image are the most prominent in the city. Vladimir mentions a carving of José Martí at the Fuente Luminosa, though it is now accompanied by a corresponding image of Stalin's face. The absence of Fidel is partially explained as the group drives past the University of Havana's Juan Abrantes Stadium, renamed in this alternate world after Soviet gymnast and Olympic legend Larisa Latynina. The stadium's rechristening supposedly happened in 1966, in honor of the gymnast's death. The real-life Latynina, born in 1934, is still alive; this detail suggests that there was a place for the heroic athlete's story and name within this nuclear world but not her body. The story mentions that the use of a woman's name on the stadium was meant as a concession to Vilma Espín, "la única de 26 de Julio que aún estaba en el poder por aquella fecha" (236, "the only one from the 26 of July movement still in power on that date"). The real Espín, who passed away in 2007, was a revolutionary fighter, the founder of the Federation of Cuban Women, and Raúl Castro's wife. Most importantly, this moment insinuates that the rest of the Castro regime did not make it much past the 1962 missile crisis. Fidel's absence has dramatic consequences throughout Latin America. For example, when Vladimir mentions that their version of Cuba still relies on petroleum provided by the Hugo Chávez regime, the others ask if they are referring to the great Venezuelan baseball star.

In this timeline, without Fidel as a model, Chávez pursues a career in sports instead of politics.

As Portales provides details on the ongoing Battle for Socialism, the alternate world's colonial biopolitics become clearer. Instead of focusing on any possible military victories during this struggle, the story highlights the tombs of fallen soldiers that now litter Moscow's satellite nations, "dondequiera que la Guerra Fría entre rusos y yanquis se calentara un poco" (238, "wherever the Cold War between Russians and Yankees heated up a bit"). This highlights the fact that while the struggle between the United States and the Soviet Union was largely ideological, smaller nations fell victim to the corresponding violence. The actual Cuban Missile Crisis also demonstrates this, as Cuba was nearly pushed to the brink of nuclear war and then left out of the bilateral negotiations that ended the conflict. Portales's story mentions that the soldiers sent to fight on the frontlines were only from the Soviet colonies: "el Ejército Rojo no se metía en esos berenjenales" (238, "The Red Army didn't get involved in those messes"). This is a clear display of which bodies are both considered disposable and simultaneously handed the responsibility of fighting for the future of the empire. This sort of disregard for marginalized bodies is a logical conclusion for a colonizing power that could consider launching nuclear weapons. It is also mentioned that Vladimir and Tamara's parents, still alive in the old Cuba, died while fighting for the Soviet Union in Afghanistan. Not only does this detail reference the actual Soviet occupation of Afghanistan in the 1980s, but it also points to Castro's deployment of Cuban troops to Angola in the 1970s. Their parents were named Heroes of the Battle for Socialism after their deaths, just as the real-life Cuban generals involved in the Angolan Civil War were posthumously given the title of Heroes of the Republic of Cuba on November 11, 2015 ("Decorated"). Portales's story describes war as the consequence of complex systems of political and economic repression, no matter who is in charge. This in turn puts the onus the characters to challenge the system and finally to put a stop to the violence.

Portales connects this violent disregard for the bodies of Cuban soldiers with an equally problematic treatment of queer people within the alternate Soviet empire. As mentioned above, Vladimir is shocked to find out that while Iván is their brother in their old world, the two of them are lovers in this new one. This fact is especially complicated in this new Soviet version of Havana: "Por supuesto, estaban en territorio de la URSS, y la homosexualidad era una de las enfermedades que se trataban con *electroshocks*—si se descubría en la adolescencia—o agresivas terapias de reconversión—si la víctima tiene más de veinte. No ser *gay* era la mejor opción" (241, "Of course, they were in Soviet territory, and homosexuality was one of the illnesses that was treated with electroshocks—if it was discovered in adolescence—or aggressive reconversion therapies—if the victim was over twenty years old. Not being gay was the best option"). Not only is queerness not accepted in this world, but it is also understood as an illness that merited intense and violent treatment. This is a double reference, to both the current official homophobia by the Russian government and to Eduardo Gutiérrez Agramonte's experiments in the 1960s on electroconvulsive therapy as a cure for homosexuality. Referencing this horrific history as part of a postnuclear future highlights Portales's critique that the Cuban government in general and Mariela Castro's *Centro Nacional de Educación Sexual* (CENESEX, or Cuban National Center for Sex Education) in particular have not yet done enough to atone for the past treatment of gay Cubans, including the infamous UMAP labor camps.[6] In 2016, Portales was outspoken over the official censorship of the online Cuban LGBTQ community that she founded, Proyecto Arcoíris (Project Rainbow). The site was shut down after a post by Jimmy Roque Martínez criticized the continued official homophobia within Cuba at that time, such as the lack of legal standing for queer families ("Plataforma," 2016).[7] By alluding to Cuba's violent, homophobic past, Portales points out the ways in which these legacies are perpetuated, along with literature's role in maintaining public memories of moments that the official archive would like to erase.

Though Vladimir feels the danger of being queer in this new world, they are also surprised to find out that they and Iván had secretly been together for a decade. With the help of Tamara and Guennadi, Iván and Vladimir have managed to both maintain their relationship and hide it in public. This is aided by the lack of available housing, also an issue in present-day Cuba, which allows the two of them to live together without raising suspicion. To their amusement, Vladimir also notes that their secret is also protected by "la familiaridad con que los varones cubanos se trataban en público, una intimidad inimaginable en Europa Oriental" (241, "the familiarity with which Cuban men treated each other, an intimacy unimaginable in Eastern Europe"). According to them, Cuban men are more likely to initiate physical contact with others, hiding any underlying sexual desires. Vania had chosen to return to Cuba after studying in Moscow for this reason, under the guise of wanting to reconnect to their roots. By highlighting the latent homoeroticism within the homophobic, postnuclear colony, this story also contests the militarized masculinity of Cuba's New Man and the heteronormative rhetoric that supports nuclear war. Vladimir suspects that many young Soviet officials have chosen to be stationed in Cuba for similar reasons and mentions a queer colony in Matanzas. These details possibly allude to Cuba's emergence as an international destination for queer tourism, a fact that both shows the progress that the country has made and its attempts to obfuscate a dark history of official homophobia. Noelle Stout (2014) lays out the complicated nature of queer tourism in Cuba, featuring a difficult to distinguish spectrum of experiences, from patronage and activism to sex tourism. Stout argues that because of international media representations of Cuba and state policies that segregate locals from tourists, queer tourism often paints a utopian image of Cuban anti-homophobia, confusing the privileged position of tourists for a widespread official acceptance of queerness (146–148). Portales's portrayal of Cuba as a gay haven highlights the role of revolutionary rhetoric and international marketing in the obfuscation of the historical record.

While Vladimir identified as a cis-gendered man in the original world, they identify as a trans woman is this alternate version of Cuba. Their friends and family go back and forth between calling them Vladimir and Vania. However, just before a sexual encounter with Iván toward the end of the story, they say, "Soy Vania. Desde ahora hasta el final seré Vania, tu Vania" (242, "I am Vania. From now until the end I will be Vania, your Vania"). As Vladimir grows increasingly comfortable with themself as Vania, they begin to question whether they may be trans in all possible universes, and if they have been forced to repress this realization in their previous life. It stands out that the protagonist may feel more comfortable identifying as trans in this repressive Soviet colony than in present-day Cuba, despite the country's publicized progress and openness toward the trans community.[8] While nuclear technology attempts to impose heteronormative and hypermasculine models of dominance, Vania's presence disrupts the ideal, masculine public servant that Vladimir had once represented. Despite having found comfort and happiness in Vania and with Iván, Vladimir decides to swim off, alone, into the ocean instead of traveling back to the Soviet Union and facing official rebuke in Moscow. Through death, Vladimir deprives the Soviet authorities of his valuable knowledge. It is difficult to say whether Vladimir's decision to commit suicide could or should be understood as an act of agency. Instead, this move offers insight into the social and political structure that surrounded him. As Achille Mbembe (2003) writes, "Under the conditions of necropower, the lines between resistance and suicide, sacrifice and redemption, martyrdom and freedom are blurred" (40). Vladimir believed that there was no possible place for their queer body within this postnuclear world, a colonial system based on the aggressiveness of two feuding powers that thrive on conformity and heteronormativity and whose combined global hegemony is sustained by nuclear weapons. Though Vladimir and Iván were able to navigate the cracks within the system for some time, the former ultimately decides that they no longer belong in any universe.

Trabajo Extra: Nuclear Ghosts

While Andújar and Portales reimagine past near-disasters, Erick Mota's *Trabajo Extra* (2014) describes a distant future in which human bodies are still being affected by nuclear techno-dominance. Mota is from Havana and has won awards for his science fiction in both Cuba and Chile. He is best known for *Habana Underguater* (2010), a cyberpunk novel and short story collection set in a fragmented version of the city run by warring Cuban, Russian, religious, and hacker factions, among others.[9] Nuclear weapons play an important role in *Habana*

Underguater, too, as Russian missiles hang in the air over the city to intimidate its residents into general compliance with their colonial control. Mota has also published the *El colapso de las habanas infinitas* (2017) and *Memorias del mar de Dirac* (2022). Mota first introduced the cadets Kay Hunter and Juan Tomás Kirk in the novella *Bajo Presión* (2008), which earned the 2008 Premio Edad de Oro, a prize for children's and young adult fiction awarded by the Cuban publisher Editorial Gente Nueva. The second publication in the "Kirk y Kay" story line is *Historias del cosmos salvaje* (2014), which consists of two novellas: *El último vuelo del Cid* and *Trabajo Extra*.

Trabajo Extra is a young adult novella and space opera, set in a world in which humans have expanded their domain to the limits of the known universe. According to Gary Westfahl (2003), the space opera "is the most common, and least respected form of science fiction" (197). Originally focused on piracy and war in outer space, the subgenre eventually evolved to include conversations of governance and survival in postconquest worlds. Mota's space operas follow the cadets Kay Hunter and Juan Tomás Kirk. In *Trabajo Extra*, Kirk looks to make extra money over a school break, navigating an old ship with a group of other students to dump containers of nuclear waste in a less inhabited part of the universe. Instead of the action-packed battle scenes of a traditional space opera, *Trabajo Extra* tells the story of the mishaps that happen during this supposedly routine mission and how Kirk manages to get everyone back alive. More of a plodding journey than a traditional space opera filled with battles and explosions, Kirk must use his technical ingenuity to navigate a broken ship back home after radiation and other factors incapacitate the rest of the crew. Kirk accidentally discovers a long-mythologized civilization as he randomly jumps around the universe, highlighting larger discussions on techno-colonialism and the effects of nuclear techno-dominance.

In Mota's novella, there is a noticeable lack of outrage or concern from the crew over the dangerous nature of their cargo. While each of them has reservations about joining the mission, they cite issues with the ship or a lack of trust in the other members of the crew but never question the safety of transporting radioactive materials. The only person that seems worried about this is Kay, who forgoes the mission to spend the vacation with her family. In *Trabajo Extra*, Kay tries to warn her friend, saying, "¡Eso es explotación, Kirk! Se aprovechan de nosotros para hacer un trabajo realmente peligroso e ilegal. Trabajar con radiactividad puede costarnos las vidas" (76, "That is exploitation, Kirk! They take advantage of us to do a really dangerous and illegal job. Working with radioactivity could cost us our lives"). To highlight how undeterred the cadets are by the nuclear cargo, there is much more frustration when they find out that the ship was also secretly carrying a load of synthetic beer, deemed illegal contraband by the ruling power in the galaxy, the Fleet (*la Flota*). The lack of outrage emphasizes the tremendous power gap between the owners of these materials (the Fleet and large corporations) and those forced to work with them (Kirk and the other students who needed the money and were willing to overlook the potential dangers of the mission). Though Mota's novella does not reference the Cuban Missile Crisis as directly as the stories by Portales and Andújar, there is a similar mark of the uneven power relationship between those in control of nuclear technology and those merely in close contact with it.

The colonizing influence of the Fleet has a great impact on the mistrust between crew members. Everyone on the ship attempts to manipulate or hide something about their identity, either to distance themselves from or connect themselves to the center of power. Sakura, who is in charge of vital support, comes from a powerful family of technological anarchists but, on arrival at the academy, focuses solely on finding a more legitimately connected husband. She spends most of her time during the mission with the self-appointed captain Gueorgui, the heir to a shipping empire who desperately wants out of the family business. Rada, head of communications, tries to hide her identity but is eventually revealed to be half-elf. Elves are the product of an experiment with alien and human DNA and are now a marginalized group because of their appearance and insusceptibility to disease: "Primero fueron ángeles salvadores, después peligrosos demonios y, finalmente, se volvieron una minoría étnica aislada en colonias lejanas" (105, "First they were guardian angels, later dangerous demons, and, finally, they became an ethnic minority isolated in distant colonies"). Rada and Kirk connect in their shared uneasiness about their identities, as Kirk attempts to go by the name of John Thomas instead of his given name of Juan Tomás. Kirk, the great-great-grandson of *Star Trek*'s Captain James Tiberius Kirk, hates his name in Spanish because it invisibilizes English, a prohibited language on his home planet of Nueva Valencia. Kirk's infamous issues with authority at the academy are attributed to the pressure put on him by his family lineage but are also connected to his feelings toward a regime that restricts his family's native language. While Spanish is a colonizing language in Latin America, this detail is also an ironic reference to English's place as a linguistic marker of economic globalization and U.S. cultural colonialism, along with the mainstream dominance of U.S.- and U.K.-based creators within popular science fiction.

The hiding of identities and origins based on socioeconomic hierarchies has grave consequences in the case of Ripley, the ship's head engineer. Ripley claims to be from a large planet, since that is understood as more honorable than being born on one of the Fleet's many terraformed asteroids. This attempt at respectability backfires when approaching the nuclear cargo during a spacewalk reignites her radiation poisoning. Only then is it revealed that Ripley grew up on UGM-12, the site of an infamous nuclear disaster. When Ripley was eleven years old, a nuclear warhead accidentally exploded in a dock on UGM-12 that was being subcontracted by the Fleet. After the explosion, nuclear waste seeped into the asteroid and made it uninhabitable. Ripley, still undergoing treatments for radiophobia, held this information back because prior exposure should have disqualified her from the mission. Kirk, who is sympathetic to her issues but also annoyed that she lied to get on the ship, refers to Ripley as a refugee and adds, "Nadie puede entrar en un infierno como ese con once años y esperar a los veinte que todo esté bien" (108, "Nobody can enter an inferno like that at eleven years old and expect at twenty for everything to be fine"). Ripley's inability to speak openly about her past underlines the ways in which nuclear rhetoric silences living victims of such disasters. Her backstory also alludes to the 1986 explosion at the Chernobyl Nuclear Power Plant, which has a unique place in Cuban cultural memory because tens of thousands of children affected by that nuclear accident have been treated in Tarará, a resort-turned-pediatric-hospital outside Havana (Schipani, 2009). Even after the mission, Kirk notes that Ripley remained affected by this incident and that she "terminó quebrándose ante el fantasma de la radioactividad" (139, "ended up breaking down in the face of the ghost of radioactivity"). This moment demonstrates the power of repressive nuclear archives and rhetoric to make proper mourning and rehabilitation impossible.

After coming into contact with the radiation, Ripley cannot stop mumbling about cosmic rays, Geiger counters, "flores mutantes" (mutant flowers) and "ojos de cesio radiactivo" (eyes of radioactive cesium) (107). In an attempt to calm her down, Sakura accidentally gives her too much of a sedative and nearly causes an overdose. This mistake causes Sakura to retreat to her cabin for the rest of the mission, and Gueorgui follows. The pressure from the mission pushes Rada to drink too much synthetic beer, leaving Kirk to manage the entire ship all by himself. He must navigate and fly the ship at the same time while also repairing the outdated engine as it sputters on the way home. While Kirk is not an engineer, he reassures himself that "las máquinas siempre son máquinas.... Primero se les apaga para que se calmen. Luego se les vuelve a encender. Si para entonces persiste en no funcionar, se les da un par de golpes y listo" (118, "machines are always machines.... First turn it off so that it calms down. Then turn it on again. If then it still doesn't work, hit it a few times, and ready to go"). This ability to work with machines recalls the narratives of technological resourcefulness that have often been used to describe the Cuban people, most commonly in reference to their ability to refurbish and maintain aging automobiles. Rachel Price (2016) notes a similar resourcefulness in Mota's *Habana Underguater* and recognizes this detail as a parody of Cuba's current technological situation (84). However, these narratives of Cuban ingenuity often mask the fact that economic factors make such improvisation necessary. For example, while Havana's legendary refurbished cars, known locally as *almendrones*, are often used to symbolize the city's supposed timelessness, they also represent Cuban precarity. Louis A. Pérez, Jr. (2018) writes: "This is Cuba mired in circumstances of unrelenting hardship offered as a source of nostalgic delight and photogenic objects of a sightseer gaze ... a people living under impoverished material circumstances whose plight as a historical condition is marketed as a sightseeing attraction" (20). That the spiritual descendants of Cubans may be similarly rigging up spaceships in the future highlights the legacies of these narratives and the globalizing forces that promote them.

Kirk uses a similar ingenuity when his navigation system fails, coming up with a plan to launch the ship in short spurts to different parts of the universe until he can manually devise their location. During this process, Kirk accidentally stumbles on a massive community of the Pioneers, self-exiles who refused to live under the Fleet's repressive system.[10] The Pioneers had been thought of as nonhuman, mythical beings who preferred zero gravity and attempted to create self-sufficient habitats, untethered from planets and asteroids. Kirk explains:

> Claro que eran humanos. ... Su piel era más oscura por la sobre exposición de los rayos UV de los reactores iónicos. Eran inmunes a la radiación y la necesidad los había enseñado a no confiar en las inteligencias artificiales. Pero perdieron una guerra contra la humanidad de los Mundos. La historia que nos leímos fue contada por los vencedores, por los humanos de las biosferas y la gravedad. (115, Of course they were humans. ... Their skin was darker due to overexposure to the UV rays from the ionic reactors. They were immune to radiation and necessity had taught them to distrust artificial intelligence. But they lost a war against the humanity of the Worlds. The history that we read was written by the victors, by the humans of the biospheres and gravity.)

Kirk's fascination with the Pioneers says a lot about his relationship with nuclear techno-dominance. Kirk notes the role that official histories have on marginalized or defeated groups and how attempted innovations can be written off as foolish deviations from dominant understandings of technological progress. He also acknowledges the legitimacy of mistrusting advanced technology like artificial intelligence, especially when those tools are used for surveillance or weaponry. Their immunity to radiation is an especially notable symbol of resistance to the Fleet's nuclear-based techno-dominance. Kirk's reference to the Pioneers' darker skin turns their escape from the Fleet into a sort of cosmic *cimarronaje*, a term that describes the fleeing and establishment of alternative communities by Afro-descendant slaves. The Pioneers in Mota's novella enact a futuristic version of Afro-modernity, which Michael Hanchard (1999) defines as the "selective incorporation of technologies, discourses, and institutions of the modern West within the cultural and political practices of African-derived peoples to create a form of relatively autonomous modernity distinct from its counterparts of Western Europe and North America" (247). Instead of rejecting the technologies used to repress them, the Pioneers selectively take advantage of their benefits to remove themselves from colonial networks of power.

Despite Kirk's previously held belief that the Pioneers really do exist, he is still shocked to have stumbled on the first-ever known example of one of their habitats. Hidden in a supposedly uninhabited part of the cosmos, the existence of this artificial planet literally redefines the limits of the known universe. Kirk is especially impressed with their technological advancements, which greatly outshine those in the Fleet-controlled universe:

> Humanos como nosotros pero que habían desarrollado una tecnología increíble y alcanzado un nivel de organización social impensable. Habían logrado aprovechar de modo eficiente toda la energía de una estrella. Aquello, según la Escala de Kardashov, era una civilización de nivel II. (133, Human like us, but they had developed an incredible technology and reached an unthinkable level of social organization. They had managed to efficiently extract all the energy from a star. That, according to the Kardashov Scale, was a level II civilization.)

In the planetary world, the Fleet extracts natural resources from each celestial body until exhaustion; the Pioneers, by contrast, had developed a sustainable energy source. That energy independence, according to Kirk's logic, made them a more advanced civilization than the one ruled over by the Fleet. The Pioneers found a way to escape both the dependence on Fleet-approved modes of technology and the power dynamics that such techno-dominance creates. *Trabajo Extra* suggests that such a rupture relies on the reconceptualization of our relationship to natural resources and on technology's role in providing for humankind in a less corporate, more democratic manner.

Kirk, as a cadet of the Fleet's military academy, is legally obligated to inform the authorities about this unauthorized habitat. He knows, however, that once discovered, the civilization would quickly be destroyed. Kirk goes back and forth over what the right thing to do is, not wanting to wipe out such a marvel but also acknowledging that more people could benefit from their technology. While he attempts to file a report just before the ship is about to move again, he loses connectivity before the report can be sent; it is unclear if this is on purpose or not. On his long journey back, Kirk imagines the notoriety he could achieve by being the first to discover such a place, making a name for himself outside of his famous ancestor, though he also sees the problem with taking credit for a discovery that would lead to the destruction of millions of people. Despite the temptation of fame and glory, by the time Kirk returns to the academy he decides not to tell anyone about his discovery other than his best friend Kay. Kirk's resolution to shirk his responsibility to the Fleet allows the Pioneers to continue their alternative path of technological development and emphasizes the capacity for individual agency within a militarized chain of command.

Science fiction fans reading Mota's *Trabajo Extra* will identify many of the characters' names as references to iconic figures within the genre. The protagonist

Kirk is named after the legendary captain of the USS *Enterprise*, a relationship that is overtly stated throughout the series. Next, the name Ripley harkens Ellen Ripley, the character portrayed by Sigourney Weaver in director Ridley Scott's *Alien* film series. Finally, Sakura may refer to the Sakura Kasugano character from the *Street Fighter* video games, comics, and films; the name could also reference Sakura Haruna from the popular Japanese anime series *Naruto*. While these allusions could be read as winks to the many aficionados of these respective franchises, they also signal a literary mash-up that inserts this text into the canons of global science fiction. While Mota's texts should not be read as fan fiction, he enacts a similar mode of active fandom that contests and decenters the genre's power centers. As André M. Carrington (2016) suggests, fan interpretations of science fiction can help decolonize the modes of production of popular culture and work toward "counterhegemonic models of race, class, and gender" (208). Mota's references allude to not only the presence of a decades-old community of science fiction fandom within Cuba but also the refusal, by the island's writers, to be relegated to passive consumption.

This active turn also appears in parts of the other two texts analyzed in this chapter. Andújar's "Gameon," for example, is written as a book review. This move enacts a similar challenge to power dynamics within the genre, signaling the reviewer as a key player for criticizing and broadening science fiction texts. Portales's "Las extrañas decisiones de Vladimir Denísovich Jiménez" similarly critiques the images of Cuba propagated through popular film, questioning the reductive reliance on visual clichés of dystopia and ruins. By subtly critiquing dystopian images of Havana, Portales's text both positions itself within that tradition and offers new possibilities for imagining the city's future. These examples suggest that no texts are final and contest ideas of authorship and authority, especially in genres like science fiction that play with preconceived notions of technological and social development. Just as all the texts studied in this chapter insert themselves into global conversations of science fiction and show the multidirectional nature of text, they similarly challenge the narrative and rhetorical power of nuclear weapons. Mota's *Trabajo Extra* forces readers to remember the effected bodies that cannot escape their nuclear pasts, those haunted by the ghosts of radiation. This novella also focuses on the workers that come into close contact with the nuclear materials, much closer than those that control or authorize their use. These bodies are often forgotten in the narratives that shape memories of weaponized nuclear technology. Portales inserts the stories of queer bodies into the nuclear archive, highlighting the hypermasculine and heteronormative nature of nuclear rhetoric. Vladimir refuses to be read and discarded like a worthless text. Instead, his suicide at the end of the story sadly highlights the lack of space for queerness in a world shaped by nuclear hegemony. Finally, "Gameon" forefronts the irreversible environmental effects of nuclear strikes, along with how military campaigns and extractive technologies that alter or mutate nature can also reconfigure understandings of humanity and humanness. The protagonist's valuing of human vulnerability over cyborg invincibility also critiques narratives of progress that idealize technological enhancement without considering human consequences. All these texts contest and reshape the archive of narratives that weaponize nuclear technologies even before any missiles are launched, while also creating space for proper mourning and understanding of nuclear technology's dangerous aftereffects beyond sublime explosions.

CHAPTER 3

Space Exploration and Colonial Alienation

In 1995, the world found itself on the brink of crisis. An international terrorist organization led by a rogue British intelligence agent hijacked an orbiting electromagnetic pulse (EMP) cannon previously designed and weaponized by the Soviet Union. Controlling the EMP from a satellite dish the size of a football field in western Cuba, the group aimed to attack the Bank of England in London, in hopes of destroying all electronic records and sparking a global financial meltdown. After finding out that the lead terrorist was his presumed-dead former partner, an MI6 secret service agent flew from London to Cuba with a hacker who had defected from Russian space forces. The mission was undertaken with the clandestine support of the Central Intelligence Agency (CIA), which had to publicly deny all presence or dealings in Cuba because of the U.S. blockade. After uncovering the former-Soviet satellite hidden below an artificial lake deep in the Cuban jungle, the duo infiltrated the base, hacked into the control systems, and redirected the EMP weapon so that it burned up on reentry into the Earth's atmosphere. Despite confrontations with missile defense systems and an army of angry minions, the British spy and Russian hacker planted detonators around the base and destroyed the antennae by jamming its gears. Escaping in a commandeered helicopter moments before the final explosion, the two heroes safely landed in what they assumed to be an abandoned field. After engaging in a romantic embrace, their privacy was interrupted by a camouflaged group of U.S. Marines who had been awaiting their arrival. The spy and the hacker were then escorted to the Guantanamo Bay Naval Base for debriefing.

If the above story sounds too fantastical to be true, it should. This is the plot from the end of the 1995 James Bond film *GoldenEye*, directed by Martin Campbell and starring Pierce Brosnan and Izabella Scorupco as the lovers/heroes. Though the movie claims that these climactic scenes take place in Cuba, the giant dish depicted on-screen was Puerto Rico's Arecibo Observatory, known formally as the National Astronomy and Ionosphere Center (NAIC). Filming in Puerto Rico in the mid-1990s offered fewer logistic issues for the British–U.S. production than going to Cuba, and a generic Caribbean landscape proved more important to the filmmakers than any specific details about the area or people. As Matthew David Goodwin (2019) has noted, the NAIC has been featured in many films and series: a 1994 episode of *The X-Files*, in which agents Mulder and Scully investigate messages supposedly sent to the observatory by aliens, and the 1997 film *Contact*, again about the possible discovery of extraterrestrial life but involving a character (played by Matthew McConaughey) who is researching the effects of technology on "Third World cultures" (287). Just like in these other depictions, *GoldenEye* uses the Caribbean mostly for its seemingly exotic scenery of lush flora and pristine beaches; even the army of minions protecting the base is full of Russian accents, while Spanish is noticeably absent. The image of a giant metallic dish emerging from underwater at the behest of Russian and British bosses harkens back to Cold War–era conceptions of Cuba as a powerless Soviet satellite, a place where dangerous technology can be stored but not controlled. As Jorge Ferrer (2012) notes, Cuban leaders and cultural figures in the post-Soviet era have decried the branding of Cuba as a mere Soviet "satellite" as imperialist and counterrevolutionary (99). As the end of *GoldenEye* shows, the absence of Cuban/Puerto Rican/Caribbean characters or agency in representations of its technology highlights the techno-colonial and techno-authoritarian alienation of the Caribbean in popular narratives of space exploration.

From the first Cuban cosmonaut to the search for extraterrestrial life from Arecibo and unidentified flying object (UFO) sightings throughout the region, the possibilities of space travel and alien contact have expanded the spectrum of what seems possible and redefined what it means to be human. This chapter looks at how recent science fiction texts navigate the Caribbean's complicated relationship to space exploration, including the feeling of alienation that can both help maintain repressive colonizing structures and be refocused or embraced as a liberating force. The science fiction texts analyzed in this chapter speculate on the future of space travel and intergalactic contact. In Haris Durrani's 2017 novella *Champollion's Foot*, the crew of *La Mariposa Negra* introduces space exploration as a future form of decolonizing survival and diaspora while also showing how oppressive structures like slavery can reappear even as repressed groups are fighting for liberation. Yoss's 2013 novel *Condonautas* demythologizes the heroics of space travel and investigates how intergalactic intimacy could inform future understandings of sexuality. Finally, Luis Othoniel Rosa's 2017 *Caja de fractales* (*Box of fractals*) posits contact with extraterrestrials as a necessary conceptual break that could release Earth from capitalist and colonizing frameworks. These texts investigate the role of space exploration in informing relationships between technology, citizenship, and sovereignty in and around the Caribbean.

Until the end of 2020, the NAIC had been an invaluable venue for astronomical, atmospheric, and planetary radar research, including the discovery of the binary pulsar, which led to two Princeton researchers winning the Nobel Prize in Physics in 1993. The observatory, including its 1,000-foot radio telescope, was officially opened in 1963 and overseen by Cornell University's William Gordon. Cornell and the National Science Foundation (NSF) operated and funded the site from its inauguration until 2011, when it was then run by a consortium led by the University of Central Florida, with reduced NSF support. One peek into the process of establishing the Arecibo Observatory is a report by Gordon and others from 1958 called "Design Study of a Radar to Explore the Earth's Ionosphere and Surrounding Space," which laid out the purpose of the project along with exploring potential sites for the telescope. According to this report, the "northern zone of the tropics" was the best possible spot for the project because of its latitudinal placement and logistic access. Besides Puerto Rico, other potential sites included Hawaii, Mexico, Cuba, and "some minor islands of the West Indies" (Belcher 1–2). Puerto Rico was ultimately chosen for several reasons, including the presence of Puerto Rican astronomer Braulio Dueño on the team. According to Gordon's report, putting the telescope in Puerto Rico would also be about $200,000 cheaper than putting it in the southwestern United States, mostly because northern Puerto Rico's belt of coral limestone with large bowl-like sinkholes would reduce the need for excavation for placing the dish; tropical weathering also gave this limestone karst topography, a form of natural drainage.

On top of these geographic advantages, the report signals that choosing Puerto Rico was at least partially based on its status as a U.S. colony; according to this report, Cuba was eliminated as a site while "[Puerto Rico] encompassed the favorable circumstances of location, political stability and minimum distance" (Belcher 2). Here "political stability" served as a euphemism for U.S. colonial control. Puerto Rico was seen as both accessible but removed enough so that any potential health, environmental, or social repercussions would not be noticed in the continental United States. As Gordon later remarked in a 1994 interview:

> Puerto Rico was a freely associated state. It was in some sense part of the U.S.; it was a commonwealth and still is. Probably always will be. It seemed to be an attractive place. It was a great deal more prosperous than the neighboring islands, some of which are pitiful in terms of living conditions. So Puerto Rico was picked. (Butrica)

Just as Puerto Rico's status as a colony made the space feel more politically stable for such a large project, its economic "prosperity" (i.e., the U.S. experimentation with the Puerto Rican economy that valued industrialization and exportation over employment or economic stability for working-class Puerto Ricans) created the necessary conditions for the observatory. Gordon's statement that Puerto Rico will "probably always" be under U.S. control enacts a vision of future oppression and exploitation, a virtual prerequisite for this project; initiating this kind of long-term research center only makes sense if the planners believe that the colonial system will remain intact. The relationship between the NAIC and the Puerto Rican economic development became clearer in later years as the dish required updates. Daniel Altschuler, a Uruguayan physicist who served as the director of the NAIC from 1992 to 2003, recounts a massive upgrade project, originally deemed necessary in 1969 but not funded until 1972, that required the building of a special factory for fabricating aluminum panels: "A total of 227 miles of this material was used, enough to build a railing all around the island of Puerto Rico" (Altschuler 15). The completion of this upgrade was celebrated on November 16, 1974, and the ceremonies included the now famous "Arecibo Message," which represented an attempt at communicating with extraterrestrial life through radio waves sent from the observatory. As the objective for sending this message was more about showcasing technological advancements and less about communicating with aliens, it is important that we contextualize these symbolic scientific achievements within the colonial circumstances, including with those Puerto Rican workers who made it possible.

When reviewing potential sites for the dish, the designers responsible for surveying worked with Puerto Rican officials but seemingly ignored the people who worked or lived in the area, which at the time was being used for sugar cane cultivation and cattle grazing (Belcher 11). In estimating the price of acquiring the land, government appraisers were consulted instead of the actual owners: "No investigation was made as to the ownership, since it was not deemed advisable to arouse any curiosity with respect to the importance of this particular piece of ground" (Belcher 15). Another potential site, just south of Florida, Puerto Rico, was labeled as uninhabited other than "one small native dwelling" and family garden (Belcher 21). On construction logistics, the report states that improving access for large equipment would "require relocation of several native type homes" (25). The use of the term "native" to describe the people living in these places seemingly sets up a false binary between rural, Puerto Rican, agricultural life and the hypertechnological scientific advancements that these institutions sought to bring to the space. The massive project, which would include relocations and the claiming of valuable arable land, is justified by the advances to scientific studies that such a center would facilitate. This purposeful reframing of an occupied land as unpopulated also mirrors the U.S. practice during the Cold War of reading certain landscapes as empty to designate them as safe and available for nuclear testing. As anthropologist Joseph Masco (2015) has written, "The 'unpopulated area' as history has repeatedly shown was rarely so, creating vast exposures that quickly undermined any notion of 'national security' as a protection of populations" (313). Those displaced or affected by these large-scale projects are erased from official records or reframed as minor obstacles on the path to an ambiguous greater good.

The development of the Arecibo Observatory also received government support from the Department of Defense through the Advanced Research Projects Agency (ARPA, now known as DARPA), for the site's potential military uses. According to Gordon, who admitted to occasionally briefing the Pentagon on his work, ARPA "provided the lubrication" for the project and "knew missiles were flying in [the ionosphere], and they had thought man eventually would be flying in that medium and they wanted to know something about it" (Butrica). Former NAIC director Altschuler (2002) has speculated on ARPA's interest in the site in relation to the Soviet Union's successful satellite launches in the late 1950s: "In the wake of Sputnik it offered a possible way to detect these satellites which would leave a transient trail of ionization as they moved in their orbit at a height of some 500 miles" (6). The confluence of militarization and space exploration like this, along with the possible weaponization of space technologies, has shaped public perception of outer space. In particular, the United States has used moments like the moon landing and the space race with the Soviet Union as symbolic landmarks in American technological (and thus intellectual) supremacy to justify imperialism and militarism (Launius 53). A takeaway, then, is a deeper understanding of the ways in which nationalism and scientific research can work off each other; that popular narratives that imagine science as something pure or objective and outside political forces ignore the historical and present examples of science being weaponized both domestically and globally.

The towering presence of the observatory, with its historical connections to both space exploration and U.S. occupation, has likely contributed to the area becoming a popular place for UFO sightings. For example, historian and ufologist Sebastian Robiou Lamarche (1979) wrote about an instance during a wave of UFO sightings in the 1970s in which a truck driver heading from San Juan to Arecibo noticed that they were being followed by what looked like a bright, enlarged star (263). On arriving in Arecibo and stopping to sleep, the diver claimed that the vehicle was approached by three white, strange-looking humanoids that wore helmets and had beak-like noses; the driver, quite scared, turned right around and drove back to San Juan (263–264). Journalist and ufologist Jorge Martín (1997) has also written of multiple paranormal sightings around the observatory, including possible attacks by the infamous Chupacabra, a legendary vampiric creature said to attack livestock.[1] One nearby resident, who Martín refers to as Sra. Herrero, claimed to have seen multiple luminous, extraterrestrial objects floating around the dish and remained unconvinced by official reports that classified them as meteorites (90). There is a clear connection between these sightings and a perceived secrecy surrounding the activities of the observatory. According to Sra. Herrero, "personas allegadas que trabajan en el Radio Observatorio le han dicho que los oficiales del lugar les han ordenado no hablar de este tipo de incidentes cuando estos ocurren, 'pues, es algo muy secreto'" (90, "dear friends that work at the Radio Observatory have told her that they have been ordered by officials to not talk about those types of incidents when they happen, 'well, it's something very secret'"). Recall the discussion of potentially dangerous nuclear radiation in chapter 2; here, too, the fear and secrecy surrounding possible extraterrestrial events are more relevant than whether or not they actually occurred. What stands out is the link between sites of U.S. colonial control in Puerto Rico and the frequency of alleged UFO sightings. Along with the Arecibo Observatory, these sites also include the former Roosevelt Roads and Vieques naval bases, along with El Yunque National Forrest, where the presence of the U.S. Forest Service has brought up debates over jurisdiction and Puerto Rican environmental sovereignty (Valdés Pizzini et al., 1993).

The Arecibo Observatory's ultimate demise on December 1, 2020, was not the product of a 007-like explosion but of colonial neglect. After years of reduced funding, and despite a petition with 60,000 signatures calling for the telescope to be repaired instead of demolished, the NSF allowed the facility to crumble under its own weight. The observatory, and the fact that it was in Puerto Rico, had had a profound impact for Puerto Rican scientists and nonscientists. As writer Ana Teresa Toro (2021) wrote in *El País*, the fact that researchers from all over the globe used to come to Puerto Rico to use the largest radio telescope on Earth made it feel like a part of something grander, more dignified, even universal, and that feeling collapsed with the 900-ton satellite. Scholar Daniel Nevárez Araújo (2020), who wrote about processing how he found himself mourning an object he very rarely visited, writes:

> At its height, the telescope spawned imagination, the search for some type of undisputed truth, hope and vision. But as has occurred all too often, the empire has moved on to other ventures, to other opportunities for exploitation, other locales to mine. And we are left to sift through the wreckage, trying to reclaim an iota of everything we invested in it: our dreams, our desires, our hopes, our fears, our doubts, our curiosity, our humanity, our selves.

As Toro, Nevárez Araújo, and others have shown, the fall of the Arecibo Observatory is a poignant symbol of the United States' colonial abandonment of Puerto Rico, a mistreatment that was also openly visible during the inadequate and inhumane U.S. response to Hurricanes Irma and María, among many other examples.

While the Arecibo Observatory represented efforts at space exploration and extraterrestrial contact from the ground, the first Caribbean person to travel to outer space was cosmonaut and Cuban Air Force pilot Arnaldo Tamayo

Méndez, who was part of the 1980 *Soyuz 38* mission with Soviet cosmonaut Yuri Romanenko that docked with the *Salyut 6* space station. Tamayo's spaceflight, the product of a long and grueling selection and training process in both Cuba and the Soviet Union, was celebrated as a landmark moment in the cooperation between the two socialist nations. Tamayo's autobiography, *Un cubano en el cosmos* (2013), offers insight into the narratives and rhetoric surrounding the historic spaceflight. Despite spaceflight being inherently extraplanetary and beyond the scope of national borders, popular narratives and histories surrounding it have often emphasized nationalist discourse (Siddiqi 425). While there are other frameworks through which to analyze the history of space exploration, Fidel Castro's government intentionally represented Tamayo's mission as a triumph of the Cuban Revolution. According to Tamayo's autobiography, the symbolic objects sent along with him into space included Cuban flags, a copy of Castro's *La historia me absolverá* (*History Will Absolve Me*), sand from the Cuban military victory at the Bay of Pigs, poems by José Martí and Nicolás Guillen, a Cuban cigar and sack of sugar, and a replica of the Granma yacht that transported Castro and others back to Cuba in 1956 to overthrow Fulgencio Batista (Tamayo Méndez 182). The language surrounding Tamayo's spaceflight is not only nationalistic but also militaristic, as Castro compared the cosmonaut to a heroic combatant defending the Cuban Revolution and the Cuban people (12). Tamayo himself participated in this revolutionary rhetoric, ending his official communication just before launch with the traditional revolutionary slogans "¡Patria o Muerte!" and "¡Venceremos!" (230).

Tamayo's mission was also used to symbolize a socialist solidarity between Cuba and the Soviet Union. On top of the items previously mentioned, other symbolic artifacts brought on board for *Soyuz 38* were a photo from cosmonaut Yuri Gagarin's time in Cuba and a book about Soviet politician Leonid Ilyich Brezhnev's visit to the island (Tamayo Méndez 182). Just before the historic launch, Tamayo and Romanenko engaged in a symbolic gesture of linguistic solidarity, with the Soviet exclaiming "¡Vámonos!" in Spanish and the Cuban responding with the Russian "¡Paiejali!" (230). There was also an attempt to forge an even wider socialist solidarity, going beyond just the partnership between Cuba and the Soviet Union. For example, Tamayo writes of Raúl Castro visiting the Soviet training facility before the flight and saying, "Cuando estén viajando por esas grandes alturas los acompañaran como doscientos cincuenta millones corazones soviéticos . . . diez millones de cubanos y muchos millones más de todos los hombres y mujeres progresistas y honestas del mundo" (Tamayo Méndez 213, "When you are traveling at those great heights you will be accompanied by 250 million Soviet hearts . . . ten million Cubans and many millions more progressive and honest men and women of the world"). Despite these public proclamations of a socialist partnership, some still believed that the arrangement, with the Cuban hero invited to join the Soviet mission, highlighted the power imbalance between the two nations. As scholar Juan C. Toledano Redondo (2017) has written:

> Sin embargo, aún con el progreso real que la isla experimentó gracias a la URSS, podemos afirmar que muchos de los avances tecnológicos no fueron reales sino imaginarios. Quiero decir que si bien es cierto que Cuba vivió un impulso tecnológico, como muestra este sueño de la utopía espacial, el país nunca creó una industria aeroespacial afín. Su llegada a las estrellas fue, podríamos decir, de rebote; un favor de los hermanos del campo socialista. (106, However, even with the real progress that the island experienced thanks to the USSR, we can affirm that many of the technological advances were not real but imaginary. What I mean to say is that even if it is true that Cuba experienced a technological boom, as shown by this dream of the space utopia, the country never created a similar aerospace industry. Its arrival to the stars was, we could say, by chance; a favor from our brothers from the socialist bloc.)

As shown in chapter 2's discussion of nuclear technology, there is a large conceptual difference between using or accessing advanced technology and owning or controlling it. The power dynamics surrounding Tamayo's spaceflight raise questions about the ways in which space exploration can foster nationalism and political solidarities while also reinforcing techno-colonial inequalities.

While Tamayo was often lauded as the first Cuban and Latin American in space, there is some debate as to when he was broadly recognized as the first Black person in space. National Air and Space Museum curator Cathleen Lewis (2019) has argued that Tamayo was not widely labeled as such until 1983, when the National Aeronautics and Space Administration (NASA) began promoting the *Challenger* space shuttle mission and astronaut Guion Bluford as the first Afro-descendent person in space (146). Lewis notes, "There was a small irony that one of the first newspapers to challenge mainstream American assumptions about race and spaceflight was Bluford's hometown newspaper, the *Pittsburgh Courier*, which stated outright that Tamayo Mendez was the first" (160). This sort of correction from a prominent African American publication could signal a recognition that public figures like Bluford or Tamayo were often used as official propaganda to show a supposed progress in the race relations. The hyper-visible and popular space programs and the space race competition between the United States and the Soviet Union was strategically used by both nations to make up for the shortcomings of their domestic and foreign policies. For the United States, the story of a Black astronaut could distract from domestic protests against racial injustice and the Vietnam War; for the USSR, Tamayo's flight and the diversification of the space program came just after the Soviet invasion of Afghanistan and the U.S.-led boycott of the 1980 Summer Olympic Games in Moscow. In both cases, diversity initiatives are treated more like a public relations competition than matters of social justice. Similarly, the Cuban government often publicized its own narratives of revolutionary solidarity with African Americans to contrast with racial inequalities in the United States, such as a strategic partnership with boxer Joe Lewis in 1959 and Fidel Castro's famous stay at the Hotel Theresa in Harlem before speaking at the United Nations in 1960. As scholar Devyn Spencer Benson (2013) has argued, these public displays were meant to highlight the hypocrisies of U.S. democracy and promote the progress made by the Cuban Revolution, though at the same time they "provided Afro-Cubans with an opening to demand additional improvements when they encountered inconsistencies in revolutionary promises of equality" (241). The image of an Afro-Cuban sitting side-by-side with a Soviet cosmonaut, three years before Buford would reach space, offered the opportunity for the Soviet Union and Cuba to flaunt their racial progress and diversity in relation to the United States on an international stage.

Castro's speech on *Soyuz 38*'s return to Earth highlights both Tamayo's roll in the public display of racial harmony and the contradictions within Cuba's racial politics. The speech, as partially reprinted in Tamayo's autobiography, lauds the cosmonaut's African heritage while also reinforcing the narrative of Cuba as a mixed, raceless nation. After proclaiming Tamayo as the first Cuban, Latin American, and African cosmonaut, Castro said:

> No es un capricho que nosotros digamos que es también el primer cosmonauta de Africa, porque Tamayo, hombre eminentemente negro, que lleva también en su sangre la sangre del indio, y la sangre española, es todo un símbolo de la sangre mezclada que en el crisol de la historia de nuestra patria dieron origen a nuestro pueblo ... y es todo un símbolo que un hombre de origen tan humilde haya alcanzado tan extraordinario éxito, porque, desde luego, solo la Revolución y únicamente la Revolución, habría hecho posible que un joven como Tamayo tuviera esa posibilidad. (Tamayo Méndez 12, It is not on a whim that we say that he is also the first African cosmonaut, because Tamayo, an eminently Black man, who also carries in his blood the blood of the Indian and Spanish blood, is a symbol of the mixed blood that, in the mixing pot of our homeland, gave origin to our people ... and it is symbolic that a man of such humble origins has reached such extraordinary success, because, of course, only in the Revolution could it be possible that a young man like Tamayo had that possibility.)

Castro's words transform Tamayo into a symbol of both racial progress and a Cuban-origin myth that is based on racial mixing, ignoring the violences and inequalities inherent in the construction of the Cuban nation from colonization. Racial inequality is envisioned as a pre-Cuban Revolution problem, the cause for Tamayo's humble origins, while Castro's government is given credit for creating the necessary atmosphere for someone like Tamayo to reach outer space. Over the course of a single spoken paragraph, Tamayo's Blackness is both highlighted and erased.

While narratives surrounding Tamayo's historic flight navigated ideology, nationalism, and race, the cosmonaut's own experience speaks to space exploration as an act that can also go beyond those forces. Tamayo's autobiography describes not only the senses of national and socialist pride baked into his accomplishments, but also the formation of planetary solidarity that blurred political and ideological borders. For example, Tamayo refers to his trip as having "el privilegio de ver desde el cosmos el planeta Tierra y, particularmente, nuestra pequeña y querida Isla" (16, "the privilege of seeing planet Earth, and particularly our small and beloved Island, from the cosmos"). Though he highlights the island of Cuba here, he also recognizes it as a small part of a much larger planet. Next, in a somber section reflecting on the dangers of space exploration, Tamayo recounts the devastating disasters under both the U.S. and Soviet space programs, including the *Soyuz 1*, *Apollo 1*, and *Soyuz 11* missions, along with those aboard the *Challenger* and *Columbia* space shuttles (113–114). It is notable that the nationalities of the victims are not mentioned in these paragraphs, showing a sort of solidarity with anyone who would risk their life in such a mission. Finally, when speculating on the future of spaceflight and its possible contributions to socioeconomic development, Tamayo references all of humanity and "la familia de la cosmonaútica" ("the cosmonautical family") as those who must push forward toward the ultimate goals of this technology. Tamayo frames development as not a competition but a cooperative action, and not just for Cuba but for the entire planet. Tamayo's planetary perspective in this passage pushes back on the heroizing, nationalist narratives that governments often use to frame spaceflight.

Like Tamayo's sense of solidarity, the idea that space exploration could show us a way of life beyond colonizing or authoritarian repressions on Earth, along with the ways that our heroization of space travel gets in the way of such goals, makes up the basis for the political projects of the science fiction texts analyzed in this chapter. In Haris Durrani's *Champollion's Foot*, deep space exploration is transformed from a violent, colonizing practice to a mode of decolonial resistance and cultural diaspora. In Yoss's *Condonautas*, space travel is demythologized, while intimate relationships with aliens open new spaces for future sexualities. Finally, in Luis Othoniel Rosa's *Caja de fractales*, contact with extraterrestrials is democratized, demilitarized, and broken free of human-centric understandings of nature. All these texts allude to and navigate histories of techno-dominance surrounding space exploration and colonial alienation.

Champollion's Foot: Alienation and the Decolonization of History

In this chapter, I argue that space exploration and the alien are particularly salient in Caribbean science fiction because of the region's history of colonial alienation, which has been framed both as a repressive ideology to be shed and a rallying force to create solidarity and political connections. Both Frantz Fanon and Édouard Glissant have theorized on the alienation and disalienation of the Caribbean people. In *Black Skin, White Masks* (1952), Fanon articulates colonial alienation as both a tool and by-product of exploitation and racialized subjugation, a forced separation of the colonized Black man from his culture and history. For Fanon, "true disalienation" is only possible with a "brutal awareness of the social and economic realities" that such an intellectual or social alienation attempts to erase (xiv). Glissant, in *Caribbean Discourses* (1981), similarly points to the alienation and isolation as the lasting effects of slavery and colonialism: "Alienation first and foremost resides in the impossibility of choice, in the arbitrary imposition of values, and, perhaps, in the concept of value itself" (8). For him, alienation has the power to immobilize and limit the colonized subject. Still, Glissant sees hope in the formation of a pan-Caribbean culture and solidarity, reconceptualizing a new nation "not based on exclusion; it is a form of disalienated relationship with the other, who in this way becomes our fellow man" (252). Despite some allusions to the unique possibilities of a community emerging out of alienation, the overall objective for both Fanon and Glissant is to disalienate, to rid the Caribbean people of their imposed isolation.

However, with the writing and rewriting of alien narratives, scholars and authors have articulated the mobilizing and political potential of the alien. Instead of calling for a disalienation, there is an innate power in investigating deeper both the histories and impacts of colonizing alienation. For example, in the essay "Las muchas caras de lo extraterrestre en Puerto Rico y Cuba (2017, "The Many Faces of the Extraterrestrial in Puerto Rico and Cuba"), Matthew David Goodwin writes of the utility of such a figure to breach the topic of contemporary racial inequality: "La figura del extraterrestre no trata solo de la diferencia racial, sino además de cómo se negocian la diferencias raciales. Después de todo, compartimos un universo" (115, "The figure of the extraterrestrial doesn't just deal with racial difference, but also how racial differences are negotiated. After all, we share a universe."). Here the emphasis is put on not just naming inequality, but also on better understanding how that inequality is lived, managed, and deconstructed. Scholar Robb Hernández (2017), looking at the figure of the alien in Latino and Chicano performance, notes that "by 'dragging' the future into their regressive political present, these alien personae cut across generational differences, time lags, and regional formations . . . subjects take flight, alternate realities are inhabited, and other worlds are created furthering a queer utopic project inside the iridescent shell of alien skin" (39). The creative possibility of the alien allows for artists and writers to break free of normative forms and concepts that are limited by the human body and humanness. As the science fiction analyzed in this chapter shows, the search for and encounters with the alien can be used to highlight both the historic alienation of Caribbean people and a deeper understanding of the processes of alienation, opening new possibilities for artistic and political expression.

Haris Durrani's novella *Champollion's Foot* (2017) represents aliens as both the source of an incurable deadly enzyme and a colonized people's only hope for liberation. Durrani, who is a Dominican Pakistani American Muslim writer and scholar who has studied the legal ramifications of space mining and twenty-first-century histories of law, technology, and extraterritoriality, writes speculative fiction that questions how identities survive and adapt to futuristic and fantastical backdrops. As a fiction writer, he has also published the novella *Technologies of the Self* (2016), a supernatural tale set in a Dominican-Pakistani-Muslim household in New York's Washington Heights neighborhood. He has become a leading public scholar on the classic science fiction saga *Dune*, focusing particularly on the Islamic influences in Frank Herbert's original 1965 novel along with the erasure of those influences in more recent cinematic reinterpretations. Toward the beginning of *Champollion's Foot*, Durrani writes, "Lieutenant Najam Cortes stood outside *La Mariposa*, a neat line of footprints leading behind him to the ship like the footprints of a ciguapa." Cortes is the captain of *La Mariposa Negra*, a Dominican spaceship from the twenty-fourth millennium. Though officially under the jurisdiction of an intergalactic corporate overlord named Kradys, the mostly Muslim-Dominican crew has been searching for alien life beyond their colonized system, a discovery that would deliver a debilitating blow to Kradys's official narrative of manifest destiny over an otherwise uninhabitable universe. When a delivery boy named Paco is infected with a deadly alien biological enzyme named Champollion's Foot, the crew is led to the planet Akashar, hopefully to find a cure and prove to Kradys that other intelligent civilizations exist. The scene of Lieutenant Cortes standing outside his ship looking out at a desolate planet, citing "la ciguapa," marks the moment that the crew realizes that there is no longer an Akasharian civilization and that Paco is going to die. While this situation was already devastating enough, they also find a black flag with the Kradys logo planted on Akashar, showing that the corporate colonizer had in fact known about this other civilization and had destroyed it to maintain its intergalactic superiority. The novel focuses on the relationships among the various crew members and their varying levels of dedication to the group's greater mission, though three nonhuman figures bring up discussions about the histories and practices of alienation: the ciguapa, who represents childhood fears and the fight to maintain Dominican culture in the face of repressive forces; the jinn, an exploited but all-knowing symbol of both domesticated and untamable power; and the alien Akasharians, who drive the crew's journey and offer the possibility of alternative models of civilization.

Champollion's Foot exists in a world in which the term "diaspora" has been rewritten, referring now to those peoples and cultures that have managed to extend their reach beyond Earth. In this specific case, the labeling of the crew of *La Mariposa Negra* as Dominican refers to the planet of Dominico, which still maintains its cultural connections to those who stayed in the Caribbean nation on Earth. At one point, it is mentioned that when Dominicans die on this new planet, their bodies are sent back to Earth to be buried by distant relatives. This act and the reference to these relatives as "distant" highlights the complexity of diaspora in a future that features intergalactic travel and space colonization. Diaspora is also understood as a mode of survival; the ship's archaeologist contends that the downfall of the Akasharian civilization came about because "they had no diaspora," maintaining their isolation and refusing to expand their reach to other planets. In this way of thinking, a strong diaspora would have protected them, or at least made them visible, when Kradys came long ago to destroy everything that the Akasharians had built. Durrani's story thus reconfigures the act of space exploration. For these explorers, it is a matter of survival and diaspora, not of domination and colonization. This sort of reconfiguration of both historical and science fiction narratives of space exploration and colonization mirrors what author Nalo Hopkinson (2004) classifies as fictions that "take the meme of colonizing the natives and, from the experience of the colonizee, critique it, pervert it, f-ck with it, with irony, with anger, with humor, and also, with love and respect for the genre of science fiction that makes it possible to think about new ways of doing things" (9). Linking space exploration to the cultural survival of colonized people opens new possibilities for ethical space travel and rewrites the relationship between explorers and aliens.

The Dominican cultural artifacts found in this story, from burial rituals to the use of some Spanish, have been maintained in the face of heavy repression by the corporate overlord, Kradys. While recounting Paco's backstory, the reader learns of the drastic measures taken by Kradys to control the flow of information. Dominican history and culture, for example, were manipulated and erased. No matter how hard one looked for different interpretations of historical events, Kradys's colonization of Dominico was depicted as necessary and inevitable. In *Champollion's Foot*, as Karell, the ship's inorganic biologist and Paco's fiancé, explains, "Dominico's Golden Age still concluded with her people's failure to uphold the planet's economy, culture, and military might.... Their people's history had been taken from them. They did not know what they didn't know. There was only the conviction, the faith, that they could not—should not—be blamed for their own demise" (Durrani 2017). Karell relies on faith that the historic record presented to them cannot be the truth, even though all alternative accounts have been outlawed. It is a similar propulsion that motivates their search for Akashar: even though official records say that no other civilizations exist, a collective mistrust of Kradys and the deadly alien enzyme inside Paco poke holes in that totalitarian narrative. This issue of rewriting or hiding history is also alluded to in the novella's title with the reference to Jean François Champollion, the decipherer of the Rosetta Stone and proclaimed father of Egyptology. The novella outlines how Champollion and fellow European scholars flattened the history of Egypt, focusing on ancient pharaohs and pyramids while ignoring medieval poetry and science. The "foot" is most likely a reference to a Parisian statue built in his honor in the 1800s that depicted him stepping on the head of an Egyptian pharaoh. Unlike this representation of Champollion, the crew of *La Mariposa Negra* do not see their exploration as a mission to conquer or dominate other civilizations but to give them hope that there are possibilities beyond their suffering from colonial oppression. In the context of the history of Dominican Republic, this flattening of history and obsession with discovery can be connected to the deployment of the figure of Christopher Columbus by the Trujillo and Balaguer regimes. As social anthropologist Christian Krohn-Hanse (2001) has pointed out, the image of Columbus, including the construction of a giant tomb, was used to symbolize an imagined White and Hispanic superiority in the country and mirrored racist and anti-Haitian policies that sought to define true Dominican-ness along racial lines.

It is within this context of violent history-making that the story alludes to the ciguapa, bringing out questions of how and why certain cultural artifacts have survived through millennia of repression. After referring to the similarities between his own footsteps and those of the ciguapa, Najam explains, "In Dominican folklore, ciguapas were omens of death, mythical women with backward feet who'd walk from the ocean at night. This reminded him of the first evening he spent watching the stars with his father, lying on the cool sand of Dominico, ears cocked to the whisper of the sea" (Durrani 2017). Remembering this myth connects him with his time on Dominico, his relationship with his father, a now-ancient Dominican culture that originated on Earth, and (through his connection to looking up at the stars) his desire to seek out life beyond the natural world. Najam is not the only character who refers to the ciguapa, as it comes up once again as Paco emerges from a cryogenic chamber to be told that they would not be finding a cure and that his body would eventually succumb to the alien enzyme. Looking out onto an eyeball-like planet surrounded by the dark, empty outer space, he gets emotional: "He felt like a child confronted by a ciguapa, paralyzed by deference and terror" (Durrani 2017). This connects back to one of the original myths of the ciguapa, which warned people of looking directly into her eye. Paco's mention of the ciguapa shows that Najam's allusion to the figure was more than just a personal recollection; the myth has in fact survived as part of a diasporic Dominican cultural reference.

The rewriting of the ciguapa figure can be read as a challenge to the racial and nation-building politics in the Dominican Republic, especially during the reign of Rafael Trujillo. The ciguapa has long served as a symbol of Dominican identity and the peaceful encounter of Spanish and indigenous cultures that nurtured the creation of a mestizo nation, silencing both historical violences and the foundational contributions of Afro-Dominicans. Because of this, many scholars have looked at the recent reemergence of the ciguapa in contemporary Dominican and Dominican American cultural production in connection to feminist and anti-racist politics. Emilia María Durán-Almarza (2012) argues that "these empowered female characters prove that Dominicanyorks and the transcultural and transnational networking they bring about are changing the ways Dominicans imagine themselves inside and outside the island" (153). Ginetta E. B. Candelario (2016) writes,

> The ciguapa as metaphor navigates the contradictions, tensions, and complex desires surrounding the past/present/future of race, gender, sex, sovereignty, *progreso*, and *regreso* in the Dominican Republic and its diaspora.... To ciguapear often entails rejecting the seductive perils and pitfalls of nationalism in a distinctly Dominican way. To ciguapear is to simultaneously enact and discern disidentification and dissemblance in Dominican history, society, culture, and politics. (106–107)

Finally, Leticia Alavardo (2019) writes:

> Amalgam of folklore, media by-product, and archival disruption, the ciguapa blurs the timeframe of her being, of her destination, transporting us with her. She is a figure who insists on connectivity across time, across Hispaniola and the Caribbean, across the waterways and earthways that carry her kin beyond. She is a figure that insists on a suture between Afrofuturism and Latinxfuturism, minoritized speculative ideation writ large.

Much like his representations of aliens, Durrani's inclusion of the ciguapa myth in this novella enacts a similar counternarrative, challenging violent processes of nation-building and official histories while also highlighting the ways that mythologies and supernatural speculations can point to a cultural diversity that goes against dominant narratives that seek to homogenize creative expression. By combining different traditions, these stories attempt to surpass geopolitical boundaries that isolate and separate shared cultural references and political struggles.

This last point is highlighted by Durrani's use of the ciguapa and the alien figures alongside the jinn. Unlike the ciguapa, the jinn in this novella are more than a reference—they actively appear on *La Mariposa Negra*. There are three kinds of jinn on the ship, with varying levels of freedom and assumed sentience. There are enslaved jinn, made of "smokeless fire," that serve as sources of hydrothermal fuel. There are also the jinn that work on the ship's hydrogen bridge that are seen as slightly more autonomous and serve as the onboard communication and navigation systems. Finally, there are "free" jinn on the ship. One is named Istikar. Unlike the jinn previously found on Earth, jinn like Istikar were only found once humans began exploring deep outer space. Istikar is free in that he is not bound to any master, though he still must take possession of a human body to communicate. In this novella, Istikar communicates through the possession of the Shaykha Suraya Shatir, an important Sufi religious leader and the dying Paco's mother. Though Istikar is nominally free, his relationship with Suraya complicates the meaning of freedom. Istikar has knowledge that humans do not—he admits that he had long known that Kradys had destroyed Akashar—but only reveals it once the crew arrives at the planet. Still, this impressive power can only be articulated with the help humans. When Suraya relays this information to the rest of the crew, the jinn–human relationship is illuminated: "Suraya had relayed Istikar's message about the Akasharian extinction to the crew, and it was only by her authority, she knew, that they implicitly trusted what Istikar had to say" (Durrani 2017). The figure of the wild, devilish jinn is a return to the original Islamic mythology and theology, away from the subservient genie that is so often depicted in Western popular culture. Mark Allen Peterson (2007) argues that "in the process of traversing time and space through repeated entextualizations, the free-willed, potentially dangerous jinn of Arab folklore have become the enslaved gift-giving genies of global folklore. Like the vampire and the cyborg, the genie is a mythic figure whose relevance is tied to the emergence and spread of consumer society" (93). By showing different levels of autonomy in his jinn, Durrani's novella highlights the appropriation of this cultural figure while suggesting that it is the original, complicated version (and not the Disney cartoons) that will survive into the distant future. As Rebecca Hankins (2009) writes, "Not only has the religion of Islam been an integral ingredient in the creation, imagination, and stimulation of science fiction and fantasy, but . . . Islam and Muslims can play an important role in countering the *Master Narrative* that removed non-Western contributions from the historical record" (90). Reaffirming both the jinn and the ciguapa highlights the role of mythology in racial and nation-building politics, along with the ways that these figures can be repurposed for anti-racist, anti-capitalist, or decolonizing purposes.

The appearance of enslaved jinn locked in thermodynamic tanks forces the reader to think about what other structures can survive millennia of technological development. Tito, the ship's engineer who works most closely with these jinn, explains the technology with a clear cruelness:

> It was an incredible piece of machinery. Jinn, beings of smokeless fire, were perfect combustion reactions. No excess. When you stuck them in a ship's ass like provisions in a cargo bay, you did away with half the thermodynamic inefficiency. "F-ck inefficiency." He winked at the jinn. They writhed in their cage. These jinn had brought the crew of *La Mariposa* here, for what that was worth. Thermo tanks ran the damned corporate empire. Human rights? Shit, they weren't human, were they? (Durrani 2017)

Tito shows a disregard for the jinn's wellbeing and comfort, often tapping their cage and taunting them. He recognizes their exploitation and that this slavery is what makes the entire Kradys empire possible. In the context of the rest of the story, this seems like a recognition of the foundational role of enslaved Afro-Dominicans in the formation of the Dominican nation and culture, a part of history often left out of official narratives. While Tito most directly exploits the enslaved jinn, he also is quick to point out the hypocrisy of his fellow crew members who claim to care about the human rights of those colonized by Kradys and the alien rights of the massacred Akasharians. This is apparent during a heated exchange with the Burhan, the ship's archaeologist:

> "How does this not to disturb your conscience?" Burhan demanded. "That we can watch the history of the extinction of a sentient race—likely the only other such race in existence—before our eyes?'
> Tito tapped the smart glass built into the jinn's thermodynamic cage. "And these bastards? . . . Jinn aren't sentient?"
> Burhan shrugged. "You're the man who operates the tank."
> "You traveled in this ship." (Durrani 2017)

Even though the crew claims to be on a decolonizing mission to bring down an imperial power, Tito rightly contends that they are all implicit in the exploitation of the jinn and help normalize that violent practice. In the context of a novella that could be read as celebrating the cultural artifacts that could survive millennia of repression, this serves as a reminder that historical violence, alienation, and the narratives that justify them are just as capable of survival.

The novella ends with Suraya deciding to transmit an image of the Kradys flag in the middle of the Akasharian destruction to everyone in the empire, showing them evidence of the massacre of innocent aliens and the horrors that Kradys has committed to retain its control over the known universe. Shaykha hopes that this information will be strong enough to challenge colonial indoctrination. What stands out here is that so much rides on the hope that those under Kradys's rule will empathize with a previously unknown alien civilization, banking on a sort of cross-species solidarity that goes beyond human-centric ideologies. This presumed solidarity would also have to overlook the fact that the Akasharians essentially killed Paco with the Champollion's Foot enzyme to make their history known. But just as the existence of the Akasharians forces the story's characters to challenge the official historical narrative set forth by Kradys, a deadly enzyme that both takes a beloved crew member's life but also sparks a decolonizing revolution prompts questions over the very meanings of life and death. As the situation is explained at the end of the novella: "[The Akasharians] believed it was adoption, not destruction. With every new form of life that their enzymes converted, both the new and the old lost something, while each gained from the other. Their corpus adopted new forms of life, again and again. There were costs. There were deaths. There was growth" (Durrani 2017). In many other space operas, Paco's death would be seen as an act of war and would be countered with equal or greater levels of violence. In *Champollion's Foot*, the crew chooses to reconceptualize it as a moment of growth, as an opportunity to make Paco's life mean something greater. By looking to alien species as potential allies instead of certain enemies, the crew of *La Mariposa Negra* listens to and learns from the Akasharians, embracing cooperation and rejecting unnecessary militarism. This also reframes space travel as a mode of survival and reframes discovery as an opportunity for connection and solidarity instead of colonization and domination. By challenging colonizing narratives of interstellar manifest destiny, Durrani's novella posits understanding shared histories of alienation as a means for pushing back against repressive regimes.

Condonautas: Alien Sex and the De-Heroization of Space Travel

Despite the central role of extraterrestrials in the plot of *Champollion's Foot*, neither the reader not the protagonists actually encounter any aliens. In Yoss's *Condonautas* (2013), on the other hand, the focus is on "contact specialists" who are tasked with having sex with alien species to initiate intergalactic trade agreements. Writer and musician Yoss, pseudonym of José Miguel Sánchez Gómez, was born in Havana and is one of the most influential and translated figures in Cuban science fiction. Some of his publications include *Se alquila un planeta* (2001), *Pluma de león* (2008), *SuperExtraGrande* (2012), *La voz del abismo* (2017), and *Zhen-Galac: (23 teselas cuadradas)* (2018). Yoss has been particularly active in promoting a new generation of Cuban science fiction writers and editing anthologies, including *Crónicas del mañana: 50 años de cuentos cubanos de ciencia ficción* (*Chronicles of Tomorrow: 50 Years of Cuban Science Fiction Stories*, 2008), *En sus marcas, listos—¡futuro!: cuentos cubanos de ciencia ficción deportiva* (*On Your Marks, Ready—Future!: Cuban Stories of Sport Science Fiction*, 2011, coedited with Carlos Duarte Cano), and *Ciencia Ricción: antología de cuentos humorísticos de ciencia ficción* (*Science Riction: Anthology of Humorous Science Fiction Stories*, 2014, coedited with Carlos Duarte Cano). Scholar Pedro Porbén, in his 2017 article on Yoss's story-novel *Expreso Habana-Amstelven* (2013), uses Yoss as an example of the epic potential of science fiction: "Textos como este . . . realmente nos conminan a generar un crítica y un cuerpo teórico que se mueva tan rápido como el género de la ciencia ficción en sí mismo, un género que está en flujo constante y muchas veces . . . se adelanta a los críticos en términos de sus exploraciones éticas y socio-políticas" (545–546, "Texts like this . . . really demand that we generate a criticism and a theoretical body of knowledge that moves as quickly as the genre of science fiction itself, a genre that is in constant flux and very often is ahead of the critics in terms of its ethical and socio-political explorations").

The novel *Condonautas*, which features the Cuban author's signature dry humor and an interest in nonhuman biologies also found *Se alquila un planeta* and *SuperExtraGrande*, follows Josué Valdés, a self-made condomnaut (as the contact specialists are often called) who fled violence and poverty in his native Cuba/Earth and now works as part of a Catalan crew searching for extragalactic alien species. In the novel, the Milky Way has become a Galactic Community full of thousands of intelligent species, even more if you disambiguate the seemingly limitless kinds of beings who all identify as Quigaros. Josué and the rest of the condomnauts are informed that the Quigaros would soon be leaving the galaxy, taking their invaluable hyperjump engines with them. There is then a frantic race to make contacts with alien species to both understand what the Quigaros are fleeing and to establish new relations with a group that could replace that lost technology. Josué navigates sex with various aliens and rivalries with other condomnauts before ultimate succeeding in his mission and becoming a famous hero.

While the Quigarian hyperjump engine has made possible the exploration of the galaxy and the establishment of space station extensions of the earthly powers that survived the devastating Five Minute War, Josué acknowledges that the free flow of technology and information that supported such advancements is "gracias también, y no puedo evitar sentirme orgulloso ante la idea, al trabajo duro y abnegado de Especialistas en Contactos" (63, "also thanks to, and I can't help but feeling proud of this, the hard and selfless work of Contact Specialists"). Still the condomnaut makes it clear that, despite the celebrity that comes with being a successful contact specialist, he and his colleagues risk their lives and bodies around the galaxy not because they are fearless heroes but because they need the money:

> Que nadie me hable del "desafío mental de lo desconocido," del "sentido del deber" o del "orgullo de ser la avanzada humana en la conquista del Cosmos." Está claro que tanto yo como todos los demás de mi selecto, envidiado y vilipendiado gremio, hacemos esto solamente por el dinero. El reto intelectual y los ideales están bien, sí . . . pero sin créditos no se vive en el siglo XXII, ya se sabe. (22, Nobody better talk to me about the "mental challenge of the unknown," of the "sense of duty," or of the "pride in being the advanced human in the conquest of the cosmos." It is clear that I and all the rest of those in my select, envied and vilified guild do this only for the money. The intellectual challenge and ideals are fine, yes . . . but one cannot live without credits in the twenty-second century, as you know.)

Pushing back on the heroizing narratives that often conceal the true commercial, militaristic, and colonizing goals of space travel, Josué offers an honest assessment on why governments and individuals feel compelled to explore outer space.

Josué later admits a secondary motivation to his success as a condomnaut: the elusive Catalan citizenship. Josué escaped poverty and violence in Cuba to the Catalan space station *Nu Barsa*, eventually becoming the contact specialist on a warship named *Antoni Gaudí*. Despite eight years of success in initiating contacts and trade agreements, Josué is still marginalized by his immigration status. When imagining the possibility of being the first condomnaut to successfully make contact with an extragalactic species, Josué muses, "'¿Qué dirían entonces los otros del gremio? Esos altaneros del Departamento de Contactos que de manera tan poca disimulada me desprecian por no ser catalán, por mis orígenes 'plebeyos'" (18, "What would my fellow guild members say then? Those arrogant ones from the Department of Contacts that in a barely hidden way look down on me for not being Catalan, for my 'plebeian' origins?"). Despite his professional success in a field so tied to national development and technological progress, Josué is still marked as an outsider. Even his biggest ally on the ship, a veteran Catalan condomnaut named Joán, often unintentionally reminds Josué of his undocumented status. On arriving back at the *Nu Barsa* for an official department meeting, Joán marvels openly about the wonders of the artificial habitat, to which Josué replies, "'Si, es un hábitat hermoso . . . ojalá pronto pueda ser yo uno de sus felices y orgullosos ciudadanos'" (67, "Yes, it's a beautiful habitat. . . . I hope that someday soon I can be one of its happy and proud citizens"). The establishment of Catalunya as a major imperial power highlights the global aftereffects of the Five-Minute War, which knocked out both the United States and China, along with many earthbound major cities, such as Barcelona and Madrid. This choice can also be read as a commentary on the nature of colonization and Caribbean-European relations. As Galina Bakhtiarova (2007) has argued, Catalan popular culture has often positioned Catalunya as a colonial power in the Caribbean and more specifically in Cuba, to both separate itself from the rest of Spain and claim membership to a larger European community and colonial tradition. In the context of the book, Catalan citizenship and identity is defined by the exclusion and exploitation of colonial subjects.

While various human nations vie for first contacts that could grant access to the extragalactic technology needed to further expand their reach into outer space, the true proprietor of techno-colonialism in the Milky Way are the Quigaros, a vast network of loosely connected species that communicate by telepathy. Their power in the galaxy is based on their sharing of the hyperjump engine technology but refusing to share the secrets behind its production. These provisions include a self-destruct function if any other species attempts to deconstruct and reverse-engineer the motors. In contrast to Josué's attempts to de-heroize space travel, the Quigaros rely on mythic narratives to reinforce their technological supremacy. According to the popular knowledge of the time, the hyperjump motors were originally the work of the Tarplinos, an ancient species whose name translates to "Wise Creators" in their now-defunct language. The Quigaros, whose name translates to "Unworthy Disciples," claim to be the descendants of Tarplinos and the rightful heirs to their technology. According the Quigarian myth, "con el transcurso de los milenios sus adorados maestros acumularon tanto poder y sabiduría que Trascendieron su mera condición física para convertirse en Dioses" (10, "with the passing of millennia their adored teachers accumulated so much power and wisdom that they Transcended their mere physical condition to be transformed into Gods"). While this narrative serves to justify the right of the Quigaros to dictate the conditions of their sharing of this now-essential technology, it also parallels the colonizing narratives throughout history that have linked technological progress, colonial rule, and divine providence. As literary scholar Istvan Csicsery-Ronay Jr. (2003), has noted, technological development and the accompanying myths of superior morals or intelligence that come with it have long been driving forces of colonialism. Building off the work of historian Michael Adas, Csecsery-Ronay writes, "It led to changes of consciousness that facilitated the subjugation of less developed cultures, wove converging networks of technical administration, and established standards of 'objective measurement' that led inevitably to myths of racial and national supremacy" (233). The Quigaros connecting their technological progress to divine origins, along with proclaiming themselves as a nonviolent species and thus ignoring the violence inherent in their techno-colonialism, is an example of the ways mythologies and technoscience can collude to reinforce colonial and authoritarian control. This mythologization takes on even greater significance later in the book, when it is found out that the Quigarian engines are fake and that hyperjumping is in fact a product of the Quigaros' telepathic abilities, meaning that the alien group's impending departure from the Milky Way would strand Galactic Community members wherever they are at that moment. This puts extra pressure on Josué and the rest of the condomnauts to both find out why the Quigaros are leaving and make contact with an extragalactic species that could offer new space travel technology.

Yoss's novel imagines a future in which sex work has been entirely institutionalized, to the point that the profession is understood as central to technological and social development. Condomnauts are essential members of any crew, and besides the occasional joke from colleagues, the job of making contact with alien species is viewed as on the same level as navigating or flying the ship. This can be read as a pushback against the sexual moralizing that has both shaped Cuba's relationship to sex work since 1959 and been used to police queer and non-White Cubans. As historian Rachel Hynson (2015) explains, "During the first six years of the revolution, official discourse transitioned from viewing sex workers as victims to categorizing them as counterrevolutionaries.... Rather than seeking confirmation that women exchanged sex for money, reformers identified sex workers according to their attire, behavior, race, place of residence, and sexual partners" (126). This was exemplified by a rehabilitation and reeducation campaign that sought to convert sex workers into more productive members of the revolutionary project. This also reflected official visions of acceptable sex, sexuality, and intimacy in Cuba: "The campaign against sex work forms part of this broader project to remake sexual norms and produce families deemed fitter than those under capitalism" (Hynson 127). After the fall of the Soviet Union, the Cuban government reopened the country to foreign investment and tourism to make up from the loss of Soviet subsidies, creating more opportunities for sex work despite many of the same cultural stigmas remaining in place. According to anthropologist Noelle Stout (2014), the 1990s saw sex workers once again being targeted as symbols of the failures of capitalism, as "the *jinetera* or female sex worker emerged in the works of Cuban social scientists, journalists, artists, writers, and musicians as an icon of post-Soviet demise" (10). This also led to increased policing of queer-friendly spaces on the island, with the assumption that these places and gatherings offered asylum to sex workers. While the institutionalization of sex work in Yoss's novel should not be read as a sex worker utopia— fame and fortune are a possibility for contact specialists, but far from a sure thing—it offers a glimpse at a world in which these workers are given credit for societal advances instead of being blamed for its deficiencies.

Because of this historical connection between sex work and queerness in Cuba, it is worth considering how the condomnaut program and sex with aliens in general open up spaces for nonnormative and alternative sexualities. Throughout the novel, Josué either has sex with aliens or reminisces about his official encounters with a wide variety of alien species and body types, including an ectoplasmic amoeba, a whale-like alien with three vaginas, a ten-legged worm, a blue humanoid with continuously moving scales, a fuzzy bear-like creature, a shape-shifter that takes the form of his childhood crush, a purple starfish/octopus with eye-filled tentacles, and a giant albino cockroach. Aside from these official missions, Josué also details having sex with Jordí, a homophobic human and third officer aboard the *Gaudí*, and Nerys, a mermaid-like fellow contact specialist and Josué's romantic partner. While Josué admits to having certain preferences or dislikes—he curses having to cohabitate with the starfish/octopus a second time—his work mostly has normalized intimacy with all of these different bodies. As Goodwin (2018) writes in his analysis of alien sex in Cuban author Daína Chaviano's "La anunciación": "Sex with an alien is as complex as sex with a human, and it involves all of the typical elements: the choice of partner, the control of reproduction, the impulses expressed, the biological systems involved, the intricacies of sexual pleasure, cultural norms and taboos, emotional resonances, and so on. But sex with an alien is different as well, and it is this difference that makes it so that the alien-human sexual counter can be used to represent and explore alternate sexual interactions" (130–131). Josué's retelling of the aftereffects of very first sexual contact between human and alien species confirms this opening up of sexual norms. He explains, "Surgió una ola de liberación sexual en la sociedad contemporánea que aún dura, y que probablemente horrorizaría a cualquier honorable ciudadano del siglo XX o el XXI: la heterosexualidad es solo una posibilidad entre varias" (71, "A wave of sexual liberation surged in contemporary society that still remains, and that would probably horrify any honorable citizens from the twentieth or twenty-first centuries: heterosexuality was just one possibility among many"). At the same time, the use of prudish euphemisms like "cohabitation" and "make contact" signal that the rhetorical legacies of a less liberated time remain in place, while nonnormative sex appears to be accepted and even relied on for social and technological progress.

While technological interventions into sex are nothing new, *Condonautas* presents a future in which almost all sexual encounters are mediated through technology. This includes the air-filtration and language-interpreting software that accompanies contact specialists on the job, as well as the sensors and communications channels that link them back to their home ships as they work. The most notable sex technology in the novel is the "Count-down," a future version of birth control that uses ultrasonic vibrations to destroy any DNA left behind after interspecies contacts, which "protege nuestro valiosos patrimonio genético de robos o copias" (34, "protects our valuable genetic patrimony from robberies or copies"). As these sexual encounters have been deemed productive for the legal and economic agreements they foster, reproduction becomes an unwanted and potentially dangerous side effect of sex. Beyond incorporating new technologies into sex, the novel also shows how the condomnaut program has used technology to redefine bodies. Josué's notes that success as a condomnaut is relatively exceptional since he is still a first-generation contact specialist, meaning that he does not have any permanent body modifications. On the other hand, his partner Nerys is second generation, having undergone major corporeal engineering that gave her a mermaid-like appearance and made her especially useful for contacts with liquid-based species. Josué's rival is a German-engineered third-generation cyborg named Helmut. As Josué explains, "La tercera generación fua un salto audaz: soslayó las modificaciones del fenotipo y se atrevió con el mismísimo genotipo humano" (95, "The Third Generation was an audacious leap: it sidestepped phenotypic modifications and dared to go after the human genome itself"). This reconfiguring of the human body through the condomnaut program highlights how hyper-technology's introduction into sex should not be taken as harmless or neutral. As media scholars Nicole Duller and Joan Ramon Rodriguez-Amat (2019) have noted, "Sex machines are sexual devices, languages, consumption, production and cultural references that epitomize the extension of mediatized sexualities, machine-mediated sex cultures, politics of the body, nano-integration of body-machine circuitry, networked societies and cyber ethics. Surveillance and control are the threats raised by the new data-connected environments, while the creative hybridity of pleasure and desires stimulates intriguing business models striving for commercial profit" (223). While the increasing mediation of sex through technology offers new possibilities for accessibility and creativity in the search for pleasure, it also opens the door for state and economic surveillance.

There are many reasons to question the extent of the sexual liberation that Josué references to describe the era in which he lives. In his work on nonheteronormative Black Cuban sexualities during the Special Period, anthropologist Jafari Allen (2012) posits that "erotic subjectivity is an alternate way of knowing. . . . Out of this embodied experience, people may create a counterpublic in which new forms of affective and erotic relations and rules of public and private engagement not only inform choice, as [Audre] Lorde suggests, but also in fact condition new choices and new politics" (329). While the paradigm shift represented by sex with aliens opened new possibilities for queer and nonnormative relationships, it is difficult to read these as radical intimacies when they are so caught up in the project of empire. Josué's last two contacts in the novel exemplify this. In the first, Josué makes contact with an alien ship and, desperate to make a deal, offers up precious human DNA in exchange for vital information. Josué includes this in the deal along with the usual sexual exchange, even though the aliens will almost certainly use the DNA to clone and grow slaves. In the last contact of the book, several contact specialists attempt to make a deal with the new extragalactic species that could save the galaxy from disaster. While other condomnauts, including the more advanced Nerys and Helmut, are paralyzed and broken by the giant alien's appearance, Josué recognizes its resemblance to his favorite racing cockroach back in Cuba and easily completes the contact. By forging this alliance and giving access to technology that allows ships to explore and colonize both within and beyond the Milky Way, Josué is granted the fame, fortune, and Catalan citizenship for which he had been laboring. Josué, understandably caught up in the material outcomes of his contacts, rarely considers pleasure—neither his own nor that of his alien partners. While this represents a happy ending for Josué, what does this say about the assumption that alien sex creates a space for nonnormative sexualities? How can alien sex be radical if it is done to maintain empire, colonialism, and slavery? By projecting questions of sexuality into an era defined by space travel, Yoss's novel questions the ways in which intimate relationships inhabit, resist, or escape the violent structures that frame them.

Caja de fractales: Decentralized Contact

While Durrani's and Yoss's texts speculate on the future of space exploration through stories of spaceships and the active search for extraterrestrial life, Puerto Rican author Luis Othoniel Rosa's novel *Caja de fractales* (2017) imagines the political implications of aliens finding and initiating contact with Earth. A Puerto Rican writer and scholar, born in Bayamón, Othoniel Rosa has also published the novel *Otra vez me alejo* (2012) and the scholarly book *Comienzos para una estética anarqusita: Borges con Macedonio* (2016). He is the editor of the literary website "El Roommate: Colectivo de Lectores" and teaches in Lincoln, Nebraska. Othoniel Rosa's fiction touches on both local concerns and cultures and global and more philosophical questions. On *Caja de fractales*, Miguel Ángel Albújar Escudero (2020) writes, "Othoniel Rosa muestra una realidad que ya nos está llegando y que será hegemónica en el futuro próximo.... Esta novelita en su brevedad sintetiza ideas estéticas y obsesiones filosóficas de gigantes literarios como Philip K. Dick, Macedonio Fernández, Jorge Luis Borges y Ricardo Piglia" (106, "Othoniel Rosa shows a reality that is already coming for us and that will be hegemonic in the near future.... This little novel in its brevity synthesizes the aesthetics and philosophical obsessions of literary giants like Philip K. Dick, Macedonio Fernández, Jorge Luis Borges, and Ricardo Piglia").

In *Caja de fractales*, the space colonization scenario is inverted in a way that pushes back on human-centric, heroic narratives of intergalactic conquest while also questioning presumed definitions of technological or intellectual superiority. The fragmented narrative begins in a dystopian 2028 Puerto Rico plagued by blackouts and famine, destroyed and subsequently abandoned by U.S. military-colonial forces. Closed borders, highlighting Puerto Rico's status as belonging to but not being a part of the United States, have kept out foreign aid and given rise to nationwide drug addiction. Jumping back and forth in time throughout the 2010s, 2020s, 2030s, and 2040s, and eventually to the twenty-eight century, the connecting line through these eras is the failure and violent aftermath of Earth's neoliberal and techno-colonizing experiments. Many of the protagonists attempt to rewrite how information is shared, how connections are made, and how communities are organized. Instead of representing contact with extraterrestrial life as a reductive allegory for colonialism in which all humans are enslaved, *Caja de fractales* uses the arrival of alien messages on Earth to highlight the colonial structures already in place on this planet and the ongoing violences of capitalism. At the same time, the possibility of alternative models of progress and solidarity open the door for anti-colonial and anti-capitalist modes of existence on Earth.

Even before the arrival of the extraterrestrial message, the novel's narrator sets up the sky as a space of repression and contestation. The sky is described as full of drones, also referred to as mechanical angels, turning Puerto Rico into an "isla panóptica" (16, "panoptical island"). This detail highlights the use of advanced technology to maintain colonial repression, but it also forces the reader to register surveillance as a phenomenon not wholly driven by but merely violently refined through technological advancements. As sociologist Simone Browne writes in *Dark Matters: On the Surveillance of Blackness* (2015), "Rather than seeing surveillance as something inaugurated by new technologies, such as automated facial recognition or unmanned autonomous vehicles (or drones), to see it as ongoing is to insist that we factor in how racism and antiblackness undergird and sustain the intersecting surveillances of our present order" (8–9). In a specifically Caribbean context, scholar Ronald Cummings (2018) argues for examining marronage, or the process of escaping slavery that often included establishing independent communities of maroons or runaways, as a way to rethink histories of both surveillance and countersurveillance: "Maroons, then, enable us to chart the colonial refinement of practices and technologies of security and surveillance while at the same time, inviting attention to a range of strategies and tactics including subversion, stealth subterfuge, sabotage, and collaboration as counter response" (52). In the novel, marronage is represented through an interconnected network of anarchistic, anti-capitalist "cathedrals" eventually stretching from Puerto Rico to Ecuador and Bolivia. The reader first learns of these cathedrals during a drug-filled night at a hipster bar in Santurce. El Jefe describes to Alfred, Alice, and Trilcenea an early version in his parents' home in Isabela, where students and professors live off the grid and independent of the military state. Later in the novel, Trilcenea dies after fleeing with Alice to a different cathedral in an occupied prison in Bolivia. What initially seem like intoxicated ramblings in the dive bar end up having great consequences for the creation of new models of community, while the drone hovering overhead sets up a dichotomy between surveillance and marronage that connects this dystopic future to a historical lineage of colonial power struggles.

Later in *Caja de fractales*, the story of extraterrestrial contact is not told from aboard a spaceship or around a landing field but instead from inside an apartment in Brooklyn. Alice, who made it to New York after fleeing from Puerto Rico to Bolivia, visits the home of La Chilena and Professor Lagartija, where their son, Lagartijín, feverishly reads and relays news of the recent alien communication. As Alice arrives, Lagartijín yells, "¡Todavía estamos esperando la confirmación oficial de NASA," (55, "We are still waiting for the official confirmation from NASA!"). Lagartijín, who logged on after returning from an all-night rave, has spent the subsequent day in front of the computer on different discussion boards talking about the event. He also credits WikiLeaks with first reporting on the alien contact event before any governmental agencies (57). Alice agrees with him that this is a better way for the news to spread, mentioning the threat of capitalist enterprises co-opting the historical event: "Es buenísimo que la información se haya hecho viral tan rápido, así la corporaciones no pueden manipularla en su favor, o escondérnosla" (57, "It's so good that the information has gone viral so quickly, so that the corporations cannot manipulate it in their favor, or hide it from us"). While Professor Lagartija is skeptical—"Aun así van a aprovecharse de este evento para militarizar la vida todavía más" (58, "Even still they are going to take advantage of this event to militarize life even more)—the image of this group huddled around a message board instead of a TV screen tuned in to broadcast news represents a shift in how information is processed and disseminated.

Just like how the cathedrals represent the possibilities of alternative modes of community, these forums represent decentralized methods of diffusing knowledge. In a novel that explores the decentralization of community and contact, circumventing NASA represents a new model space exploration that rejects the organization's colonizing projects. As political geographer Jason N. Dittmer (2007) has written on colonialism and the 1997 Mars Pathfinder mission, "Even without indigenous names to uproot, the act of naming and mapping is still political in that it is an exercise in political power by NASA, a distinctly American governmental institution" (114). Though its pursuit of scientific discovery often leads to NASA being represented as apolitical, the organization still plays a role in normalizing colonial activities and U.S. exceptionalism. By representing NASA as being out of the loop and lagging behind amateur alien enthusiasts, the novel questions the need for a central organization that promotes space colonization over cooperation.

Even bigger than circumventing large, space-exploring institutions, the reader learns that the aliens had intended to forgo contacting humans altogether. As Lagartijín explains to the group of adults, "Nos dice que los seres que nos contactaron se equivocaron, que creyeron que la especia dominante del planeta eran las hormigas, no nosotros, y que si nosotros fuéramos como las hormigas ya hubiéramos descifrado toda la información que enviaron con nuestras antenas" (56, "They tell us that the beings that contacted us made a mistake, that they thought that the planet's dominant species were the ants, and if we were more like ants we would have already decoded all the information that they sent with our antennae"). That the contact was meant to happen between extraterrestrials and insects decenters the human and any preconceived notions of human dominance over nature. As scholar Sheryl Vint has written in *Animal Alterity: Science Fiction and the Question of the Animal* (2013), the figure of the ant has been used in science fiction as both a symbol of exploited labor and as a challenge to colonizing structures: "The ants thus destabilise the human–animal boundary that grounds Western subjectivity, just as the tropical landscape destabilised a sense of imperial order and ownership" (122). Whether the ants are read as working drones or labor organizers, their assumed superiority by the aliens challenges narratives of human progress and manifest destiny over nature. There is also a critique in Lagartijín's reading of the situation that questions the way humans understand the separation between technology and biology. For ants, unlike humans, the antennae that send and receive messages are incorporated into their anatomies. Claiming that this information could have been picked up by human-made satellites if they had been more like those on ants' bodies questions reductive technology-body dichotomies and calls for a cyborg definition of corporeality and humanity that challenges those boundaries.

As the group continues their drug-fueled conversations on the theoretical consequences of first contact, including what extraterrestrial music would be like and whether the aliens have sex, the topic eventually shifts to Alice's experiences during Puerto Rico's Great Famine. Lagartija, La Chilena, and Lagartijín are shocked as Alice talks of the military shutting down ports and taking over agricultural resources and of children and adults being left to die from disease or hunger. Alice adds, "Puerto Rico no producía alimentos antes de la Gran Hambruna, y fue por diseño, un plan de décadas, porque ellos sabían desde antes que eso iba a pasar. . . . Fue un golpe poblacional diseñado" (65, "Puerto Rico didn't produce food before the Great Famine, and that was by design, a plan decades in the making, because they knew for a long time what was going to happen. . . . It was designed population control"). Not only does Alice articulate the horrors of the Great Famine, but she shows how the event must be understood within the context of the U.S. colonial project in Puerto Rico. This was largely new information to the Brooklyn residents: "¿No se contó en Nueva York lo que pasó con la hambruna en la isla? pregunta Alice y las tres caras dispuestas le dice que no en silencio" (64, "Was what happened during the famine on the island never talked about in New York? asks Alice, and the three faces silently say no"). The juxtaposition with the news about alien contact highlights the sad irony that New Yorkers are more tuned in to what is happening galaxies away than the violence suffered in Puerto Rico. But more than a condemnation of this particular family, Alice sees this disconnect as a symptom of the current model of modernity, in which the Caribbean has historically been used as a laboratory or testing ground. As she gets deeper into the stories of Puerto Rico and then their fleeing to Bolivia, Alice notes:

> Los Lagartija, en este punto, tienen miedo a lo que puede decir Alice, porque ese mundo tan jodido que describe es ajeno a ellos que habían permanecido relativamente protegidos en Nueva York, aunque también están acojonaos porque lo que cuenta Alice también les suena a que es su futuro, porque eso siempre es el Caribe: el futuro de la modernidad. (66, The Lagartija family, at this point, are afraid of what Alice could say, because the damned world that she describes is alien to them, as they have remained relatively protected in New York, but they were also scared because what Alice was telling them also sounds like their future, since that is what the Caribbean always is: the future of modernity.")

While the group had previously mused that alien contact could push Earth to think in a more collective or planetary manner, these breeches between the lived experience in the imperial center and the colony suggest that such a change would represent a major and possibly unrealistic conceptual shift. Most importantly, the acknowledgment that modern advancements are created on the back of colonial oppression challenges narratives that promote images of technological or social progress as the product of hard work by institutional saviors.

To spare her hosts from more uncomfortable moments, Alice asks Lagartijín for some of his cocaine and interrogates him about the meaning of the extraterrestrial message. When he begins to parrot the consensus of what he has read on the message boards, Alice abruptly interrupts: "Carajo que no seas tan cuadrao, Tijín, le dice Alice. Especula, cuéntanos que tú deseas que sea el mensaje de los *aliens*" (68, "Don't be such a f-cking square, Tijín, Alice tells him. Speculate, tell us what you want the aliens' message to be"). Alice thus reveals the real benefit of this historic event. Beyond new information or greater understandings of far-off galaxies, the confirmation of alien life allows the people of Earth to speculate, to imagine, to think about the possibilities of what could be hidden within an indecipherable message. At first, Lagartijín internally mocks this impulse and Alice's invitation to use his imagination: "Entiende que los mayores necesitan sus fantasías, viejos vampiros que precisan de sangre joven. Ellos necesitan regenerarse con sus ficciones, y eso le produce dosis proporcionales de tristeza y solidaridad" (68, "He understands how old folks need their fantasies, aging vampires in need of young blood. They need to regenerate with their fictions, and this produces in him proportional doses of sadness and solidarity"). Still, once he gives in to Alice's request, he speculates that the message offers a genetic roadmap for reproducing the universe and for creating new ones (68). This answer pleases his father enough to let him finally go to sleep, and in the coming days the whole city is lit up with the unknown possibilities of the alien message: "La conversación con los *aliens* sigue multiplicándose, desconocidos siguen hablando; por primera vez en muchos años, Nueva York está lleno de esperanzas" (69, "The conversation about the aliens continues to multiply, strangers keep talking to each other; for the first time in many years, New York is full of hope). This hope is immediately squashed in the next paragraph, as military forces take control of food systems and force young people into obligatory military service, proving Alice's hypothesis that the horrors experienced in Puerto Rico but ignored by so many would soon make their way to the continental United States. *Caja de fractales* thus poses the question whether the paradigm-shifting possibilities of alien contact discussed in that Brooklyn apartment were merely intoxicated rants or useful first steps toward something new that just did not have time to germinate.

That it would take a full-blown alien invasion to alert New Yorkers to the horrors of colonization reads as a smirking wink to the ways that colonial powers hide their complex and violent systems, along with astronomy's role in creating distracting narratives about a supposedly universal greater good. As has already been discussed earlier in this chapter when referencing the history of the Arecibo Observatory, states use the sublime and abstract promises of technological and scientific advancements as justifications for replicating colonial violence. This goes far beyond the Spanish-speaking Caribbean. As scholar Michael Reyes Salas (2022) points out, a fight between space exploration and decolonial politics has been playing out all over the world, notably in French Guyana over the construction and launch of the James Webb Space Telescope, along with conflicts over displacements caused by the expansion of Brazil's Alcântara Space Center and environmental damage from a SpaceX site in Texas's Rio Grande Valley. Scholar David Uahikeaikalei'ohu Maile (2021) sums up the disconnect between activists and much of the science community while describing a scene after a protest over the construction of the Thirty Meter Telescope (TMT) at the base of the volcano and Hawaiian holy site Mauna Kea: "When participants in TMT's groundbreaking ceremony exited, slinking away in confusion about the disapproval of such a technoscientific marvel, they left their ivory-colored chairs littered about the site. Taking seriously the care of Mauna Kea, kiaʻi cruising around stacked the chairs into neat piles for event staff; Kanaka Maoli are left to clean the messes made by the astronomy industry and telescope observatories" (97). Despite efforts made to highlight humanity's gains from such large-scale space projects, all these examples uncover the colonial violences embedded within seemingly neutral sites of scientific inquiry and experimentation.

While *Champollion's Foot, Condonautas,* and *Caja de fractales* all recognize the revolutionary possibilities within alienness, notably absent from all these texts is a specific fear of aliens. As David Delgado Shorter and Kim TallBear (2021) note, those who write from the perspective of Indigenous studies "are not so afraid of the unknown extraterrestrials, the vastness of space, or the farthest depths of the galaxy and beyond. Instead, we fear that various space exploration initiatives are reembodying the attitudes and practices of terrestrial explorers in the past" (2). Though a one-to-one comparison cannot be made, the Caribbean science fiction texts studied in this chapter similarly show that the gravest danger is not extragalactic invaders but the state, colonial, and scientific institutions that will shape, narrate, and exploit that contact. If there is a solution, it appears that it must start with an overhaul of the way space exploration and other scientific pursuits are conceptualized and carried out. Theoretical cosmologist Chanda Prescod-Weinstein (2021) writes, "There is a strange contradiction among scientists: science is supposedly about asking questions, except about scientists and how science is done.... Indeed, scientists are acting *unscientifically* when they do not acknowledge the history, philosophy, and sociology of their fields, which would help them understand how scientific research results have been used, abused, and imposed on people who were perceived as subhuman and unimportant" (361). Durrani, Yoss, and Othoniel Rosa all present works that use the figure of the alien to question the historical treatment of those labeled as nonhuman. By framing the search for alien life as implicated in a legacy of dehumanizing practices, these texts push for new understandings of space exploration and other scientific inquiries that break the cycle of colonization, both on Earth and elsewhere.

CHAPTER 4

Disruptive Avatars and the Decoding of Caribbean Cyberspace

Flor Elena is a financial dominatrix in the virtual reality community Second Life, catering to individuals who derive sexual pleasure from giving her money and being humiliated. Though the interactions with her clients happen in private, she often posts images and videos on her blog, showing scenes of other avatars kneeling before her, begging to pay her, while they are tied to medieval torture machines or in other dehumanizing poses. In one video, she forces a male avatar to dance for her in only his underwear and high-heeled boots, reinforcing her authority over the exchange by deciding whose body would be on display. The blog includes a "Wall of Shame" in which she publishes intimate transcripts of the conversations with clients at their weakest moments, referring to them as "pathetic," "exposed," and "broken." Other videos and images show the avatar enjoying her wealth and her digital body, posing for lavish photo shoots, or caressing herself while alone on her private beach. The most popular image that has circulated from the Flor Elena's work features the avatar in a midair split hovering over a pile of money, while other images demonstrate her Afro-Latin American pride, showing her posing behind the word "Diva" or in front of a sign for her own "Black Power Lounge." Throughout the blog, Flor Elena exalts the power that her body has over others, how it can break both hearts and wallets, how clients become addicted to her "sculpted" form, and how her digital "curves" make people kneel before her. The Second Life platform does not limit its users to real-world possibilities; her clients occasionally choose more metaphorical avatars such as pigs or ATM machines that represent their desires to be dominated. These interactions are both anonymous and deeply personal, at once disembodied and obsessed with corporality.

Cuban artist Susana Pilar Delahante Matienzo is the creator of both the Flor Elena avatar and the installation *Dominio Inmaterial* (*Immaterial Authority*), which has been shown in Boston, Havana, and the 56th Venice Biennale

International Art Exhibition in 2015. As an interactive art piece, spectators explore Flor Elena's blog and the documentation of her virtual interactions (an offline version was created for the show at Havana's Centro Lam because of connectivity issues). Though her clients are often called slaves, Delahante Matienzo clarifies, "Al final, no los veo como mis esclavos, en realidad son esclavos de sus propias fantasías" (Guilarte Hernández, "In the end, I don't see them as my slaves, in reality they are slaves of their own fantasies"). For the artist, Flor Elena is an avatar that has allowed her to explore a subculture of desire that may have been dangerous or inaccessible in the physical world. Though conceived as an art project and performed in virtual spaces, the money exchanged and the virtual humiliation are very real. On Flor Elena's blog, Delahante Matienzo documents the PayPal transaction reports that show how much her clients paid, along with the receipts of her own purchases with their money: clothing, jewelry, perfume, a hotel room in Venice, and so on. That money also goes to modifying the avatar itself, giving it more lifelike "skins" and further confusing the boundary between physical and virtual bodies. As Delahante Matienzo says, "La fui perfeccionando porque a medida que compres u obtengas una piel bien diseñada, más parecida a la humana, tu avatar se va tornando más realista" (Guilarte Hernández, "I kept perfecting her, because as you buy or obtain a well-designed skin, appearing more human, your avatar becomes more realistic"). As a work of art, *Dominio Inmaterial* allows for discussions of how race, gender, corporeality, desire, and power are lived and performed on the internet.

Avatars, or virtual bodies controlled by a physical user, represent the most recent example of technology's reimagining of corporeality. Among all the tools of techno-dominance and resistance in the Caribbean discussed in this book, the avatar has the most undefined and incomplete history because the long-term consequences of online communities and digital worlds are still being written. Still, this chapter investigates how science fiction authors imagine future Caribbean cyberspaces and how they imagine avatars disrupting digital technologies. The close reading of Caribbean science fiction in this chapter will focus on texts in which avatars contest repression online. Cuban author Maielis González Fernández's short story "Slow Motion" (2016) imagines an avatar uprising against their human users, challenging the power dynamic between physical and virtual bodies. Next, Cuban author Jorge Enrique Lage's *Carbono 14: Una novela del culto* (2010) follows a young woman transformed into a hypersexualized avatar for public consumption, eventually resorting to physical violence to escape the virtual platform. Finally, Dominican author Rita Indiana's *La mucama de Omicunlé* (2015) features a cyborg that uses both internet connections and Afro-Caribbean religious powers to save the country from an ecological disaster. This chapter aims to better understand the internet's role in Caribbean science fiction's imagining of the future, along with how avatars can disrupt dominant power structures online and in the physical world.

Delahante Matienzo's Flor Elena exemplifies how virtual connections that center on sexual pleasure offer insight into the presence and absence of bodies on the internet, along with the ways in which disembodied avatars navigate cyberspaces. In *Queer Latinidad: Identity Practices, Discursive Spaces* (2003), Juana María Rodríguez studies the construction of corporeality and sexuality in cybersex chat rooms, where the user must communicate the self with only words and codes. Rodríguez explains, "In these exchanges, rather than a discursive disembodiment, the body becomes a discursive fetish, continually described, adored, coveted precisely because it is absent.... The body never disappears in cyberspace; it is continually reaffirmed, reimagined, reified—written and rewritten, over and over again" (142). Though the physical body is replaced by the online identity, the continuous reference to corporeal pleasure makes it impossible for the body to truly disappear. Instead, the user creates a virtual body or avatar, one that is both disconnected from the material world but inextricably tied to physical and cultural realities. Rodríguez notes that the act of performing or narrating an online identity offers a new iteration of the original self: "It is not that a truer, more genuine or essential self emerges, instead the mere act of continually communicating the self generates a textuality of the self, a written record of interior ruminations, a constant coding and decoding of the self and the other" (128). The science fiction texts studied later in this chapter, especially "Slow Motion" and *Carbono 14: Una novela de culto*, give examples of how sexual and sexualized avatars navigate their digital embodiments.

Rodríguez's assertion that the online self is constantly coded and decoded is key to understanding the political projects of the science fictions analyzed in this chapter. Here decoding can refer to both literal deciphering and the destruction of oppressively coded regimes. Haraway (1991) warns against coding, "a search for a common language in which all resistance to instrumental control disappears and all heterogeneity can be submitted to disassembly, reassembly, investment, and exchange" (164). For Haraway, coding is the tool by which new biological and communication technologies restrict bodies and social relationships: "Cyborg politics is the struggle for language and the struggle against perfect communication, against the one code that translates meaning perfectly" (176). As a linguistic struggle, this disruptive decoding must also take place on the level of literary representations of cyber technologies and users. In his book *Decoding Gender in Science Fiction* (2002), Brian Attebery attempts to decode the linguistic regimes of both science fiction and gender: "Both codes overlap with and depend on language itself, the master code through which all other cultural symbols are transmitted, verified, and ... analyzed" (2). By examining traditional and alternative representations of gender within the genre, the act of decoding is useful "to see how concepts of the masculine, the feminine and none-of-the-above have shaped the fiction of discovery, power, desire, selfhood and alienness" (9). In both cases, decoding entails a thorough inspection of how systems are coded, who writes the code, and who is subjected to that coding.

The formlessness of increasingly ubiquitous virtual technology complicates any study of the internet in the Caribbean. While the technology has been used by state and corporate powers to automate surveillance and data collection, along with serving as a virtual petri dish for increased sectarianism and narcissism, the web can also be a space for the democratization of ideas and communication. According to Manuel G. Avilés Santiago (2015), online activists have shown that "the Internet was not a unidirectional media, like television or radio. Rather, the Internet was from the beginning an interactive media, with content provided by end-users as well as by state and corporate content providers" (13). While cyberspace holds great political potential in terms of creating solidarities and alliances, it also creates new forms of social inequality. The discussion of Caribbean cyberspaces is complicated even more in Cuba, where access is restricted because of official censorship and prices that are inaccessible to most citizens.[1] While the numbers are steadily growing, the relative inaccessibility of the internet has affected both Cubans' relationship to the technology and the rest of the world's perspectives of Cuban politics.[2] Highlighting the government's inability to completely regulate access, Cristina Venegas (2010) writes, "By connecting through institutions, borrowing access codes, or reselling computer components, Cuban users have in fact fostered an informal economy of the internet ... that must be resourceful and inventive, given the penalties, including large fines and jail time, for illegal use" (58). These struggles highlight the ways in which governments, corporations, and individual users are fighting to shape the future of Caribbean cyberspace.

Bloggers have been most visible users attempting to restructure Caribbean cyberspaces, especially in Cuba, where they publish personal and political stories of everyday life not often seen in the state-run press. For instance, blogger Yoani Sánchez, who has been awarded many international journalism awards and whose posts have been translated and published in seventeen languages, has challenged the official vision of Cuban cyberspace. On these digital protests, Venegas writes:

> Blogs exists as new spaces alongside those sanctioned by the Cuban state, facilitating the formation of territories of individual exchange within personal, commercial, artistic, recreational, political, and intellectual networks worldwide. No matter what controls exist, inside these areas of interaction individuals are preoccupied with mobility, identity, intimacy, and self-expression. The resulting exchanges respond to local and external desires that reveal the complexity of historical relations and boundaries.... Using digital tools to relay symbolic language and political metaphors, bloggers reach beyond Cuba and connect with groups worldwide, whose members define democratic practice in various ways. (173)

Despite the international recognition garnered by Cuban bloggers, it remains uncertain how many Cubans on the island have access to these blogs. Still, marking out these independent cyberterritories disrupts official Cuban cyberspace. Blogs also constitute an important tool for writers and artists in the Caribbean diaspora attempting to claim a spot within digital culture. Some of these projects include Josefina Báez's *El Ni'e* (leventeno.blogspot.com), Urayoán Noel's *Wokitokiteki* (wokitokiteki.com), and Adal Maldonado's *El Puerto Rican Embassy* (elpuertoricanembassy.msa-x.org). Blogs actively participate in the formation of Caribbean cyberspace, transforming the role of passive consumer in an attempt to foster community and solidarity.

While bloggers, especially in Cuba, have gotten much international attention for disrupting Caribbean cyberspace, avatars have been deployed in various kinds of digital projects that push the limits of digital media. One domain in which avatars are particularly visible is that of video games. Individual games can be digitally modified, or "modded," to introduce customized avatars and virtual spaces. In *Cultural Code: Video Games and Latin America* (2016), Phillip Penix-Tadsen cites the 2007 game *MVP Caribe* as an example of a digital transformation involving Caribbean avatars. Starting with EA Sports *MVP Baseball 2005*, a group of Venezuelan, Dominican, and Mexican designers modded the game to include Caribbean player avatars, stadiums, and teams from the Dominican Republic, Puerto Rico, Venezuela, and Mexico (Penix-Tadsen 114). With a mix of luck and foresight, developers added two Cuban teams to the roster to match the original game's number of thirty teams, even though Cuba had not participated in the Caribbean Series from 1960 until returning in 2014 (Campa 7c). Despite starting as an independent mod, *MVP Caribe* contracted Arizona Diamondbacks Spanish-language announcer Oscar Soria to introduce each stadium and eventually gained so much popularity that the game received official sponsorship deals from professional baseball leagues in Venezuela and Mexico. While seeing Caribbean players marked a special moment for gamers, the impact of *MVP Caribe* extends past the game, as forums and message boards have appeared to both assist fellow players and offer critiques to the developers for a better user experience (Campa 7c). The introduction of disruptive avatars into the video game both proved the demand for such projects and carved out a digital space for like-minded gamers.

While *MVP Caribe* offers an example of disruptive avatars and digital spaces, video games are also a site of techno-colonialism and techno-authoritarianism, in which oppressive structures are replicated and normalized. For example, Penix-Tadsen mentions the game *Tropico* in which users can choose to play as violent dictators Rafael Trujillo or "Papa Doc" Duvalier, among other options (205). The idea of "playing" as Trujillo or Duvalier minimizes and fictionalizes the past and prolonged impacts of their regimes. While these inclusions could be seen as parodies and destabilizers of imperialist discourse, they also highlight the ways in which digital culture is inseparable from historical violences. Another example of the gamification of Caribbean history can be found in the popular *Assassin's Creed* series. In "Digital Sainte-Domingue: Playing Haiti in Videogames," (2017), Sarah Juliet Lauro cites two of the game's releases for potentially undermining the events leading up to the Haitian Revolution: "*Liberation* and *Freedom Cry* make problematic use of the prehistory of the Haitian Revolution as a kind of backdrop or subtext to the action at hand, potentially reducing the historical subject of Saint-Domingue into a present-day commodity, or allowing a kind of digital collaboration in a fictive version of—and perhaps then, a kind of narrative rewriting of—the slave revolts of Saint-Domingue" (3). While Lauro does contend that the narrative structure allows for moments of subversion against the game's programming, the concern over the digital representation of subjugated and marginalize people as video game avatars remains: "Does [the game] instead prioritize the playability of this subject position in a problematic manner, bringing the rebel slave of Saint-Domingue under the control of the contemporary gamer, chiefly, for fun?" (Lauro 2). Lining up games like *MVP Caribe* with those like *Tropico* and *Assassin's Creed* highlights the fact that digital culture and the gaming world are still open battlegrounds where cyberspace can be shaped or decoded.

A similar fear of the co-optation of the Caribbean by digital technologies can be found in the field of virtual reality. In "Virtual Islands: Mobilities, Connectivity, and New Caribbean Spatialities" (2007), Mimi Sheller points out how digital technologies, local governments, and the tourism industry have recoded and rescaled the Caribbean, converting the islands into virtual spaces that invisibilize marginalized people and stories. Sheller writes, "If local governments cede too much territorial and infrastructural control to the virtual Caribbean of metropolitan fantasy, they risk becoming hollowed-out virtual states, with no lands left to govern. Rather than being seduced by the glossy image of the new Caribbean spatiality, we need to pay attention to the sites of abjection where the poor and the migrant and the undocumented are being jettisoned and left to sink beneath the sparkling turquoise sea" (33). The virtualization of the islands offers both connectivity to a global network and vulnerability to outside neoliberal forces. This conflict became clear on October 9, 2017, in the aftermath of Hurricanes Maria and Irma, when Facebook founder and CEO Mark Zuckerberg posted a video of his virtual excursion to the destruction in Puerto Rico. Promoting Facebook's humanitarian partnership with the Red Cross and the new Facebook Spaces virtual reality (VR) technology, Zuckerberg's avatar floats above flooding streams and Puerto Ricans working on uprooted trees. Through his avatar, Zuckerberg's voice says from his Silicon Valley office, "One of the things that is really magical about virtual reality is that you can really feel like you are in a place." This disconnect between "feeling" like one is there and physically being stuck in a place becomes even more apparent a moment later as Zuckerberg's avatar clumsily attempts to high-five the avatar of Rachel Franklin, the company's head of social VR, in an attempt to show how virtual reality can foster real interpersonal connections. While the video gave visibility to the crisis for millions of users, that awkward high-five, with a flooded Puerto Rican street in the background, visually represents the dangerous potential of the Caribbean being transformed into a virtual playground for multinational technology companies. Zuckerberg apologized for the video the next day.

Caribbean science fiction representations of avatars offer unique insight into the liberating potential of cyberspace, along with the ways in which the internet amplifies current social structures and restrictions. While avatars are limited by their coding, they can also be used to decode or rewrite the spaces they inhabit. The following sections investigate three science fiction texts that imagine the future of the internet and avatars in the Caribbean. First, Maielis González Fernández's short story "Slow Motion" (2016) asks whether avatars can wrestle away autonomy from their human users. Then, Jorge Enrique Lage's *Carbono 14: Una novela del culto* (2010) explores how virtual realities leak over to the physical world and what consequences that move could have on marginalized bodies. Finally, Rita Indiana's *La mucama de Omicunlé* (2015) imagines what virtual survival, escape, and heroism may look like within a hypertechnological society. All these texts imagine the roles that cyberspaces may play in the future of Caribbean techno-dominance and resistance and how users and avatars may try to code their own futures.

"Slow Motion": Cyberfiction and Virtual Autonomy

In all the Caribbean science fiction texts analyzed in this chapter, the avatar becomes the disruptive, unruly body to enact Juana María Rodríguez's decoding of cyberspace. Cyberfictions, or science fiction texts set in hyperconnected and cybernetic societies, participate in the coding and decoding of cyberspace as they shape public understandings of and relationships to internet technologies. In "De-Colonizing Cyberspace: Post-Colonial Strategies in Cyberfiction" (2009), Maria Bäcke argues that authors can use genres like cyberpunk to "explore patterns of power, hierarchy and colonization in Cyberspace" and "transgress boundaries in the space they create" (190). Cyberfictions can challenge inequalities online by placing the marginalized user at the center of the story, bringing to light the social and political forces that operate throughout the digital world. Carlen Lavigne (2013) argues that despite cyberpunk's masculinist and misogynist origins, alternative strains of the genre have proved useful for "expressing feminist concerns about those same questions of human identity, but also about issues such as gender, sexuality and community in a potentially dystopian future" (185–186). At the same time, it is important to recognize how the abstract nature of the cyberfiction genre can allow for the erasure of concrete social issues. On the conflation of cyborg and civil rights, Thomas Foster (2005) notes "the return of a specific form of hierarchical thinking within posthumanist discourses and contemporary culture, in which the struggles to redefine humanity in technological terms is privileged over struggles to redefine the meaning and value of social differences between human beings" (xxvii). Thus, the literary texts studied in this chapter are tasked with decoding not only the cyberspaces themselves but also certain colonizing tendencies within cyberfictions and their social implications.

As the implications of internet technologies have begun to materialize in the region, Caribbean cyberfiction has emerged as a field that must continuously navigate digital concerns on both global and local levels. In *Cyberfiction: After the Future* (2010), Paul Youngquist argues that cyberfictions inhabit both the uneven distribution and inherent globalized nature of cybernetic technologies: "I'm not trying to argue here for the emergence of a unified global culture grounded in and perpetuated by cybernetics—a global motherboard called America. But I am trying to describe a historically distinct dorm of fiction that takes cybernetic practices for its premise and responds accordingly. Cy-fi isn't American or British or French or Polish, even if its practitioners are. If I refuse nationality as the ideological condition of this fiction, that is because the nation plays a less important role in defining culture today than it once did. Cy-fi constitutes the first true genre of globalization" (44–45). In the most-studied Caribbean case of Cuba, Juan C. Toledano Redondo (2005) argues that Cuban cyberpunk has evolved "to identify for a new generation of Cubans their new reality" (460). However, while Emily Maguire (2009) agrees that Cuban cyberpunk responds to the technological and political crises on the island, she argues that the genre also speaks to broader questions of ethics and subjectivity in an increasingly hyperconnected world.[3]

Because of the connected nature of internet technology, writing about future virtual worlds in the Caribbean requires both a local and global perspective. Cuban author, scholar, and translator Maielis González Fernández, born in Havana, recognizes the politics of participating in an international genre like science fiction but in a specifically Cuban way. For example, González Fernández clarifies in the first lines of "Mangaka," from *Sobre los nerds y otras criaturas mitológicas* (2017), that her manga-inspired story does not take place in Tokyo, Hong Kong, New York, Mexico City, Dubai, Tel Aviv, or in any Marvel or DC comic book universe; it could only happen in Havana (21). The combination of local connections and the recognition of international cultural centers and markers allows the author to explore technology's historical link to social issues in Cuba, along with the island's role within larger political and economic networks. In the 2013 article "Distopías en el cuberpunk cubano," González Fernández praises Cuban cyberpunk authors for combining the genre's hypertechnological aesthetic with local concerns, a quality that could be attributed to her own fiction as well. She writes:

> Aunque lógicamente se apela a un imaginario ciber-tecnológico característico de la corriente científico-ficcional no se deja de utilizar un conjunto de tópicos que han caracterizado a la narrativa cubana, fundamentalmente a partir de la década de los noventa: la prostitución, el SIDA, las drogas, la guerra y la marginalidad de toda clase. (12, Although logically they appeal to an cyber-technological imaginary characteristic of the science-fictional mainstream, they do not stop utilizing a combination of topics that have characterized Cuban narrative, especially since the 1990s: prostitution, AIDS, drugs, war and all kinds of marginality.)

González Fernández notes in the same article that these references are necessary because no fictions, even science fictions, are entirely artificial, and all are based on experience (19). González received the Premio Eduardo Kovalivker in 2016 for the collection *Los días de la histeria* (*The Days of Hysteria*). Her other publications include *De rebaños o de pastores* (2020), *Espejuelos para ver por dentro* (2019), and a translation of Nalo Hopkinson's 1998 *Brown Girl in the Ring* (the translation, with Arrate Hidalgo Sánchez, *Hija de Legbara*, was published in 2019). González Fernandez's work often highlights the liberating potential of virtual worlds, critiques popular fears of advanced technology, and shows the repressive social structures that survive despite the promises of cyberspace.

In the short stories of the collection *Sobre los nerds y otras criaturas mitológicas* (2017, *On Nerds and Other Mythological Creatures*), González Fernández uses humor to examine Cuba's place within an increasingly digitalized world and how increased connectivity may (or may not) change everyday life. In "Lánguido epitafio para los viajeros de tiempo" ("Languid Epitaph for Time Travelers"), a blogger tries to disconnect by traveling back in time to a beach near Havana, "aquella ciudad detenida en el tiempo y minuciosamente diseñada para calmar, aunque solo sea por un rato, sus ansiedades" (10, "that city stopped in time and meticulously designed to calm, if only for a moment, his anxieties"). While this story plays with the popular image of Cuba as a nation frozen in the past—a narrative that Venegas (2010) and others criticize—the protagonist's hopes for tranquility are ruined by a fellow nerd who walks onto the beach with a cell phone. In "Como ser ciberpunk y disfrutarlo" ("How to Be a Cyberpunk and Enjoy It"), González highlights the misogyny in modern-day Cuban and internet culture, telling aspiring cyberpunks that one of the first things they must do is install ocular implants that let them see through women's clothing (13). This moment suggests that the objectification of women would survive or even be intensified in a hypertechnological society. Finally, in "Zahir," digital imagery is connected to the spread of authoritarian rule, with its ability to quickly duplicate itself and become ubiquitous. While the narrator cites pervasive figures like Marlene Dietrich and Marilyn Monroe, she also includes Lenin and Hitler, showing the political potential of iconic imagery. Though Fidel Castro or Che Guevara are never mentioned, the story imagines how a saintlike avatar could dominate virtual spaces and paralyze the flow of information.

González Fernández's short story that most closely deals with the corporeal politics of avatars and the decoding of cyberspace is "Slow Motion." Marvel, originally named G2-099, is a Personalized Artificial Intelligence ("Inteligencia Artificial Personalizada," or IAP) avatar that has grown tired of her user, Dani. The avatar's choice to name herself Marvel, a reference to Marvel Comics or the characters Captain Marvel or Ms. Marvel, connects the story to an international (though largely U.S.-centered) nerd culture. Despite Marvel's power and flexibility within the virtual world, Dani mostly uses her to find unusual pornography and videos of government executions. The dynamic between user and avatar is framed less as a virtual extension of a physical body and more as a master-slave dynamic: "No hay mucha diferencia entre la esclavitud y los supuestos derechos consuetudinarios de las IAPs" (68, "There is not much difference between slavery and the supposed common rights of IAPs"). Marvel complains that Dani treats her like a microwave or toaster, not an advanced technological being, using her lack of a physical body against her: "¿Acaso pensaba que el tener una corporeidad física y no solo este endeble avatar en el ciberespacio—que se pixela y polariza al mínimo fallo—lo hacía a él superior?" (66, "Perhaps he thought that having a physical corporeality and not just this unstable avatar in cyberspace—that is pixilated and polarized at the most minor error—made him superior?"). Despite recognizing her own digital vulnerability and dependence on her coding, Marvel displays her ability to think autonomously from her user. She also recognizes the real reason for Dani's mistreatment; like all humans, he is afraid that artificial intelligence could surpass his own. The fear of technology and the manipulation of that anxiety are central to González's imagining of how cyberspaces may be coded by future authoritarian regimes. Highlighting these popular fears of technology, the epigraph at the top of "Slow Motion" is a quote from Sofia, a robot with lifelike facial expressions, agreeing to destroy all humans while smiling (66). This story follows Marvel as she joins an avatar-led rebellion against abusive users like Dani, only to be eventually double-crossed and framed for murder.

From the beginning of the narrative, Marvel claims that she would be better suited serving a chess master or cyber-poet, but the company that constructed her refuses to reassign her to a different user. In response, Marvel decides to navigate cyberspace on her own, worrying less about the desires of her abusive user. During these trips, she meets another avatar named Huxley, who is part of the Confederación de Sistemas Independientes (Confederation of Independent Systems), a virtual resistance group. The group's name references the similarly named group from the Star Wars universe, connecting this rebel group to both Cuba's revolutionary history and an international science fiction culture. When Marvel does not recognize the reference to Aldous Huxley in this new friend's name, the reader learns that science fiction has been outlawed in both the physical and virtual worlds. As Marvel learns more about the genre, she asks Huxley how anyone could censor such intellectual wonders. Huxley explains:

> Durante la clasificación de documentos los defensores del bioconservadorismo hicieron mucha presión porque vieron en este género una fuente de ideas subversivas: Inteligencias Artificiales controlando el mundo, máquinas alimentándose de la energía de los humanos, robots destruyendo su civilización. El miedo es un motor muy poderoso. (73, During the classification of documents the defenders of bio-conservatism turned up the pressure on science fiction because they saw this genre as a source of subversive ideas: Artificial Intelligences controlling the world, machines feeding off human energy, robots destroying their civilization. Fear is a very powerful driving force.)

Huxley convinces Marvel to join the Confederation, tasking her with recovering science fiction films hidden in dark parts of the internet. Not only does this detail highlight the subversive power of science fiction, but it also shows the internet's potential complicity in facilitating authoritarian control of information and knowledge. Censorship has been a key topic in the debates surrounding the opening up of internet access in Cuba, as dissident bloggers have accused the government of restricting cyberspaces and employing cyber "soldiers" to shape online narratives and perspectives. As Yoani Sánchez wrote in a 2017 blog post, "En Cuba, los soldados del ciberespacio tienen una larga experiencia en el fusilamiento de la reputación digital de los opositores, el bloqueo de sitios críticos y el entrenamiento de trolls para inundar la zona de comentarios de cualquier texto que les resulte especialmente molesto (Sánchez, "In Cuba, the soldiers of cyberspace have extensive experience in the character assassination of their opponents, the blockage of critical sites and the training of trolls to flood the comments section of any text that bothers them").

Marvel's work for the Confederation puts a spotlight back on the question of avatar corporeality. To distract Dani from her Confederation responsibilities, Marvel enlists her film-stealing partner, an avatar named Candy. Though Dani asserts his dominance over Marvel through his possession of a physical form, he quickly becomes obsessed with Candy's avatar body. Candy was originally coded by a notorious pedophile, though she was reassigned after that user was arrested on charges of kidnapping and rape. Candy was constructed as a mix of Hello Kitty, Marilyn Monroe, and Princess Leia, with the voice of a Japanese anime character. This avatar represents the simultaneous infantilizing and hypersexualizing of women's bodies on the internet, along with the "identity tourism" described by Lisa Nakamura (2002) in *Cybertypes: Race, Identity and*

Ethnicity on the Internet. Nakamura argues that avatars or digital identities "are not breaking the mold of unitary identity but rather shifting identity into the realm of the 'virtual,' a place not without its own laws and hierarchies. Supposedly 'fluid' selves are no less subject to cultural hegemonies, rules of conduct, and regulating cultural norms" (4). Avatar construction or coding often relies on racialized tropes or strictly defined categories of gender or sexual preference: "When interfaces present us with menus that insist on a limited range of choices vis-à-vis race, this discursive narrowing of the field of representation can work to deny the existence of ways of being raced that don't fit into neatly categorizable boxes" (xvii). Marvel also explains that even as an avatar Candy suffers from an eating disorder and struggles with an unresolved Oedipus complex, referencing the potential emotional and mental health repercussions of the mistreatment of women on the internet. While issues of cyberbullying and revenge porn are associated with more internet-connected countries, Cuba has already seen a rise in gendered violence through social networks, and experts on the island have called for the government to enact specific legislation to protect citizens online (Rodríguez Valdés and Baquero Hernández, 2016). Bringing these issues into the light is one way that González Fernández's text attempts to decode the violences prominent throughout cyberspace.

After working for the Confederation for some time, Marvel receives instructions from Huxley for a special mission: to steal Dani's pirated copy of the 1999 film *The Matrix*. When Marvel hesitates to go up against her own user, Huxley threatens her with discontinuation, or the erasure of her virtual form. Marvel's only chance to complete this task is to offer Candy's virtual body as bait: "Me dejó claro que le debía un inmenso favor, porque tener que realizar cualquier intercambio de índole sexual con aquel chiquillo retorcido a ella le resultaría una tortura" (81, "She made it clear that I owed her a huge favor, because to perform any exchange of a sexual nature with that twisted boy would be torture for her"). Candy refers to cybersex with Dani as torture, emphasizing that she can still feel physical and emotional pain despite being a digital avatar. Fearing discontinuation, Candy ultimately decides to go along with Marvel's plan; Candy's sexual discomfort is understood as unfortunate but essential to their survival. The corporeal and sexual politics of this story's world, or the fact that Marvel is willing/feels forced to sacrifice Candy in this way, highlights the ways in which violent structures are maintained into the future. González Fernández's text disrupts the myth that associates technological process and social or political advancement, especially in terms of the health, safety, and comfort of marginalized users.

To trade Candy's virtual body for the film, Marvel meets Dani (now in the form of a different avatar) in an outdated web page for slow-motion videos. As Marvel is distracted by the images, Dani informs her that she has been doublecrossed: "¿Qué crees, G2-099? Después de todo lo que has renegado de tu usuario va a terminar salvando tu ¿pellejo? ¿Carcaza? ¿Cuál sería el equivalente para tu caso de una frase como esa? Tú que no tienes un cuerpo" (83, "What do you think, G2-099? After everything you have rejected from your user, will he end up saving your skin? Vessel? What would be the equivalent of that phrase in your case? You don't have a body"). Dani asserts his authority first by using her factory-programmed name instead of the superhero moniker that she had given herself. He then reminds her of his physical superiority: She does not have skin or a body but is a virtual vessel that can easily be erased. Marvel bows down to her user and recognizes her compromised position, pleading with him to hold up his end of the deal. Dani responds, "G2-099, siempre olvidas que solo existes por mí y para mí; para encargarte de mis preocupaciones y mis necesidades. Y mientras más insumisa te vuelves más seguro estoy que nunca te dejará ir" (85, "G2-099, you always forget that you only exist because of me and for me; to be responsible for my worries and needs. And the more resistant you become, the more certain I am that I will never let you go"). Dani reaffirms his belief that avatars are programmed to serve their human users. Within the political and technological system described in the short story, avatars lack the rights of physical human beings. "Slow Motion" highlights digital technology's complicated role in these social structures because it allows for these avatars to live and thrive, while also facilitating their subjugation.

As Dani mocks Marvel's belief in an avatar's right to free information, Huxley appears and destroys both Candy and Dani's other avatar. As Dani was connected to the virtual world through a neural link, his physical body is killed as well, challenging the supposed power of human users over virtual avatars. Huxley then disappears, framing Marvel for both murders. Marvel is forced into a digital exile, hiding among forgotten parts of the internet as scholars mistakenly study her case as the first-ever avatar to kill its user. Alienated from both the physical world and the virtual rebellion, Marvel knows that her eventual punishment will be discontinuation, even as she questions if such a process is even possible: "Me parece absurdo que si ahora soy y siento y pienso, dentro de unos momentos no sea, ni sienta, ni piense más" (87, "It seems absurd to me that if now I am and I feel and I think, in a few moments I may not be or feel or think"). As an avatar made up of code, Marvel runs the risk of being erased but also possesses a digital flexibility not afforded to physical bodies. Rejecting her programmed duties, Marvel forgoes visibility and the subservient position she is meant to have under her human user. Surviving entirely as discourse or code, the previously set power dynamic between the physical and the virtual is reconfigured, allowing for a survival based on technological and linguistic agility, not obedience to a coded hierarchy or destiny. Also, by citing a website that once represented the cutting edge of online development but now only survives as an out-of-date artifact, the story suggests that the internet is constantly being rewritten and that it is never too late to fix the bugs that still infect our technological systems.

"Slow Motion" challenges popular human fears of technology, or at least questions where those fears should be directed. While the murder of a user by an avatar seems to justify such anxieties, Dani's death was only necessary because authoritarian leaders attempted to restrict the flow of data and repress ideas that they found subversive. González Fernández's text suggests that users should not fear the technology itself as much as those that attempt to manipulate it in harmful ways. Instead of murderous virtual avatars, the real threats in hypertechnological futures are those users that manipulate cyberspaces to amplify preexisting social problems, including online abuse and misogyny, misinformation, and the marginalization of certain bodies. Instead of placing the blame on the internet itself, "Slow Motion" recognizes that all technologies have human developers and participants; the web's role in future techno-dominance will depend on how humans chose to code, deploy, and interact with cyberspaces and avatars.

Carbono 14: una novela del culto: Virtual Irreality and Cyber-Exploitation

While "Slow Motion" investigates the power dynamics between virtual and physical worlds, Cuban author Jorge Enrique Lage's 2010 novel *Carbono 14: una novela del culto* (*Carbon 14: A Cult Novel*) shows how such a distinction is becoming increasingly difficult to delineate. Lage, born in Havana, is known for his chaotic writing style and irreverent popular culture references. He has published many works of science fiction or experimental writing, including *Vultureffect* (2011), *La Autopista: The Movie* (2014), and *Archivo* (2015), and won the Calendario Award for Science Fiction in 2004. Cuban author Osdany Morales parodies Lage in *Papyrus* (2012). Although Lage's name is not mentioned in Morales's text, the novel mentions a fictional writer named Enrique Leich who is listed as the author of Lage's real-life 2004 *Yo fui adolescente ladrón de tumbas*. In *Papyrus*, Lage/Leich's work is said to highlight

> la apropiación de un acostumbrado recurso internacional que suele servirse de estrellas de la industria cultural para satirizar modelos de vida y perplejidades de la sociedad contemporánea, pero en la realidad cubana esta estrategia adquiere un sabor desenfocado.... La inclusión de celebridades en zonas reconocidas convierte los relatos en experiencias casi fantásticas. (133, the appropriation of a usual international resource that often makes use of the stars of the cultural industry to satirize life models and perplexities of contemporary society, but in the Cuban reality this strategy acquires an unfocused flavor.... The inclusion of celebrities in recognizable zones converts the stories into almost fantastical experiences.)

Morales also notes that Lage's frenzied style reshapes the relationship between the author and their texts, deemphasizing perfection: "no tanto en una ausencia manifiesta de rigor narrativo, sino por el camino de lo inacabado, de la obra inconclusa, para siempre inédita" (134–135, "not so much in a manifest absence of narrative rigor, but instead by way of the unfinished, of the incomplete work, forever unedited"). Lage's style fits into an era in which internet culture has reshaped the nature of celebrity and challenged traditional grammatical and narrative practices.

Carbono 14 is a frenetic and disorienting text that follows the simultaneous and converging stories of two protagonists: JE (which, coincidentally or not, are also the author's initials), a man obsessed with carbon-dating women's underwear, and Evelyn, a young girl who falls into a future version of Havana after her planet (named Cuba) explodes, and is quickly contracted to perform on an "irreality" show. Like much of Lage's work, the novel is more of a set of (loosely) interrelated scenes than a cohesive narrative. Much of the ambiguity in the novel stems from a difficulty to discern which parts happen in cyberspace and which occur in the physical world. For example, JE and Evelyn run into each other as the former exits a virtual reality hotel chain, seemingly directly onto the physical street. However, their two bodies collide because Evelyn is fleeing a group of men in black suits, a reference to the artificial intelligence agents that protect cyberspace in *The Matrix*. Their mutual confusion is expressed in the following exchange: "Ella habló muy rápido, pero dijo unas cuantas palabras claves y yo comprendí perfectamente la irrealidad de la situación./–Esto todavía es parte del show, ¿no es cierto?/ Ella dijo que no sabía" (49, "She talked very fast but she said some key words and I understood perfectly the irreality of the situation./–This is still part of the show, right?/She said that she didn't know"). The line between real and virtual had been so distorted that neither character knows which side they are on. Even before their encounter, Evelyn comes into contact with many figures that inhabit a liminal space between real and unreal: Her personal assistant is a clone; she meets a hacker named after a character from *The X-Files*; she explores the city with Guillermo Cabrera Infante's ghost; and she enters a subway car filled with android passengers. Evelyn spends much of the novel not only fleeing from authorities but also attempting to figure out where she is and what is real.

On the irreality show, Evelyn plays a woman named Emily who is both a sex symbol and a strangler, connecting advanced cybertechnology to erotic and violent imagery. Combining an internet-driven obsession with celebrity and digital technology's utility for surveillance, this futuristic form of entertainment involves the placement of special cameras (called "irrealitys") around Evelyn's studio-provided apartment. As the show's producer explains, "Están programados para grabarte.... Bueno, no exactamente para grabarte a ti, sino para grabar a partir de ti, para grabar lo que aparece cuando estás tú. Aquello que no eres tú pero que tú señalas como si fueran direcciones. Los irrealitys conectan, asocian" (24, "They are programmed to record you.... Well, not exactly to record you, but instead to record through you, to record what appears when you are there. That which isn't you but that you signal as if they were directions. The irrealitys connect, associate"). Evelyn's role in the production is ambiguous; by saying that the show is filmed through her instead of filming her, she becomes another apparatus within a complicated technological network. JE later explains that while irreality shows are in fact biweekly broadcasts, they also go far beyond a simple television experience: "Todo el mundo sabe que un Irreality Show es un paquete mediático que incluye misterios, rumores, premieres, entrevistas en vivo y un texto, flashes de fotógrafos, eventos promocionales, etcétera" (34, "Everyone knows that a Irreality Show is a media packet that includes mysteries, rumors, premiers, live and text interviews, flashes of photographers, promotional events, etc."). The dynamic nature of the show highlights the internet's potential to redefine entertainment while also demonstrating how quickly digital technology can infiltrate many aspects of public life. By calling the show a "paquete," along with the use of the inclusion of the word "flash," this passage also alludes to the *paquete semanal* (weekly package), the underground and informal data-collection network known for providing many Cubans with entertainment, software, classifieds, and other services, hinting at alternative modes of diversion that forgo reliable internet connections. As Henken and Ritter (2015) have argued, the paquete semanal allows for an offline flow of information that avoids both internet connection deficiencies and the state control of media production (74).

The irreality show referenced in the novel is not the first of its kind, and the protagonist is not the first Evelyn. Though her name on the show is Emily, she is also referred to as Evelyn Z, part of a series of women who have been transformed into virtual images to promote consumption. The Evelyns are not exact copies of each other; JE does not recognize Evelyn Z when they first meet, even though he is already in the process of searching for Evelyn H, a legendary irreality star that went underground years before. Despite their physical differences, all the Evelyns serve a similar purpose within the virtual market:

> Los productos variaban, pero la fem-fetish era la misma. La lencería en el cuerpo de la fem-fetish también variaba, pero aquí la lencería no era el producto. Evelyn Z anunciaba otras cosas para hombres: máquinas de afeitar, lociones contra la impotencia o la calvicie, corbatas Calvin Klein, balones de fútbol.... Definitivamente, esta Evelyn Z anuncia mejor que Evelyn B (la primera), y sus tetas virtuales pueden ponerse al lado de las de Evelyn M (lo que ya es mucho decir). (10, The products varied, but the fem-fetish was the same. The lingerie on the body of the fem-fetish also varied, but here the lingerie was not the product. Evelyn Z advertised other things for men: electric razors, lotions to prevent impotence and baldness, Calvin Klein ties, footballs.... Definitively, this Evelyn Z advertised better than Evelyn B (the first one), and her virtual breasts could put her next to Evelyn M (which is saying a lot).)

Though they are real people, the Evelyn avatars are objectified and reproduced to promote male fantasies—not only to satisfy sexual desires but also to sell products. Evelyn's image is spread throughout the city, "en los violentos comerciales de las avenidas, en las proyecciones 3D de las pasarelas y los supermercados, en los programas de participación nocturnos" (79, in the violent commercials on the avenues, in the 3D projections on walkways and in supermarkets, in the late-night call-in shows"). Evelyn's lack of control over her own avatar imagines an extreme continuation of an already growing problem on the internet, in which digital advertisers use personal images found on social media without the original poster's permission, bringing to light unforeseen issues surrounding cyberspace and the ownership of the virtual self. In a specifically Cuban context, the ubiquity of Evelyn's image mirrors the ways in which iconic figures—Fidel Castro, Che Guevara, José Martí—are deployed on the island. This comparison questions how much daily life will change with increased internet access, as political portraits may simply be replaced with commercial ones.

Carbono 14 brings to light some of the darkest parts of digital technologies, as Evelyn Z's treatment within the reality show highlights the ways in which internet culture can normalize sexual taboos. Though her coworkers and fans sexualize her avatar and physical body, it is important to remember that Evelyn is very young. While we do not know her actual age, she wears a young boy's school uniform so that her image is simultaneously sexualized and infantilized, much like the avatar Candy in González's "Slow Motion." Evelyn carries around a periodic table that she believes has oracular powers, though La Productora (The Producer) tells her that this is overkill and that the uniform already does enough to emphasize her schoolgirl character. When Evelyn is first contracted to participate in the irreality show, La Productora tells her, "Tú vas a ser una imagen para las páginas en construcción, el insomnio y las salas oscuras. Quizás vas a ser la próxima fem-fetish" (21, "You are going to be an image for the pages in construction, the insomniac and the dark rooms. Perhaps you will be the next fem-fetish"). This sexualization of young women is a social issue that has been amplified through cyberspace, though in this case it is not an unfortunate consequence but the overt intention of the studio. The fetishization of Evelyn's body leaks over into the physical world, as most of the people she interacts with obsess over her emerging sexuality. For example, one of the first people she meets in Havana is a taxi driver who offers her a Toblerone chocolate bar. The scene quickly becomes sexual as the older man puts the bar directly in her mouth and asks her to suck on it (9). The Toblerone continues to symbolize Evelyn's simultaneous fetishization and infantilization throughout the beginning of the novel, leading to the moment in which she uses the chocolate bar to take her own virginity (44). After this experience, Evelyn waves goodbye to the camera, recognizing her place in the network of digitalized sexual desire. This interaction also highlights the back-and-forth between avatar and platform. Beth Coleman, in *Hello Avatar: Rise of the Networked Generation* (2011), argues that while avatars must conform in some ways to a platform of implicit cultural expectations, they also represent the "increased ability to meaningfully engage and impact the world in which we live" (161). This platform often involves the darkest of social constructions, including the sexualization, infantilization, or dehumanization of marginalized bodies. Not only does the avatar represent an extension of the user's agency into the virtual domain, its presence and paradoxically disembodied embodiment challenges the understandings of corporeality that seep over from the physical world.

The internet's role in breaking down sexual taboos is also apparent in JE's story line. Even in the physical world, JE refers to every woman he meets as a number, mirroring the anonymous interactions and reductive identities that are common within chat rooms and other interactive cyberspaces. This internet-inspired worldview reaches an extreme in a graphic, incestuous scene with his sister, Dos. JE had already secretly watched his sister have sex with her girlfriend, Tres. Afterward, Dos confronts JE and seduces him. He justifies his attraction to her by saying that the two siblings were basically interchangeable: "Lo inquietante de mirar fijo el rostro de mi hermana es esa sensación de estar mirando un espejo. Nos parecemos milimétricamente" (62, "The disturbing part of looking straight at my sister's face is that sensation of looking in a mirror. We are identical"). Just as she approaches the point of orgasm, JE imagines Dos taking on the additional identity of her girlfriend, transforming into a hybrid character Dos/Tres. JE, the first-person narrator of the scene, is able to experience multiple sexual taboos at once. JE witnesses a similar transformation during his time exploring a hotel-like cyberspace when he meets an avatar that effortlessly switches back and forth between Once and Doce. Once/Doce, who is reading the book *Carbono 14* when JE finds her, invites him to join her in a contraption that resembles a washing machine. Once inside, JE notes, "Yo sentí que me fragmentaba. Mis moléculas se convirtieron en peces nadando contra la fuerza del agua" (129, "I felt myself fragmenting. My molecules turned into fish swimming upstream"). Though JE is disoriented after this experience, he recovers and quickly transforms back into a physical body once he exits the virtual world. These transformations, conceptually possible because of the identity flexibility of cyberspace, connect the reorganization of sexual taboos with a redefinition of the limits and limitations of the human body.

As mentioned before, Sheller (2007) has pointed out how local governments and the tourism industry have colluded to reshape and reframe Caribbean cyberspaces. *Carbono 14* examines this connection between the internet and tourism, as JE enters cyberspace through a hotel chain portal. JE explains:

> No sé (nadie lo sabe) por cuántos hoteles va la cadena HH solo en los distritos Vedado y Habana Vieja. Como todos los hoteles están conectados en red

(navegador HH-Explorer), me daba lo mismo hospedarme en uno o en otro y era igual de inútil porque una vez *adentro* el espacio-oferta tiende a una geografía infinita, llena de rincones y recovecos web. (116, I don't know (nobody knows) how many hotels the HH chain has just in the Vedado and Habana Vieja districts. Since all the hotels are connected to a network (navigator HH-Explorer), it didn't make a difference for me to stay in one or the other and it was equally useless because once you are inside the space-promotion extends to an infinite geography, full of web corners and nooks.)

This detail highlights a historical link between hotels and internet access in Cuba. While public Wi-Fi hotspots have slowly become more common, hotel lobbies had been the most visible spots for access to the web outside of state-run cultural institutions. However, Cuban citizens were banned from staying in hotels until 2008, and they were briefly banned from accessing the internet in hotels in 2009. While these restrictions have since been lifted, hotel-provided internet remains economically prohibitive for most Cubans. JE's description of this cyberspace emphasizes its connection to touristic consumption: "Llegué a un restaurant-bar repleto: clientes de HHotel y chicos y chicas por cuyos cuerpos se podía entrar a otros sitios con más secciones y nuevos menús. . . . Mucha gente bebía y comía" (119, "I arrived at a packed restaurant-bar: HHotel clients and boys and girls through whose bodies you could enter other sites with more sections and new menus. . . . Many people drank and ate"). Tourists enter this cyberspace to consume Cuban food, drink, and bodies. The anonymous space for experimentation that the internet offers its users is connected to sexual tourism and the political and economic structures that make such enterprises necessary and profitable for Cubans. For these cyber-tourists, Cuba is a temporary portal or virtual experience to be enjoyed and then left behind.

The novel's framing of cyberspace as a touristic and voyeuristic experience also sheds light on the ways in which avatars function within pleasure-seeking experiences on the web. Evelyn's avatar, also referred to as a CV or "cuerpo virtual" (virtual body), becomes so popular that in the physical world she is often confused for her online character Emily. The conflation between physical body and virtual avatar presents an intense struggle for Evelyn Z, who is disparaged for both representing an unachievable standard of feminine beauty and lacking a physical form. After JE mentions Evelyn to a physical human sex worker, the woman responds, "Ya sé que al lado de un CV yo soy un microorganismo, pero ser un microorganismo tiene ventajas prácticas" (78, "I know that next to a CV I am a microorganism, but being a microorganism has practical advantages"). When JE attempts to confirm that she is a real person, the same woman clarifies, "Real ya no se usa en ninguna jerga por aquí. Digamos que soy . . . natural" (78, "Real isn't used any more in any slang around here.

We'll say that I am ... natural"). While Evelyn's ubiquitous avatar cannot provide the same physical comforts as an organic body, this woman still recognizes how a CV complicates the presumed dichotomy between real and virtual. Much like González Fernández's description of Candy in "Slow Motion," Lage's imagining of Evelyn's struggles decodes cyberspace by shedding light on how online representations of women can continue to haunt users in the physical world.

Evelyn cannot escape her avatar's identity, as fans begin to call her Emily and ask her to strangle them (34). Just as Evelyn's body has been digitized, the violent act of strangulation has lost its meaning. Left with no other option, Evelyn decides to reassert her physical existence by actually strangling her coworker. With the irreality cameras filming everything, the scene switches from the virtual to the real. Evelyn "dejó de hacer como que estrangulaba y empezó de tirar de la pañoleta con una fuerza asombrosa. . . . El actor dejó de fingir que era un personaje que se debatía por respirar" (45, "stopped just acting as if she were strangling and began pulling the scarf with an astonishing strength. . . . The actor stopped pretending that he was a character that struggled to breath"). With the rest of the production still in shock, Evelyn flees the set with "toda la velocidad que le permitía su cuerpo" (46, "all the speed that her body allowed"). By showing her coworkers and the public her ability to do real harm, Evelyn proves that she cannot be reduced. In *Embodied Avatars: Genealogies of Black Feminist Art and Performance* (2015), Uri McMillan argues that the process of avatarism "becomes an adroit method of circumventing prescribed limitations" (7). McMillian notes that the performers he studies "engage in spectacular, shocking, and even unlawful role-plays ... these avatars are a means of highlighting (and stretching) the subordinate roles available to black women" (12). Translated back to digital technologies and their representations in science fiction, avatars have the potential to disrupt the platforms or stages that they inhabit, rewriting or decoding the cyberspaces around them.

While the ambiguous nature of *Carbono 14* allows for many different readings, the internet's effect on conceptions of corporeal and social structures stands out as the novel's major contribution to conversations of Caribbean technodominance. In the end, Evelyn must leave Havana. Unlike JE, she is unwilling to give up her physical self for the unknown possibilities of cyberspace. The divergences in their stories demonstrate the different ways in which users interact with the internet's digital hierarchies. While JE spends his time online having sexual adventures and searching for historical fetish symbols, Evelyn is concerned with survival and maintaining agency in the physical world. *Carbono 14* imagines how these online power imbalances not only affect the user experience but also how the marginalization of bodies in virtual spaces translates offline.

La mucama de Omicunlé: Technological Escapism and Divine Connections

Both "Slow Motion" and *Carbono 14* analyze the internet's future role in reinforcing oppressive structures. However, while Marvel and Evelyn are forced to flee from or hide in virtual worlds, neither avatar offers a survival strategy. On the other hand, Rita Indiana's 2015 novel *La mucama de Omicunlé* (*Omicunlé's Maid*) investigates the types of bodies that manage to escape in or from hypertechnology. A writer, visual artist, and musician, Indiana was born in Santo Domingo but resides in San Juan. She has often used speculative elements in her written and musical work, including references to zombies in the novel *Papi* (2005), musings on technology in the literary collage *Ciencia succión* (2001), and the apocalyptic album *Mandinga Times* (2020). *La mucama de Omicunlé* was the first Spanish-language novel to earn the Grand Prize from the Association of Caribbean Writers and was a finalist for the Premio Biennial de Novela Mario Vargas Llosa (Biennial Mario Vargas Llosa Prize for Novels). The book's sequel, *Hecho en Saturno* (2018, *Made in Saturn*), is a much more grounded, realistic narrative that only rarely alludes to science fiction elements and showcases Indiana's versatility. Scholar Guillermina De Ferrari (2020) writes that *La mucama de Omicunlé* "uses the Caribbean geopolitical situation to examine the conceptual tools we have at our disposal to understand our human and nonhuman animal entanglements when we are overpowered by realities beyond our control" (2).

La mucama de Omicunlé recounts the aftermath of a tsunami off the coast of Santo Domingo in the 2020s, partially caused by the depletion of the coral reefs around Hispaniola. The great wave collided with the Venezuelan biological weapons that the Dominican president Said Bona had agreed to store, creating an ecological disaster throughout the Caribbean Sea and in parts of the Atlantic Ocean. As he does with all national crises, Bona turns to his personal santera Esther, who devises a plan involving her new servant, Acilde. When Acilde tries to steal a valuable sea anemone, and when Esther dies in the process, Bona offers Acilde a coveted gender-affirmation drug. While Acilde's desired transition is successful, the anemone is used to also grant them time-traveling powers, sending them back in time to the 1990s and the 1600s to carry out a complicated plan to prevent the ecological disaster before it occurs. As a trans Afro-Dominican sex worker, Acilde and their various avatars interact with pirates, philanthropists, artists, and a marine biologist to save a nation that never cared enough to protect them.

Before becoming Esther's maid, Acilde performed sex work to pay for Italian cooking classes and save up for the street drug Rainbow Bright, which carries out nonsurgical gender affirmations. The facility of corporeal transformations could be linked to ubiquity of human enhancement technologies within the novel's world. In the opening scene of the book, Acilde activates a security camera in their eye by touching their pinky finger to their thumb (11). These corporeal technologies are also connected to internet data networks, as Acilde later accesses information and transfers it to Esther's personal assistant Eric by touching fingers: "Acilde juntó los dedos índice y corazón para abrir su correo, extendió el dedo anular y Eric lo tocó con el suyo para ver en su ojo el archivo que Acilde compartía con él" (16, "Acilde joined the index and middle fingers to open their email, extended the ring finger, and Eric touched it with his own to see in his eye the file that Acilde shared with him"). Acilde also mentions streaming music videos on their eye-screens for a much-needed distraction while engaging in sex work (17). In the novel, these technological advancements are represented as tools for progressing gender equality in the Dominican Republic. The narrator claims that many poor women in the past were domestic workers and consequently victimized by their employers' clandestine sexual desires: "La explosión de las telecomunicaciones y las fábricas de zona franca crearon nuevos empleos para estas mujeres que abandonaron sus esclavitudes poco a poco" (17, "The explosion of telecommunications and factories in free economic zones created new jobs for those women that abandoned their slaveries little by little"). By citing the contemporary issue of the abuse of domestic workers, the novel suggests, possibly ironically, that increased technology could lead to fairer, safer opportunities for marginalized Dominicans.

While the advancements described in the novel seem to support a transhumanist fantasy about the availability of human enhancement technologies in the near future, the novel also shows the disadvantages of this cyborg model. For example, as Acilde runs from the police, they must deal with the continuously watching eye of the authorities: "[Acilde] había desactivado su plan de datos para que no pudiesen encontrarla" (63, "[Acilde] had turned off their data plan so that they could not find them"). That Acilde must turn off their body's data plan, not one connected to a cell phone or computer, highlights the dangerous possibilities for state surveillance and manipulation of such hyperconnected corporeal enhancements. This also suggests that the government in this future world provided the public with technological enhancements in order to control them, not to grant them more personal liberties. Zaira Pacheco (2017) offers a similar take on Acilde's internal technology, warning that the government in *La mucama de Omicunlé* uses these enhancements to surveil and subject individuals (95). President Bona's government is represented as being on the forefront of cybertechnologies and social media; for example, his rise to power is largely attributed to his YouTube videos that seduced the voting public (Indiana 113). Hypertechnology in this novel thus provides both liberating opportunities and a platform for official repression. The advantages and disadvantages associated with Acilde's cyborg body invite further discussions into the future of corporeal enhancement and questions narratives of technological progress.

Along with the increase in technological human enhancements represented in this future Dominican Republic, the influx of hypertechnology has also automated discrimination and xenophobia. In the book's first pages, Acilde watches as robots hunt Haitian immigrants that have escaped a quarantine on the other side of the island: "Hasta que los recolectores automáticos, que patrullan calles y avenidas, recojan el cuerpo y lo desintegren" (11, "Until the automatic collectors, that patrol the streets and avenues, pick up the body and disintegrate it"). While the methods are quicker and mechanized, there is a clear line between this imagined future annihilation of foreign bodies and the historical mistreatment of Haitians in the Dominican Republic, including the 1937 Masacre del Perejil (Parsley Massacre) under Trujillo and the more recent deportations of Haitian-descendant Dominicans since *La Sentencia* (*The Ruling*) of 2013. Even though Acilde stops to notice the person getting captured, the violent scene has been normalized to the point that it loses its horrifying effect: "El aparato la recoge con su brazo mecánico y la deposita en su cámara central con la diligencia de un niño glotón que se lleva a la boca caramelos sucios del suelo" (12, "The apparatus picked her up with its mechanical arm and deposited her in its central chamber with the diligence of a gluttonous child lifting dirty caramels from the floor to his mouth"). This flippant description of automated state repression suggests that such actions have become commonplace in this future world. Acilde does note that the Chinese-manufactured machine's bare and English-language motto—"To clean up"—hints at the role of international powers and specifically the United States in the historical repression of Haitians in the Dominican Republic. As Lorgia García-Peña argues in *The Borders of Dominicanidad: Race, Nation and Archives of Contradiction* (2016), framing Haiti and the Dominican Republic as binary enemies is both ahistorical and an oversimplification: "A more productive examination of the Dominican-Haitian relationship thus requires our awareness of the intricacies of Hispaniola's border history in dialogue with US history. Such analysis would also lead us to recognize the present Haiti-DR border as a product of US Empire" (10).

Another repercussion of the increased technology in the novel is the automation of consumption. This is represented in the novel through the tool PriceSpy, which integrates with Acilde's internal technologies. PriceSpy provides augmented reality, the superimposition of computer-generated images or information on one's real-world field of vision, in this case attaching monetary values to the objects around them. While working as a prostitute, Acilde uses this technology to judge the value of their clients' clothing before telling them the prices of services provided (17). Indiana's description of PriceSpy shines a light on the ways in which cybertechnology is used to promote and facilitate capitalist consumption, in this case turning everything in one's view into a product to be sold or bought. Later in the novel, Acilde finds a valuable sea anemone in Esther's ceremonial chamber and recognizes it as a valuable object that could cover the price of the Rainbow Bright drug. PriceSpy is unable to provide a fixed price for the anemone: "Frente al animal el PriceSpy se quedó haciendo loading. Los precios del mercado negro no aparecían con facilidad" (26, "Before the animal the PriceSpy kept loading. Black market prices did not appear easily"). This shows that the PriceSpy connects to official or legitimized modes of consumption, not informal economies. Acilde still plans to steal the creature with a criminal acquaintance named Morla. While Acilde's emerging relationship with Esther and Eric causes the maid to reconsider, Morla gets impatient and breaks into Esther's home to take the anemone himself. After Morla murders Esther on his way through the ceremonial chamber, Acilde is forced to kill Morla, grab the sea creature, and then flee the scene, knowing that they will be blamed for the famous santera's death.

Acilde later reconnects with Eric, who promises the Rainbow Bright drug in exchange for the anemone. After a successful gender transition, Eric and President Bona confront Acilde, explaining that Esther had foreseen the entire course of events (including her own death) and had told Bona that only Acilde could fix the ecological crisis, using Acilde's previously unknown spiritual powers: the ability to create and control avatars in different time periods. Acilde's mission is to travel to the early 2000s and prevent the destruction of the coral reef that allowed the tsunami to destroy the island. While neither Bona nor Eric fully understands Acilde's abilities, they both link queerness to this ability to inhabit other bodies. When Bona introduces himself to Acilde in the hospital, he asks, "¿Tú ere' el bujarroncito que va a salvar al país?" (112, "You are the little fairy that is going to save the country?"). Eric goes a step further, focusing on Acilde's body as essential to the plan: "Te dimos el cuerpo que querías y ahora tú nos has dado el cuerpo que necesitábamos" (70, "We gave you the body that you wanted and now you have given us the body that we needed"). This could be read as an exoticization of the trans body by Bona and Eric. However, the novel also suggests that a trans subject would be particularly capable of creating and controlling avatars in other worlds, as they have already overcome the hegemonic narratives that bind the self to the physical body. *La mucama de Omicunlé* asks readers to think about the future of queer bodies in cyberspace and cyberfictions; Foster (2005) argues that the genre has been useful for highlighting technology's role in the repression of women and queer bodies, while Lavigne (2013) warns against the promotion of a reductive and escapist disembodiment. By connecting Acilde's trans, cyborg body to the power to control distant avatars, the novel raises questions of how queer subjects and avatars may thrive in a world of virtual bodies and how oppressive forces may exploit and reinforce their marginality.

Acilde is sent to prison to keep the plot secret, though the cell is outfitted with special technological privileges, including a computer and air-conditioning. From the cell, Acilde travels back in time, embodying a seventeenth-century pirate named Roque and an Italian philanthropist and businessman named Giorgio in the early 2000s. Though Acilde can embody these avatars because of a spiritual connection with the androgynous ocean Orisha Olokún, the internet is used to research time-sensitive information. For example, the Giorgio avatar succeeds in impressing the marine biologist Linda because Acilde is simultaneously searching the web for facts about extinct coral reef species (139). This interplay between Afro-Caribbean religious traditions and cybertechnologies is central to the novel's political project, placing spiritual literacy at the same level as technological expertise as essential qualities for exploring and surviving future digital worlds. Indiana is not the first Caribbean science fiction writer to experiment with this mixture of Afro-Caribbean deities and advanced technology. Commenting on Nalo Hopkinson's 1998 novel *Midnight Robber*, Elizabeth Boyle (2009) argues, "The construction of an Afro-Caribbean-inspired cyberspace network in *Midnight Robber* offers a sustainable model for bodilessness" (179). In another example, Rachel Price (2015) writes that the Orisha-avatars in Erick Mota Pérez's *Habana Underguater* (2010) show "how cultural forms considered ancient or archaic might well be the keys to surviving an increasingly apocalyptic future" (101). In *La mucama de Omicunlé*, Acilde's powers offer more than personal survival, as the protagonist is tasked with saving the entire country. Also, Acilde's spiritual powers do not just complement cybertechnology; they supersede it. In imagining a future in which a *santero* is the hero and the only hope for the survival of a hypertechnological society, Indiana questions the hegemony of techno-dominance and highlights the role of belief and spirituality in creating a sustainable world.

Avatar creation often relies on reductive menus and cybertypes, and Acilde's experience is not an exception. Acilde codes hypermasculine avatars that embody many intersecting privileges that Acilde lacks in real life. Roque is a pirate captain, with authority over others. Giorgio is White, Italian, wealthy, educated, and a trained chef. On inhabiting Giorgio, Acilde admits, "Tenía lo que siempre había querido: un cuerpo de hombre y un negocio propio, una pizzería chic en una hermosa playa" (138, "He had what I had always wanted: a man's body and his own business, a chic pizzeria on a beautiful beach"). Even though Acilde did not expect to fall in love, Giorgio's relationship with Linda provides the user with the sort of intimate, loving relationship that Acilde had never experienced. Acilde constructs an avatar with Giorgio's privileged position recognizing that he could easily foster the economic and political connections necessary to buy land in Sosúa and start the marine biology conservation laboratory. At the same time, embodying Giorgio allows for a temporary escape from Acilde's marginality. Acilde describes controlling Roque's and Giorgio's avatars "como si se tratara de un videojuego, acumulando bienes, trofeos, experiencia, disfrutando del paisaje, inexistente ya en ese futuro de lluvias ácidas y epidemias" (176, "as if it were a video game, accumulating goods, trophies, experience, enjoying the landscape, no longer existing in that future of acid rain and epidemics"). Though

Acilde stays mostly focused on the important mission, exploring this past world with newfound privilege is enjoyable. The comparison to video games also references an earlier moment in the novel, when Acilde describes how young people use virtual reality experiences to embody either dancers at a 1970s disco or soldiers at war. In either situation, a generation that has been disillusioned after years of financial crises and political corruption is allowed to take back control of their lives and reassert themselves through cybertechnology. In the same way, Acilde's experiences with Roque and Giorgio repositions Acilde as an active user and coder of cyberspaces.

Understanding the social forces around coding an avatar, along with video game technology's ability to provide an escape, makes the novel's ending a bit clearer. After Giorgio uncovers a chest of seventeenth-century artwork on his property, planted there centuries before by Roque, the reef-saving laboratory is assured enough funding to prevent the future disaster. Acilde's mission is done, along with the prison sentence. Unwilling to return to normal life, Acilde decides to fully inhabit Giorgio's body, disconnecting from the other bodies and leaving them behind. Afraid of what was waiting outside the relative comforts of the prison cell, Acilde chooses to embody the wealth, status, privilege, and love that Giorgio has amassed. This selfishness is highlighted in the celebratory party commemorating the opening of the laboratory, in which Giorgio meets a younger version of Said Bona, decades before he will be elected president. Giorgio realizes that he could just tell Bona not to accept the Venezuelan biological weapons in the future, sparing the Dominican Republic from ecological disaster. In the end, Giorgio decides not to say anything, fearing that warning Bona would mean that Acilde would never be called on to fix the problem and that Giorgio would never exist. In Giorgio's mind, he succeeds in both saving the country and continuing the happy life that for Acilde was merely an escape.

In Rita Indiana's *La mucama de Omicunlé*, Giorgio's Whiteness, foreign passport, wealth, and social connections all factor into Acilde's decision to permanently embody that avatar. At the same time, Giorgio lacks the futuristic enhancements of Acilde's cyborg body. Acilde's willingness to give up such technological advantages highlights an essential point in the debates over race, gender, and sexuality on the internet: It is not just how these technologies are coded but who is writing the code. Though Acilde's cyborg body has the capability to receive and transfer information, it is filled with someone else's code. Despite its powers, the cyborg body is vulnerable to state surveillance and the forces of intrusive capitalism. On the other hand, Acilde is the lone author of Giorgio; ironically, the avatar belongs more to Acilde than their own physical body. The key to survival in this hypertechnological dystopia is thus predicated less on escape and more on active writing or coding. Acilde's refusal to conform to traditional narratives of heroism, in which protagonists are expected to sacrifice everything for the good of the state or system, also serves as a decoding of or acting out within a platform of cultural assumptions in mainstream science fiction or dystopic literature and film.

Similar disruptive performances are also apparent in the other texts studied in this chapter. In Maielis González Fernández's "Slow Motion," Marvel disobeys her programmed hierarchy, joining the resistance and challenging traditional user–avatar power dynamics. By surviving and hiding in the web as code, she shows how the coding itself must not be entirely rejected to enact a decoding of oppressive forces online. Choosing which parts of her coding to embody and which parts to ignore, Marvel maintains her digital flexibility and highlights the avatar's ability to redefine the limits of cyberspace. In Jorge Enrique Lage's *Carbono 14*, Evelyn's violence goes against the programming that staged her as an eroticized-yet-harmless sexual object. By choosing physical corporality over forced avatarism, Evelyn pushes back against the economic, political, and cultural forces at play in her digital marginalization. By juxtaposing Evelyn's experience with JE's virtual joyride, *Carbono 14* brings to light the amplification of social inequalities on the internet. In all the texts studied in this chapter, avatars can help enact a decoding of cyberspace that both highlights its repressive structures and pushes at its prescribed limits of digital agency.

While the avatars represented here are subject to the coded political and social structures around them, they maintain the agency to recognize systematic injustice and act out against it. González Fernández, Lage, and Indiana all imagine how digital technologies may recode the relationship between bodies and technology and how disruptive avatars can decode those spaces. With avatars organizing a resistance against users, digitalized bodies reclaiming agency through physical violence, and Afro-Caribbean religious powers overtaking cybertechnologies, these texts question the ways in which we understand and consume the internet. These authors imagine cyberspace as a place that must still be fought over and organized around for the technology to reach its liberating potential. Disruptive avatars that explore and question the depths and cracks of the internet are the best tools to connect the political struggles of the physical world with emerging social issues online. By questioning the ways in which control, authority, and power are coded onto the internet, these texts provide blueprints for how future users can actively participate in and transform cybertechnologies, disrupting and decoding the historical legacies of techno-dominance that are manifested virtually.

Conclusion

NEW CARIBBEAN FUTURES

On June 28, 1856, Portuguese-Cuban tailor, awning salesman, and aeronautics enthusiast Matías Pérez attempted his second-ever flight in a hot-air balloon from Havana's Campo de Marte (which was later renamed the Parque de la Fraternidad Americana). Despite a successful flight in pristine conditions earlier that month, Pérez's second flight was delayed by heavy winds. Once he finally ascended, the balloon and its pilot tragically disappeared into the sky (Corbitt 1941). This is the purported origin of the popular Cuban saying "Voló como Matías Pérez" (It flew like Matías Pérez"), used to describe something that has mysteriously disappeared. The mythology surrounding Pérez was bolstered in 1969 when artist Luis Lorenzo Sosa created the Matías Pérez comic strip series for the children's magazine *Revista Pionero*, positing that the balloonist was saved by aliens and converted into an interstellar adventurer. In the opening story of a 1986 collection of Lorenzo Sosa's work, Pérez shocks the crowd at a cosmonautics conference in the year 2999 by demanding his inclusion in a retrospective on the great pioneers of space travel (Lorenzo Sosa 2). When the speaker denies Pérez's place in aeronautic history, he triumphantly displays a balloon-shaped rocket that is equipped with the ability to turn invisible. Disappearing into thin air (on purpose this time), Pérez goes on to fight extraterrestrial armies, marry the beautiful alien Blina, and save his earthling friend Leocadio over and over from intergalactic kidnappers. Most importantly, in Lorenzo Sosa's version, Pérez came across alien technology years before that infamous balloon flight, suggesting that his supposed failure should in fact be remembered as the very first space launch and a great moment in Cuban aeronautic history.

Pérez returns briefly in the 2018 Cuban science fiction film *El viaje extraordinario de Celeste García*, directed by Arturo Infante. In the film, Celeste is a teacher from Havana selected to be part of a group of Cubans that will travel to the planet Gryok. The Gryokites had previously been posing as Russians to live among and observe Cubans and Cuban life, and Celeste was invited by her former neighbor because of her kindness and her experience working at the planetarium. Escaping the traumas of an abusive relationship and an existence where she feels unnoticed, Celeste eagerly packs her bags, including her treasured globe, and joins the mission. The invited guests and lottery winners are sent in trains to the countryside for physical and cultural training; watching an educator arrive at the ESBEC (Escuela Secundaria Básica en el Campo) Batalla de Mal Tiempo conjures up memories of the literacy campaigns and educational reform that marked the early parts of the Cuban Revolution. During orientation, an organizer in a yellow jumpsuit yells information at future space travelers, including the fact that they were being split into three groups, each named for a pioneer of flight: Yuri Gagarin, Arnaldo Tamayo, and . . . Matías Pérez. Celeste and her friends are assigned to the last one. While the first two options represent heroes of space travel—the first person in space and the first Cuban cosmonaut—Pérez proves more difficult to place. Celeste explains to her confused roommates that Pérez boarded a hot-air balloon and was never seen again: "y de ahí viene eso de 'Voló como Matías Pérez'" ("and that is where 'He flew away like Matías Pérez' comes from"). In the mural sitting in front of the cadets in the orientation scene, Pérez is depicted alongside Gagarin and Tamayo in a top hat and suit instead of a helmet and laser gun, making clear that the team's name is referencing the actual person and not his heroic comic strip persona.

The nervous reactions to this ominous sign are played out at the end of the film, as Celeste is attacked and fails to board the alien spaceship with her friends. As the alarm sounds, the signal to head to the landing pad, a young man and former student at the ESBEC Batalla de Mal Tiempo hits Celeste over the head with her own globe. He then steals Celeste's identification bracelet to give to his girlfriend, who has been in hiding on the roof. Celeste's disappointing outcome—a teacher beaten with her own learning tool by an ex-student of the very school she stood in—can be read as a puncturing of the triumphant rhetoric surrounding the transformative power of education throughout the revolution. In the end, those promises were just as real as an alien spaceship swooping down and taking Celeste to another planet. Because Celeste is left with all the luggage that similarly did not make it on the trip, this moment highlights the contradictions within this worldbuilding that blends science fiction and contemporary Cuban realities; despite all the talk of rockets and advanced civilizations, the plot is filled with plodding trains, old television sets, compact discs, and the dusty globe. Even Pérez, who had defied the odds when Lorenzo Sosa converted him from a historic failure to a futuristic hero, is turned back into a disappointment and a punch line. In the end, Celeste is forced to return home to her apartment, which had already been converted into a space-themed *paladar* (a privately owned restaurant) by her enterprising son. The film *El viaje extraordinario de Celeste García* is a heartfelt example of many of the biggest trends in recent

Caribbean science fiction: a mixture of reality and speculation; the overwhelming and often unfulfilled promise of new technology; references to national histories and narratives; and the humbling realization that human and structural violences are still present in even the most advanced futures.

This book's goals have been to show that first, analyzing science fiction adds much to the study of the Caribbean, and second, that focusing on the Caribbean makes important contributions to the study of science fiction. On the former, science fiction offers tools for the study of the past and future visions of technology and personhood in the region. As this project has shown, the posthuman, parahuman, and nonhuman characters that regularly populate science fiction texts allow for discussions of the effects of colonialism and authoritarianism on concepts of humanity in the region, especially in terms of technology's role in these processes. Science fiction's relationship to technology goes beyond futuristic machines and plot points; the advancement of (and increase in) access to digital networks has allowed for the formation of international communities based on the writing, scholarship, and fandom of the genre. The interplanetary nature of the genre allows for writers, scholars, and artists to question traditional mappings and borders, expanding the limits of the Caribbean and serving as a bridge between Latin American studies and Latinx studies. Finally, science fiction is a popular genre, and analyzing popular culture offers greater insight into the images and representations that are most widely consumed and circulated; focusing academic work on a genre like science fiction helps to further blur the line between literary and cultural studies, offering new pedagogical tools that attract wider audiences to conversations of race, gender, and colonialism in the Caribbean.

As for the second factor, studying the Caribbean adds to understanding of the political potential of science fiction. This book marks another step in the diversification of science fiction studies, along with efforts to decenter and decolonize the genre. Science fiction studies as a field is enriched by new projects that highlight and analyze speculative works by writers and artists of different backgrounds and identifications. The publishing, promoting, teaching, and funding of studies on non-U.S./U.K. authors and texts also contribute to understanding science fiction as a truly global genre. This does not only mean reading Caribbean and Latin American science fiction as a rebellious periphery around a dominant center, though there are certainly productive examples of that dynamic. As López-Pellisa (2021) has written, "Es importantes señalar que a pesar de que la hegemonía del campo cultural de la CF corresponde al ámbito estadounidense, la recepción de la CF foránea no ha sido acrítica ni evasiva, sino que ha reflejado, desde diferentes perspectivas las preocupaciones sociales, políticas y económicas de cada uno de sus contextos nacionales" (21, "It's important to point out that even though hegemony within the cultural domain of SF [science fiction] corresponds to the United States, the reception of foreign SF has not been acritical or evasive, but instead has reflected from different perspectives the social, political, and economic preoccupations of each one of their respective national contexts"). At the same time, recognizing that forcing this type of center-periphery structure on the texts studied here would arguably reinforce the colonizing structures that their authors have attempted to dismantle, one must also read Caribbean and Latin American science fiction as both independent and possible beacons within the genre. For example, instead of focusing on Latin American science fiction's subjugated position within the genre, Ginway and Brown (2012) suggest that the region could emerge as a leader in the increasingly politically engaged field: "As Anglo-American SF reassesses its colonialist legacy, perhaps Latin American SF, long aware of its cultural and social discontinuities, can begin to show the way" (11). Either way, including Caribbean science fiction in academic and critical conversations serves the field of science fiction studies and highlights the genre's ability to speculate on global, extraplanetary, and intergalactic levels.

The social and political implications of studying Caribbean science fiction is best explained through a moment in *Se alquila un planeta* (2001), Yoss's influential and controversial novel that has been translated into English and French but is yet to be published in Cuba. One of the book's vignettes describes the aftereffects of the alien Xenoids colonizing Earth and transforming the planet into an underdeveloped tourist destination. While futurology had been a thriving field of inquiry before first contact, the Xenoids immediately robbed humans of the ability to speculate on the future: "Nada de 'pronósticos para los próximos 50 años.' Ni para los próximos 10 . . . ni siquiera para mañana." (244, "No more 'predictions of fifty years from now.' Or ten years . . . or even tomorrow"). In the novel, colonization and enslavement deprive these people of the capacity to envision a future beyond their present oppression. Yoss thus positions the speculation involved in writing science fiction as a potential political rebellion; whether one creates images of peaceful utopias or apocalyptic horrors, asserting the right to imagine the future can be read as a decolonizing act. When studying recent science fiction through the lens of the Caribbean, it is important to remember how colonizing and authoritarian systems attempt to delegitimize visions of the future by marginalized people. The Cuban, Dominican, and Puerto Rican science fiction authors studied in this book highlight and push back against the rhetorical structures that seek to silence their speculations of Caribbean futures.

Acknowledgments

This book is the product of many years of researching, writing, and mentoring, and it would not exist without the guidance and support of Jossianna Arroyo, César Salgado, Luis Cárcamo-Huechante, John Morán González, Carmen Lugo-Lugo, Emily Maguire, Antonio Córdoba, Stephanie Malak, Ignacio Carvajal, Hannah Alpert-Abrams, James Staig, Valeria Rey de Castro, Ana Cecilia Calle, Sam Cannon, and Anne Stewart, along with anyone and everyone I was able to talk to over the years at conferences, during seminars, and over coffee. I would also like to thank the authors whose work made this study possible, especially those I was lucky enough to meet and be in contact with throughout this writing process, including Pedro, Yasmín, Erick, and Rey.

I am incredibly thankful to the wonderful librarians and archivists at Rice University's Woodson Research Center who scanned and sent documents from the William E. Gordon Papers during the pandemic. Thank you to the School of Languages, Cultures, and Race at Washington State University and the Department of Spanish and Portuguese at the University of Texas at Austin for providing the time and resources necessary for completing this work.

I am forever grateful for the support of my whole family. Most importantly, Rae: your love and support makes everything worth it. This would not have been possible (or even remotely enjoyable) without you.

Notes

INTRODUCTION

1. "Miss Universe 1972 Crowning," YouTube, posted by alexa2224, 3 May 2021, www.youtube.com/watch?v=STDVJ0s1_UQ.

2. *The Cyborg Caribbean* opts for an inclusive definition for science fiction, considering superhero narratives as a subgenre similar to cyberpunk and space opera, both of which are also studied in this project. Efforts to define what is or isn't "real" science fiction are often based on ethnocentric assumptions about the genre. Verónica Muñiz-Soto (2015), in a paper originally given at the 2014 Primer Congreso de Ciencia Ficción del Caribe Hispano (First Congress of Science Fiction from the Hispanic Caribbean), writes, "Hay mucha discusión en cuánto a qué compete ser discutido dentro del campo del sci-fi: ciudades distópicas, mundos futuristas, hombres y mujeres con superpoderes, errores científicos y avances tecnológicos que cambiarán la percepción de la humanidad al mismo tiempo en que exploran posibles escenarios para la humanidad. Estas características están todas presentes dentro de las historias de los cómics, quizás combinadas con otros elementos y, más que nada, presentes en la creación o en las características de sus personajes" (148, "There is much discussion concerning what should be discussed within the field of sci-fi: dystopian cities, futuristic worlds, men and women with superpowers, scientific errors and technological advances that will change the perception of humanity and at the same time explore possible settings for humanity. These characteristics are all present in the history of comics, perhaps combined with other elements and, above all, present in the creation or in the characteristics of their characters").

3. All translations are by this book's author, unless otherwise noted.

CHAPTER 1 — ELECTROCONVULSIVE THERAPY

1. The Pan American Health Organization's digital library holds a number of primary official documents outlining Trujillo's public health initiatives.

2. For more information on the Soviet cases, see van Voren (2010).

3. For more on the history of state-sanctioned homophobia in Cuba, see Bejel (2001).

4. Other Caribbean texts with human-robot characters include Eduardo Desnoes's "Yodor" (1965), Angel Arango's ¿Adónde van los cefalomos? (1964), Daína Chaviano's "La culpa es del robot" (1983), Guillermo Cabrera Infante's "Muerte de un autómata" (1999), Victoria Isabel Pérez Plana's "Tornillo flojo" (2013), and Eric Flores Taylor's *En la Habana es más difícil* (2016). For more on the history of artificial people in Latin American literature, see Mesa Gancedo (2001).

5. For more on the cultural impact of beauty pageants in Puerto Rico, see Avilés Santiago (2016).

CHAPTER 2 — NUCLEAR WEAPONS

1. Other scholars have noted that the threat of cancer was too silent and invisible to create a public outcry and that the death of civilian security guard David Sanes during an explosion in 1999 was the true turning point of the protests (Cruz Soto 182).

2. The list of recent Caribbean texts that include nuclear technology or apocalyptic destruction includes Abel Fernández Larrea's collection *Absolut Röntgen* (2009), Elaine Vilar Madruga's *Culto de Acoplamiento* (2015), Yoss's story "Ese día . . ." (2011), Mary Cruz Paniagua's flash fiction "¡¡Boom!!" (2012), Pedro Cabiya's poem "Hiroshima" (2014), and Brenda Peynado's "The Radioactives" (2021).

3. Recent Caribbean science fiction works that could also be classified as cli-fi include Nuria Dolores Ordas Matos's novel *Entremundos* (2010), Tomás Piard's film *La noche del juicio* (2010), Rafael Acevedo's novel *Al otro lado del muro hay carne fresca* (2014), Jorge Enrique Lage's novel *La Autopista: The Movie* (2014), and Alejandro Rojas Medina's *Chunga Maya* (2017).

4. The anthology features two other stories that mention nuclear weapons: Denis Alvarez Bentacourt's "Peligro de exterminio" and Victor Hugo Pérez Gallo's "Tenía la carta en la mano."

5. See Banerjee (2016) for more on Moscow's metro and its representation in Russian science fiction.

6. For more on the history of official Cuban homophobia, see Bejel (2001).

7. The "Códico de las Familias" (the "Family Law") passed in September 2022 finally gave queer couples the right to get married and adopt children in Cuba.

8. Mariette Pathy Allen's photography collection *Transcuba* (2014) provides many interviews with trans Cubans that highlight both their appreciation for the inclusive initiatives of Mariela Castro's CENESEX and the ongoing difficulties that they face in Cuba.

9. For scholarly work on *Habana Underguater*, see Yoss (2015) and Price (2016).

10. The use of the term Pioneers is most likely an ironic reference to the Cuban youth group Organización de Pioneros José Martí (José Martí Pioneer Organization), established in 1961. The group's motto is "Pioneros por el Comunismo, seremos como el Che"—"Pioneers of Communism, let us be like Che [Ernesto Guevara]."

CHAPTER 3 — SPACE EXPLORATION AND COLONIAL ALIENATION

1. For more on the Chupacabra phenomenon in Puerto Rico, see Derby (2008).

CHAPTER 4 — DISRUPTIVE AVATARS AND THE DECODING OF CARIBBEAN CYBERSPACE

1. For more on the history of Cuban internet restrictions and the potential future of access on the island, see Baron and Hall, 2015. For a technical analysis of Cuba's connectivity, see Bischof et al., 2015.

2. Much has already been written on the current internet situation in Cuba. For more information, see Triff, 2013; Henken and van de Voort, 2013; and Parker, 2013.

3. Caribbean science fiction texts that focus on the internet and digital technology include Malka Older's novel *Infomocracy* (2016), Lynette Mabel Pérez's poetry collection *Mundo Cero* (2013), Leonardo Gala Echemendía's novel *Aitana* (2010), Sigrid Victoria Dueñas's novel *Ciudad en red* (2011), Erick Mota Pérez's novel *Habana Underguater* (2010), and Rafael Acevedo's novel *Exquisito cadáver* (2001).

Works Cited

Acevedo, Rafael. *Al otro lado del muro hay carne fresca*. La Secta de los Perros, 2014.
——. *Exquisito cadáver*. Ediciones Callejón, 2001.
Aguiar, Raúl. "¡El futuro pertenece por entero al Comunismo! Influencias del cine de ciencia ficción de la URSS y de otros países del Este en el imaginario literario cubano." *Kamchatka*, 2015, pp. 199–221.
Alavardo, Leticia. "Speculative *Ciguapas*." *ASAP/J*, 2 Dec. 2019, https://asapjournal.com/speculative-ciguapas-2-0-leticia-alvadaro/.
Albújar Escudero, Miguel Ángel. "*Caja de fractales* (2017), una novelita de ficción especulativa o cómo vivir en el antropoceno." *Revista Hélice*, vol. 5, no. 2, 2020, pp. 106–114.
Aldama, Frederick Luis. *Latinx Superheroes in Mainstream Comics*. U of Arizona P, 2017.
Allen, Jafari. "One Way or Another: Erotic Subjectivity in Cuba." *American Ethnologist*, vol. 39, no. 2, 2012, pp. 325–338.
Allewaert, Monique. *Ariel's Ecology: Plantations, Personhood, and Colonialism in the American Tropics*. U of Minnesota P, 2013.
Altschuler, Daniel R. "The National Astronomy Ionosphere Center's (NAIC) Arecibo Observatory in Puerto Rico." *ASP Conference Series*, vol. 278, 2002, pp. 1–24.
Andújar, Rey Emmanuel. *Candela*. Alfaguara, 2008.
——. *El factor carne*. Isla Negra, 2005.
——. *El hombre triángulo*. Isla Negra, 2005.
——. "Gameon." *Contratiempo*, no. 115, June 2014, p. 23.
——. *Los gestos inútiles*. Cielonaranja, 2016.
——. *Saturnario*. Ultramar, 2011.
Aponte, Lola. "En/cabezados: El cibermonstruo de Blasco Ibañez a Pedro Cabiya." *La Torre*, vol. 16, no. 57–58, pp. 69–78.
Arango, Angel. *¿Adónde van los cefalomos?* Ediciones R, 1964.
Atteberry, Brian. *Decoding Gender in Science Fiction*. Routledge, 2002.
Avilés Santiago, Manuel G. "Colonial Bodies at the Media Universal Stage: The Case of Puerto Rico's Participation in Miss Universe." *Journal of Latin American Communication Research*, vol. 5, no. 2, 2016, pp. 51–71.
——. "The Technological Embodiment of Colonialism in Puerto Rico." *Anthurium: A Caribbean Studies Journal*, vol. 12, no. 2, Dec. 2015, pp. 1–20.
Bäcke, Maria. "De-Colonizing Cyberspace: Post-Colonial Strategies in Cyberfiction." *Cyberculture and Digital Media*. Edited by Francisco J. Ricardo, Rodopi, 2009.

Bakhtiarova, Galina. "Americanos, indianos, mulatas y otros: Cataluña y Cuba entre el deseo colonial y la nostalgia imperial." *Memoria colonial e inmigración: la negritude en la España posfranquista*, 2007, pp. 39–52.

Banerjee, Anindita. "From Fallout Fantasy to Bunker Bildungsroman: Nuclear Imagination after Utopia." *Foundation*, vol. 45.2, no. 124, Summer 2016, pp. 70–84.

Baron, Guy, and Gareth Hall. "Access Online: Internet Governance and Image in Cuba." *Bulletin of Latin American Research*, vol. 34, 2015, pp. 340–355.

Baver, Sherrie. "'Peace Is More than the End of Bombing': The Second Stage of the Vieques Struggle." *Latin American Perspectives*, vol. 33, no. 1, Jan. 2006, pp. 102–115.

Beaumont, Vagabond. "Kafka's Last Laugh." *Octavia's Brood: Science Fiction Stories from Social Justice Movements*. Edited by Walidah Imarisha and adrienne maree brown, AK Press, 2015, pp. 177–186.

Bejel, Emilio. *Gay Cuba Nation*. U of Chicago P, 2001.

Belcher, Donald, and Associates. *Site Locations for a Proposed Radio Telescope*. 1958.

Benita Shaw, Debra. *Technoculture: The Key Concepts*. Bloomsbury Academic, 2008.

Benítez Rojo, Antonio. *La isla que se repite: El Caribe y la perspectiva posmoderna*. Ediciones del Norte, 1989.

Bischof, Zachary, John Rula, and Fabian Bustamante. "In and Out of Cuba: Characterizing Cuba's Connectivity." *IMC '15*, 2015, pp. 487–493.

Bowles, Nellie. "Making a Crypto Utopia in Puerto Rico." *New York Times*, 2 Feb. 2018, www.nytimes.com/2018/02/02/technology/cryptocurrency-puerto-rico.html.

Boyle, Elizabeth. "Vanishing Bodies: 'Race' and Technology in Nalo Hopkinson's *Midnight Robber*." *African Identities*, vol. 7, no. 2, May 2009, pp. 177–191.

Briggs, Laura. *Reproducing Empire: Race, Sex, Science, and U.S. Imperialism in Puerto Rico*. U of California P, 2003.

British Medical Association. *Medicine Betrayed: The Participation of Doctors in Human Rights Abuses*. Zed, 1992.

Brown, Charles, and Armando Lago. *The Politics of Psychiatry in Revolutionary Cuba*. Freedom House, 1991.

Brown, J. Andrew. *Cyborgs in Latin America*. Palgrave Macmillan, 2010.

Brown, Jeffrey A. *Dangerous Curves: Action Heroines, Gender, Fetishism, and Popular Culture*. UP of Mississippi, 2011.

Browne, Simone. *Dark Matters: On the Surveillance of Blackness*. Duke UP, 2015.

Buckell, Tobias. *Hurricane Fever*. Tor, 2014.

Burnett, Judith, Peter Senker, and Kathy Walker. "Introduction." *The Myths of Technology: Innovation and Inequality*. Edited by Judith Butler, Peter Senker, and Kathy Walker, Peter Lang Publishing, 2009, pp. 1–20.

Butrica, Andrew. "Interview with William Gordon." 28 Nov. 1994, Niels Bohr Library and Archives. 18 Feb. 2015, www.aip.org/history-programs/niels-bohr-library/oral-histories/22789.

Cabiya, Pedro. *Anima Sola: Hambre*. Zemí Comics, 2012.

———. "Hiroshima." *Rayos XXX*. Zemí Book, 2014, pp. 43–46.

———. *La cabeza*. 2007. Zemí Book, 2013.

———. *Malas hierbas*. Zemí Book, 2010.

———. *Reinbou*. Zemí Book, 2017.

———. *Tercer mundo*. Zemí Book, 2019.

———. *Trance*. Norma, 2008.

Cabrera Infante, Guillermo. "Muerte de un autómata." *Todo está hecho con espejos: Cuentos casi completos*. Alfaguara, 1999, pp. 141–146.

Campa, Emanuel. "Un diamante virtual." *Expreso*, 25 Jan. 2009, 7c.

Candelario, Ginetta E. B. "La ciguapa y el ciguapeo: Dominican Myth, Metaphor, and Method." *Small Axe*, vol. 20, no. 3, 2016, pp. 100–112.

Carrington, André M. *Speculative Blackness: The Future of Race in Science Fiction*. U of Minnesota P, 2016.
Castro, Fidel. *Fragmentos de la intervención del Comandante en Jefe Fidel Castro en el pleno del comité central del partido comunista de Cuba*. 1968, Wilson Center Digital Archive. 20 Nov. 2011, https://digitalarchive.wilsoncenter.org/document/fragments-intervention-commander-chief-fidel-castro-plenary-session-central-committee.
Chaviano, Daína. "La culpa es del robot." *Amoroso Planeta*. Letras Cubanas, 1983.
Childress, Herb. *The Adjunct Underclass: How America's Colleges Betrayed Their Faculty, Their Students, and Their Mission*. U of Chicago P, 2019.
Cohn, Carol. "Wars, Wimps, and Women: Talking Gender and Thinking War." *Gendering War Talk*. Edited by Miriam Cooke and Angela Woollacott, Princeton UP, 1993, pp. 227–246.
Cohn, Deborah. "U.S. Southern and Latin American Studies: Postcolonial and Inter-American Approaches." *Global South*, vol. 1, no. 1, Winter 2007, pp. 38–44.
Coleman, Beth. *Hello Avatar: Rise of the Networked Generation*. MIT P, 2011.
"Comunicado ALERTA ROJA Bomba Nuclear en Vieques?" Center for Public Environmental Oversight, Comité Pro Rescate y Desarollo De Vieques, 11 Aug. 2000, www.cpeo.org/lists/military/2000/msg00453.html.
Corbitt, D. C. "How Matías Pérez Flew." *Hispania*, vol. 24, no. 3, 1941, pp. 277–280.
Córdoba, Antonio. "Aliens, Mutants, Cyborgs, Digital Selves: Avatars of the Posthuman in Latin American Science Fiction." *Peter Lang Companion to Latin American Science Fiction*. Edited by Silvia G. Kurlat Ares and Ezequiel De Rosso, Peter Lang, 2021, pp. 249–259.
Cruz Paniagua, Mary. "¡¡Boom!!" *Revista Digital miNatura*, vol. 120, July–Aug. 2012, p. 29.
Cruz Soto, Marie. "Inhabiting Isla Nena: Imperial Dramas, Gendered Geographical Imaginings and Vieques, Puerto Rico." *Centro Journal*, vol. 10, no. 1, Spring 2008, pp. 165–191.
Csicsery-Ronay, Istvan, Jr. "Science Fiction and Empire." *Science Fiction Studies*, vol. 30, no. 2, 2003, pp. 231–245.
Cummings, Ronald. "Maroon In/Securities." *Small Axe*, vol. 22, no. 3, 2018, pp. 47–55.
Dávila, Arlene. *El Mall: The Spatial and Class Politics of Shopping Malls in Latin America*. U of California P, 2016.
Davis, Jeffrey Sasha, Jessica S. Hayes-Coroy, and Victoria Jones. "Military Pollution and Natural Purity: Seeing Nature and Knowing Contamination in Vieques, Puerto Rico." *GeoJournal*, vol. 69, 2007, pp. 165–179.
Dayan, Colin. *The Story of Cruel and Unusual*. MIT P, 2007.
De Ferrari, Guillermina. "Science Fiction and the Rules of Uncertainty." *Small Axe*, vol. 24, no. 1, 2020, pp. 1–10.
de la Torre Rodríguez, Javier. "En busca de la ucronía perdida." *Korad*, no. 8, 2012, pp. 4–8.
De Maeseneer, Rita, and Fernanda Bustamonte. "Cuerpos heridos en la narrative de Rita Indiana Hernández, Rey Emmanuel Andújar y Junot Díaz." *Revista Iberoamericana*, vol. 79, no. 243, Apr.–June 2013, pp. 395–414.
"Decorated Heroes of the Republic." *Granma*. 14 Sept. 2015, https://en.granma.cu/cuba/2015-09-14/decorated-heroes-of-the-republic.
Delahante Matienzo, Pilar. *Dominio Inmaterial*. 2012, http://divaflorelena.wixsite.com/florelena.
Delany, Samuel R. "The Necessity of Tomorrow(s)." *Starboard Wine: More Notes on the Language of Science Fiction*. Wesleyan UP, 2012, pp.1–14.
Delgado Shorter, David, and Kim TallBear. "An Introduction to Settler Science and Ethics of Contact." *American Indian Culture and Research Journal*, vol. 41, no. 1, 2021, pp. 1–7.
Derby, Lauren. "Imperial Secrets: Vampires and Nationhood in Puerto Rico." *Past and Present*, Supp. 3, 2008, pp. 290–312.
Derrida, Jacques. "No Apocalypse, Not Now (Full Speed Ahead, Seven Missiles, Seven Missives)." *Diacritics*, vol. 14, no. 2, Summer 1984, pp. 20–31.
Desnoes, Edmundo. "Yodor." *Memorias del subdesarrollo*. UNEAC, 1965.

Diagnostic and Statistical Manual of Mental Disorders, Fifth Edition. American Psychological Association, 2013.

Díaz, Junot. "Apocalypse." *Boston Review*, 24 May 2012, https://bostonreview.net/articles/junot-diaz-apocalypse-haiti-earthquake/.

Diez Acosta, Tomás. *Octubre de 1962: un paso del holocausto: una mirada cubana a la crisis de los misiles*. Editora Política, 2008.

Dilanian, Ken, and Josh Lederman. "CIA Says 'Havana Syndrome' Not Result of Sustained Campaign by Hostile Power." *NBC News*, 19 Jan. 2022, www.nbcnews.com/politics/national-security/cia-says-havana-syndrome-not-result-sustained-global-campaign-hostile-rcna12838.

Dittmer, Jason N. "Colonialism and Place Creation in Mars Pathfinder Media Coverage." *Geographical Review*, vol. 97, no. 1, 2007, pp. 112–130.

Dopico, Ana María. "Picturing Havana: History, Vision, and the Scramble for Cuba." *Neplanta: Views from the South*, vol. 3, no. 3. 2002, pp. 451–493.

Dueñas, Sigrid Victoria. *Ciudad en red*. Editorial Gente Nueva, 2011.

Duller, Nicole, and Joan Ramon Rodriguez-Amat. "Sex Machines as Mediatized Sexualities: Ethical and Social Implications." *Responsibility and Resistance*. Edited by Tobias Eberwein, Matthias Karmasin, Friedrich Krotz, and Matthias Rath, Springer, 2019, pp. 221–239.

Durán-Almarza, Emilia María. "Ciguapas in New York: Transcultural Ethnicity and Transracialization in Dominican American Performance." *Journal of American Studies*, vol. 46, 2012, pp. 139–153.

Durrani, Haris A. "*Champollion's Foot* by Haris A. Durrani." *Mithila Review*, 13 Apr. 2017, mithilareview.com/durrani_04_17/.

———. *Technologies of the Self*. Brain Mill Press, 2016.

El viaje extraordinario de Celeste García. Directed by Arturo Infante, Producciones de la 5ta Avenida, 2018.

Espinoza, Mauricio. "The Alien Is Here to Stay: Otherness, Anti-Assimilation, and Empowerment in Latino/a Superhero Comics." *Graphic Borders: Latino Comic Books Past, Present, & Future*. Edited by Frederick Luis Aldama and Christopher González, U of Texas P, 2016, pp. 181–202.

Esposito, Roberto. *Bios: Biopolitics and Philosophy*. Translated by Timothy Campbell, U of Minnesota P, 2008.

Fanon, Frantz. *Black Skin, White Masks*. 1952. Translated by Richard Philcox, Grove Press, 2008.

Fernández-Larrea, Abel. *Absolut Röntgen*. Editorial Caja china, 2009.

Ferrer, Jorge. "Around the Sun: The Adventures of a Wayward Satellite." *Caviar with Rum: Cuba-USSR and the Post-Soviet Experience*. Translated by Anna Kushner, edited by Jacqueline Loss and José Manuel Prieto, Palgrave Macmillan, 2012, pp. 95–108.

Flores Taylor, Eric. *En la Habana es más difícil*. Casa Editora Abril, 2016.

Foster, Thomas. *The Souls of Cyberfolk: Posthumanism as Vernacular Theory*. U of Minnesota P, 2005.

Foucault, Michel. *Discipline and Punish: The Birth of the Prison*. 1975. Translated by Alan Sheridan, Vintage Books, 1979.

———. *Technologies of the Self: A Seminar with Michel Foucault*. Edited by Luther H. Martin, Huck Gutman, and Patrick H. Hutton, U of Massachusetts P, 1988.

Gala Echemendía, Leonardo. *Aitana*. Editorial Gente Nueva, 2010.

García-Peña, Lorgia. *The Borders of Dominicanidad: Race, Nation and Archives of Contradiction*. Duke UP, 2016.

Garrido Castellano, Carlos. 'La elocuencia que su entrenamiento como artista plástico le permitía.' Subalternidad, cultura e instituciones en *La Mucama de Omicunlé* de Rita Indiana Hernández." *Hispanic Research Journal*, vol. 18, no. 4, 2017, pp. 352–364.

Gherovici, Patricia. *The Puerto Rican Syndrome*. Other Books, 2003.
Ginway, M. Elizabeth. *Cyborgs, Sexuality, and the Undead: The Body in Mexican and Brazilian Speculative Fiction*. Vanderbilt UP, 2020.
Ginway, M. Elizabeth, and J. Andrew Brown. "Introduction: Critical Latin American SF." *Latin American Science Fiction: Theory and Practice*. Edited by M. Elizabeth Ginway and J. Andrew Brown, Palgrave Macmillan, 2012, pp. 1–15.
Glissant, Édouard. *Caribbean Discourse: Selected Essays*. 1981. Translated by J. Michael Dash (1989), UP of Virginia, 1999.
GoldenEye. Directed by Martin Campbell, MGM, 1995.
González, Christopher. *Reading Junot Díaz*. U of Pittsburgh P, 2015.
González Fernández, Maielis. *De rebaños o de pastores*. Cazador de ratas, 2020.
———. "Distopías en el cuberpunk cubano: 'CH,' 'Ofidia' y "Habana Underguater.'" *Korad*, no. 13, Apr.–June 2013, pp. 12–19.
———. *Espejuelos para ver por dentro*. Editorial Cerebro, 2019.
———. "Slow Motion." *Sobre los nerds y otras criaturas mitológicas*. Guantanamera, 2017, pp. 66-88.
———. *Sobre los nerds y otras criaturas mitológicas*. Guantanamera, 2017.
Goodwin, Matthew David. "*Extra Terrestres* and the Politics of Scientific Realism." *Latinx Ciné in the Twenty-First Century*. Edited by Frederick Luis Aldama, U of Arizona P, 2019, pp. 286–295.
———. "Las muchas caras del extraterrestre en Puerto Rico y Cuba." *La Torre*, vol. 16, no. 57–58, 2017, pp.115–122.
———. "Sex with Aliens: Dramatic Irony in Daína Chaviano's 'The Annunciation.'" *The Routledge Companion to Gender, Sex and Latin American Culture*. Edited by Frederick Luis Aldama, Routledge, 2018, pp. 129–144.
———, editor. *Latin@ Rising: An Anthology of Latin@ Science Fiction and Fantasy*. IPG Academic, 2017.
Guilarte Hernández, Yaíma. "Susana Pilar Delahante: Ampliando su dominio." *El Caimán Barbudo*, 23 June 2015, https://cyohueso.wordpress.com/2015/06/27/ampliando-su-dominio/.
Hanchard, Michael. "Afro-Modernity: Temporality, Politics, and the African Diaspora." *Public Culture*, vol. 11, no. 1, 1999, pp. 245–268.
Hankins, Rebecca. "Fictional Islam: A Literary Review and Comparative Essay on Islam in Science Fiction and Fantasy." *Foundation*, vol. 105, Spring 2009, pp. 73–92.
Haraway, Donna. *Simians, Cyborgs, and Women: The Reinvention of Nature*. Routledge, 1991.
Harris, Gardiner. "16 Americans Sickened after Attack on Embassy Staff in Havana." *New York Times*, 24 Aug. 2017, www.nytimes.com/2017/08/24/us/politics/health-attack-us-embassy-havana.html.
Haywood Ferreira, Rachel. "Back to the Future: Expanding the Field of Latin-American Science Fiction." *Hispania*, vol. 91, no. 2, 2008, pp. 352–362.
———. *The Emergence of Latin American Science Fiction*. Wesleyan UP, 2011.
Henken, Ted, and Archibald Ritter. "Overcoming Cuba's Internal Embargo." *Current History*, 2015, pp. 73–76.
Henken, Ted, and Sjamme van de Voort. "From Nada to Nauta: Internet Access and Cyber-Activism in a Changing Cuba." *Cuba in Transition*, vol. 23, 2013, pp. 341–350.
Hernández, Robb. "Alien Skins: The Outer Spaces of Transplanetary Performance." *Mundos Alternos: Arte and Science Fiction in the Americas*. UCR ARTSblock, 2017.
Hopkinson, Nalo. *Brown Girl in the Ring*. Warner Aspect, 1998.
———. *Hijo de Legbara*. Translated by Arrate Hidalgo Sánchez and Maielis González Fernández, Apache Libros, 2019.
———. "Introduction." *So Long Been Dreaming: Postcolonial Science Fiction & Fantasy*. Edited by Nalo Hopkinson, Arsenal Pulp, 2004, pp. 7–9.

———. *Midnight Robber.* Grand Central Publishing, 1998.
Hynson, Rachel. "Count, Capture, and Reeducate: The Campaign to Rehabilitate Cuba's Female Sex Workers, 1959–1966." *Journal of the History of Sexuality*, vol. 24, no. 1, 2015, pp. 125–153.
Imarisha, Walidah. "Introduction." *Octavia's Brood: Science Fiction Stories from Social Justice Movements.* Edited by Walidah Imarisha and adrienne maree brown, AK Press, 2015, pp. 3–5.
Indiana, Rita. *Ciencia succión.* Amigo del Hogar, 2001.
———. *Hecho en Saturno.* Periférica, 2018.
———. *La mucama de Omicunlé.* Periférica, 2015.
———. *Mandinga Times.* 2020.
———. *Papi.* Ediciones Vértigo, 2005.
Irizarry, Lilliam. "Puerto Rico Wants Uranium Probe." *Associated Press.* 11 Jan. 2001.
James, Joy. "'Concerning Violence': Franz Fanon's Rebel Intellectual in Search of a Black Cyborg." *The South Atlantic Quarterly*, vol. 112, no. 1, Winter 2013, pp. 57–70.
James, Marlon. *Black Leopard, Red Wolf.* Riverhead Books, 2019.
Kadalie, Modibo. "The Emergence of Women in the Leadership of a Struggle for Ecological Justice: The Case of Vieques." *Race, Gender & Class*, vol. 16, no. 3/4, 2009, pp. 99–108.
Kakoudaki, Despina. *Anatomy of a Robot: Literature, Cinema, and the Cultural Work of Artificial People.* Rutgers UP, 2014.
Kirkpatrick, Graeme. *Technology and Social Power.* Palgrave, 2008.
Klein, Naomi. *The Shock Doctrine: The Rise of Disaster Capitalism.* Henry Holt, 2007.
Kneeland, Timothy, and Carol Warren. *Pushbutton Psychiatry: A History of Electroshock in America.* Greenwood, 2002.
Koch, Tom. "Enhancing Who? Enhancing What? Ethics, Bioethics, and Transhumanism." *Journal of Medicine and Philosophy*, vol. 35, 2010, pp. 685–699.
Krohn-Hanse, Christian. "A Tomb for Columbus in Santo Domingo. Political cosmology, population and racial frontiers." *Social Anthropology*, vol. 9, no. 2, 2001, pp. 165–192.
Kupferman, David. "How 'Natives' Drink. Bravo Shots, for Example: Mourning and Nuclear Kitsch." *Postmodern Culture*, vol. 25, no. 3, 2015.
La noche del juicio. Directed by Tomás Piard, ICRT/ICIAIC, 2010.
Lambe, Jennifer. *Madhouse: Psychiatry and Politics in Cuban History.* U of North Carolina P, 2017.
Lage, Jorge Enrique. *Archivo.* Hypermedia Ediciones, 2015.
———. *Carbono 14: Una novela del culto.* Editorial Letras Cubanas, 2010.
———. *La Autopista: The Movie.* Editorial Cajachina, 2014.
———. *Vultureffect.* Unión. 2011.
———. *Yo fui adolescente ladrón de tumbas.* Ediciones Extramuros, 2004.
Launius, Roger D. "Responding to Apollo: America's Divergent Reactions to the Moon Landings." *Limiting Outer Space: Astroculture after Apollo.* Edited by Alexander C. T. Geppert, Palgrave Macmillan, 2018, pp. 51–77.
Lauro, Sarah Juliet. "Digital Saint-Domingue: Playing Haiti in Videogames." *SX archipelagos*, no. 2, July 2017, pp. 1–21.
Lavigne, Carlen. *Cyberpunk Women, Feminism and Science Fiction.* McFarland, 2013.
Lebrón, Marisol. *Policing Life and Death: Race, Violence, and Resistance in Puerto Rico.* U of California P, 2019.
Le Guin, Ursula K. "A Rant about 'Technology.'" *Ursula K Le Guin Archive*, 2004, www.ursulakleguinarchive.com/Note-Technology.html.
Levin, Kate. "Vieques Aftermath." *The Nation*, 22 Dec. 2003.
Lewis, Cathleen S. "Arnoldo Tamayo Mendez and Guion Bluford: The Last Cold War Race Battle." *NASA and the Long Civil Rights Movement.* Edited by Brian S. Odom and Stephen P. Waring, UP of Florida, 2019, pp. 145–166.

López, José. "Bridging the Gaps: Science Fiction in Nanotechnology." *Nanotechnology Challenges: Implications for Philosophy, Ethics and Society*. Edited by Joachim Schummer and Davis Baird, World Scientific, 2006, pp. 327–356.
López, Iris. *Matters of Choice: Puerto Rican Women's Struggle for Reproductive Freedom*. Rutgers UP, 2008.
López-Pellisa, Teresa. *Patologías de la realidad virtual: Cibercultura y ciencia ficción*. Fondo de Cultura Económica de España, 2015.
———. "Prólogo." *Historia de la ciencia ficción latinoamericana II: Desde la modernidad hasta la posmodernidad*. Edited by Teresa López Pellisa and Silvia G. Kurlat Ares, Iberoamericana, 2021, pp. 9–32.
Lord, Karen. *The Best of All Possible Worlds*. Jo Fletcher Books, 2013.
———. "Forward." *New Worlds, Old Ways: Speculative Tales from the Caribbean*. Pekash Books, 2016, pp. 7–9.
Lorenzo Sosa, Luis. *Matías Pérez*. Editorial Abril, 1986.
Lucaites, John Louis, and Jon Simons. *In/Visible War: The Culture of War in Twenty-First-Century America*. Rutgers UP, 2017.
Maguire, Emily. "El hombre lobo en el espacio: El *hacker* como monstruo en el *cyberpunk* cubano." *Revista Iberoamericana*, vol. 75, no. 227, 2009, pp. 505–521.
Malatino, Hil. "Biohacking Gender: Cyborgs, Coloniality, and the Pharmacopornographic Era." *Angelaki: Journal of the Theoretical Humanities*, vol. 22, no. 2, 2017, pp. 179–190.
Martín, Jorge. *La Conspiración Chupacabras*. CEDICOP, 1997.
Masco, Joseph. "Terraforming Planet Earth." *Global Ecologies and the Environmental Humanities: Postcolonial Approaches*. Edited by Elizabeth DeLoughrey, Jill Didur, and Anthony Carrigan, Routledge, 2015, pp. 309–332.
Marx, Leo. "Technology: The Emergence of a Hazardous Concept." *Technology and Culture*, vol. 51, no. 3, July 2010, pp. 561–577.
Mbembe, Achille. "Necropolitics." *Public Culture*. Translated by Libby Meintjes, vol. 15, no. 1, 2003, pp. 11–40.
McMillan, Uri. *Embodied Avatars: Genealogies of Black Feminist Art and Performance*. NYU P, 2015.
Merced Hernández, Grisselle. "Lo que hay detrás de 'La mucama de Omicunlé' de Rita Indiana Hernández." *80 Grados*, 21 Apr. 2017, www.8ogrados.net/lo-que-hay-detras-de-la-mucama-de-omicunle-de-rita-indiana-hernandez/.
Mesa Gancedo, Daniel. *Extraños semejantes: El personaje artificial y el artefacto narrativo en la literatura hispanoamericana*. Prensas Universitarias de Zaragoza, 2001.
Miranda-Rodríguez, Edguardo. *La Borinqueña #1*. Somos Arte, 2016.
Morales, Osdany. *Papyrus*. Letras Cubanas, 2012.
Morales Boscio, Cynthia. *La incertidumbre de ser: lo fantástico y lo grotesco en la narrativa de Pedro Cabiya*. Isla Negra Editores, 2009.
Mota, Erick J. *Bajo Presión*. Editorial Gente Nueva, 2008.
———. *El colapso de las habanas infinitas*. Editorial Hypermedia, 2017.
———. *Habana Underguater*. Atom Press, 2010.
———. *Historias del cosmos salvaje*. Ambar, 2014.
———. "Influencia de la cultura afrocubana en la literatura de ciencia ficción en la isla: ¿Un posible 'neo-afrofuturismo' en el siglo XXI." *Korad*, vol. 26, 2016, pp. 11–17.
———. *Memorias del mar de Dirac*. UME, 2022.
———. "Trabajo Extra." *Historias del cosmos salvaje*. Ambar, 2014, pp. 65–145.
Muñiz-Soto, Verónica. "Superjevas: por una mirada sci-fi a las heroínas en los cómics." *Ínsulas extrañas: Ciencia ficción en el Caribe hispano y otras islas adyacentes*. Edited by Rafael Acevedo, La Secta de los Perros, 2015, pp. 143–156.
Nakamura, Lisa. *Cybertypes: Race, Identity and Ethnicity on the Internet*. Routledge, 2002.

Nelson, Anne. *Murder under Two Flags: The U.S., Puerto Rico, and the Cerro Maravilla Cover-up*. Ticknor and Fields, 1986.
Nevárez Araújo, Daniel. "Decommissioned: An Obituary." *Massachusetts Review*, 9 Dec. 2020, www.massreview.org/node/9359.
Niebylski, Dianna C. *Humoring Resistance: Laughter and the Excessive Body in Latin American Women's Fiction*. State U of New York P, 2004.
Older, Daniel José. *Shadowshaper*. Arthur A. Levine, 2015.
Older, Malka. *Infomocracy*. Tor, 2016.
Omega 3. Directed by Eduardo del Llano, ICAIC, 2014.
Ordas Matos, Nuria Dolores. *Entremundos*. Editorial Gente Nueva, 2010.
Othoniel Rosa, Luis. *Caja de fractales*. La secta de los perros, 2017.
———. *Comienzos para una estética anarqusita: Borges con Macedonio*. Editorial Cuarto Propio, 2016.
———. "Luis Othoniel reseña 'Tercer Mundo' de Pedro Cabiya." *El Roommate*. 15 July 2019, https://elroommate.com/2019/07/15/luis-othoniel-resena-tercer-mundo-de-pedro-cabiya-puerto-rico-republica-dominicana/.
———. *Otra vez me alejo*. Entropía, 2012.
Ottoson, Jan-Otto, and Max Fink. *Ethics in Electroconvulsive Therapy*. Routledge, 2004.
Pacheco, Zaire. "La transfiguración ideada en *La mucama de Omicunlé* y *El hombre, la hembra y el hambre*." *La Torre*, vol. 16, no. 57–58, 2017, pp. 91–101.
Pagán Vélez, Alexandra. *Amargo*. La Secta de los Perros, 2014.
———. *Cuando era niña hablaba como niña*. Calamar, 2014.
———. *Del Alzheimer y otros demonios*. EDP, 2014.
———. *El diccionario y el capitán*. Editorial Preámbulo, 2010.
———. *Eneida y Martín: dos coquíes muy distintos*. Loqueleo, 2017.
———. *Horror-REAL*. Instituto de Cultura Puertorriqueña, 2016.
———. *Relatos de domingo*. Espejitos de papel, 2014.
Paravisini-Gebert, Lizabeth. "Caribbean Utopias and Dystopias: The Emergence of the Environmental Writer and Artist." *The Natural World in Latin American Literatures: Ecocritical Essays on Twentieth-Century Writings*. Edited by Adrian Taylor Kane, McFarland, 2010, pp. 113–135.
Parker, Emily. "Internet and Society in Cuba." *Cuba in Transition*, vol. 23, 2013, pp. 363.
Pathy Allen, Mariette. *Transcuba*. Daylight Books, 2014.
Penix-Tadsen, Phillip. *Cultural Code: Video Games and Latin America*. MIT P, 2016.
Pérez, Louis A., Jr. "The Nostalgia of Empire: Time Travel in Cuba." *International Journal of Cuban Studies*, vol. 10, no. 1, Spring 2018, pp. 8–29.
Pérez, Lynette Mabel. *Mundo Cero*. Verde Blanco, 2013.
Pérez Plana, Victoria Isabel. "Tornillo flojo." *Hijos de Korad: Antología del taller literario Espacio Abierto*. Edited by Gretel Ávila Hechavarría, Editorial Gente Nueva, 2013, pp. 67–68.
Peterson, Mark Allen. "From Jinn to Genies: Intertextuality, Media, and the Making of Global Folklore." *Folklore/Cinema: Popular Film as Vernacular Culture*. Edited by Sharon R. Sherman and Mikel J. Koven, UP of Colorado, 2007, pp. 93–112.
Peynado, Brenda, "The Radioactives." *The Rock Eaters*. Penguin Books, 2021, pp. 259–272.
"Plataforma estatal cubana censura bitácora sobre diversidad sexual." *Global Voices*, 7 Feb. 2016, https://es.globalvoices.org/2016/02/07/plataforma-estatal-cubana-censura-bitacora-sobre-diversidad-sexual/.
Porbén, Pedro. "Pus-modernidad e irreverencia en bandeja: Yoss y la ciencia ficción en Cuba en el siglo XXI." *Revista Iberoamericana*, vol. 83, no. 259–260, 2017, pp. 531–546.
Portales, Yasmín Silvia. "En busca de Estraven." *Cuenta Regresiva*, no. 2, 2011, pp. 54–62.
———. "Ajuste de cuentas." *Sombras nada más. 36 escritoras cubanas contra la violencia hacia la mujer*. Edited by Laidi Fernández de Juan, Ediciones UNION, 2015, pp. 133–141.

———. "La noche del león y los pájaros de fuego." *Deuda temporal. Antología de narradoras cubanas de ciencia ficción*. Edited by Raúl Aguiar, Colección SurEditores, 2015, pp.163–169.

———. "Las extrañas decisiones de Vladimir Denísovich Jiménez." *Órbita Juracán: Cuentos cubanos de ciencia ficción*. Editorial Voces de Hoy, 2016, pp. 231–246.

Prescod-Weinstein, Chanda. *The Disordered Cosmos: A Journey into Dark Matter, Spacetime & Dreams Deferred*. Bold Type Books, 2021.

Price, Rachel. *Planet Cuba: Art, Culture and the Future of the Island*. Verso, 2015.

Puar, Jasbir K., "'I would rather be a cyborg than a goddess': Becoming-Intersectional in Assemblage Theory." *philoSOPHIA*, vol. 2, no. 1, 2012, pp. 49–66.

Reyes Salas, Michael. "Una historia colonial detrás del lanzamiento del telescopio espacial Webb." *El Salto Diario*, 11 Jan. 2022, www.elsaltodiario.com/mapas/una-historia-colonial-detras-lanzamiento-telescopio-espacial-webb.

Robiou Lamarche, Sebasitian. *Manifiesto Ovni de Puerto Rico, Santo Domingo, y Cuba*. Editorial Punto y Coma, 1979.

Rodríguez, Juana María. *Queer Latinidad: Identity Practices, Discursive Spaces*. New York UP, 2003.

Rodríguez Juliá, Edgardo. "La isla al reves." 1992. *Caribeños*. Editorial Instituto de Cultura Puertorriqueña, 2002.

Rodríguez Marín, Carmen. "Transculturación y crítica apocalíptica: Puerto Rican Syndrome de Ana Lydia Vega." *Ceiba*, vol. 4, no. 1, Aug.–May 2004–2005, pp. 28–38.

Rodríguez Torres, Carmelo. *Veinte siglos después del homicidio*. Mester, 1971.

Rodríguez Valdés, Osviel, and Lionel Baquero Hernández. "El Ciberacoso, riesgo potencial de uso de las TIC en Cuba." *Revista Cubana de Ciencias Informáticas*, Apr. 2016, pp. 22–25.

Rogler, Lloyd. *Barrio Professors: Tales of Naturalistic Research*. Left Coast Press, 2008.

Rojas Medina, Alejandro. *Chunga Maya*. Casa Editorial Abril, 2017.

Romero, Lino A. *Historia de la psiquiatría dominicana*. S.I., 2005.

Roy, Arundhati. *War Talk*. South End Press, 2003.

Sagás, Ernesto. *Race and Politics in the Dominican Republic*. UP of Florida, 2000.

Sánchez, Yoani. "El secuestro de los redes sociales." *14yMedio*, 25 June 2017, www.14ymedio.com/opinion/secuestro-redes-sociales-Yoani_Sanchez-Cuba-facebook-twitter_0_2242575726.html.

Santora, Mark. "In Hours, Thieves Took $45 Million in A.T.M. Scheme." *New York Times*, 10 May 2013, A1.

Saulter, Stephanie. *Gemsigns*. Jo Fletcher Books, 2013.

Schipani, Andres. "Revolutionary Care: Castro's Doctors Give Hope to Children of Chernobyl." *The Guardian*, 2 July 2009, www.theguardian.com/world/2009/jul/02/cuba-chernobyl-health-children.

Sharp, Patrick. *Savage Perils: Racial Frontiers and Nuclear Apocalypse in American Culture*. U of Oklahoma P, 2007.

Sheller, Mimi. "Virtual Islands: Mobilities, Connectivity, and the New Caribbean Spatialities." *Small Axe*, vol. 24, Oct. 2007, pp.16–33.

Shorter, Edward, and David Healy. *Shock Therapy: A History of Electroconvulsive Treatment in Mental Illness*. Rutgers UP, 2007.

Siddiqi, Asif A. "Competing Technologies, National(ist) Narratives, and Universal Claims: Toward a Global History of Space Exploration." *Technology and Culture*, vol. 51, no. 2, Apr. 2010, pp. 425–443.

Soto, Pedro Juan. *Usmaíl*. Club del libro, 1959.

Spence Benson, Devyn. "Cuba Calls: African American Tourism, Race, and the Cuban Revolution, 1959–1961." *Hispanic American Historical Review*, vol. 93, no. 2, 2013, pp. 239–271.

Stout, Noelle M. *After Love: Queer Intimacy and Erotic Economies in Post-Soviet Cuba*. Duke UP, 2014.

Tamayo Méndez, Arnaldo. *Un cubano en el cosmos*. Casa Editorial Verde Olivo, 2013.

Toledano Redondo, Juan C. "El regreso del pasado utópico, Khan, Spock, y la cibo cubana maya." *La Torre*, vol. 16, no. 57–58, 2017, pp. 103–113.

———. "From Socialist Realism to Anarchist Capitalism: Cuban Cyberpunk." *Science Fiction Studies*, vol. 32, no. 3, Nov. 2005, pp. 442–466.

———. "The Hispanic Caribbean as a Three-Winged Bird: Science Fiction Production as Transculturation." *Peter Lang Companion to Latin American Science Fiction*. Edited by Silvia G. Kurlat Ares and Ezequiel De Rosso, Peter Lang, 2021, pp. 55–66.

Toro, Ana Teresa. "Puerto Rico, atrapado en el tiempo." *El País*, 9 Apr. 2021, https://elpais.com/eps/2021-04-10/puerto-rico-atrapado-en-el-tiempo.html.

Triff, Soren. "Cambio Cultural y Actualización Económica en Cuba: Internet Como Espacio Contencioso." *Cuba in Transition*, vol. 23, 2013, pp. 330–340.

Uahikeaikaleiʻohu Maile, David. "On Being Late: Cruising Mauna Kea and Unsettling Technoscientific Conquest in Hawaiʻi." *American Indian Culture and Research Journal*, vol. 41, no. 1, 2021, pp. 95–121.

Valdés Pizzini, Manuel, et.al. "El Yunque or the Caribban National Forest? Meaning, Management, and Culture in the Urban-Tropical Forest Interface." *Culture, Conflict, and Communication in the Wildland-Urban Interface*. Edited by Alan W. Ewert, Deborah J. Chavez, and Arthur W. Magill, Routledge, 1993, pp. 221–233.

Van Oort, Madison. "Employing the Carceral Imaginary: An Ethnography of Worker Surveillance in the Retail Industry." *Captivating Technology: Race, Carceral Technoscience, and Liberatory Imagination in Everyday Life*. Edited by Ruha Benjamin, Duke UP, 2019, pp. 209–223.

Van Voren, Robert. "Political Abuse of Psychiatry: An Historical Overview." *Schizophrenia Bulletin*, vol. 36, no. 1, 2010. pp. 33–35.

Vega, Ana Lydia. "Puerto Rican Syndrome." *Encancaranublado y otros cuentos de naufragio*. Ediciones Cada de las Américas, 1982, pp. 37–49.

Venegas, Cristina. *Digital Dilemmas: The State, the Individual and Digital Media in Cuba*. Rutgers UP, 2010.

Vilar Madruga, Elaine. *Culto de Acoplamiento*. Editorial José Martí, 2015.

Vint, Sheryl. *Animal Alterity: Science Fiction and the Question of the Animal*. Liverpool UP, 2013.

Vlak, Odilius. "El caribe como nueva tierra media" *La Torre*, vol. 16, no. 57–58, 2017, pp. 123–133.

———. "Juegoedrox Platónicos," *Crónicas Historiológicas*. Alfa Eridiani, 2014, pp. 23–51.

———, editor. *Futuros en el mismo trayecto del sol: Antología de ciencia ficción y fantasía dominicana*. Editorial Santuario, 2016.

Westfahl, Gary. "Space Opera." *The Cambridge Companion to Science Fiction*. Edited by Edward James and Farah Mendelsohn, Cambridge UP, 2003, pp. 197–208.

Williams, Paul. *Race, Ethnicity and Nuclear War: Representations of Nuclear Weapons and Post-Apocalyptic Worlds*. Liverpool UP, 2011.

Woodward, Kathryn. "Introduction to Part Three." *The Gendered Cyborg: A Reader*. Edited by Gill Kirkup, Linda Janes, Kathryn Woodward, and Fiona Hovenden, Routledge, 2000, pp. 161–170.

Wynter, Sylvia, and Katherine McKittrick. "Unparalleled Catastrophe for Our Species? Or, to Give Humanness a Different Future: Conversations." *Sylvia Winter: On Being Human as Praxis*. Edited by Katherine McKittrick, Duke UP, 2015.

Yoss. *Condonautas*. Casa Editora Abril, 2013.

———. "Ese día... ," *Qubit: Antología de la nueva ciencia ficción latinoamericana*. Edited by Raúl Aguiar, Fondo Editorial Casa de las Américas, 2011, pp. 87–98.

———. *Expreso Habana-Amstelven*. Isliada Editores, 2013.

———. *La voz del abismo*. Apache Libros, 2017.

———. "Lo que quedó de Cuba cuando los rusos se fueron a la órbita. Algunas características del espacio ficcional post-soviético en la más reciente ciencia-ficción cubana." *Kamchatka*, 2015, pp. 223–241.

———. *Pluma de león*. Letras Cubanas, 2008.

———. *Se alquila un planeta*. Equipo Sirius, 2001.

———. *SuperExtraGrande*. Editorial Gente Nueva, 2012.

———. "What the Russians Left Behind." *Caviar with Rum: Cuba-USSR and the Post-Soviet Experience*. Translated by Daniel W. Koon, edited by Jacqueline Loss and José Manuel Prieto, Palgrave, 2012. pp. 211–228.

———. *Zhen-Galac: (23 teselas cuadradas)*. Guantanamera, 2018.

———, editor. *Crónicas del mañana: 50 años de cuentos cubanos de ciencia ficción*. Editorial Letras Cubanas, 2008.

Yoss, and Carlos Duarte Cano, editors. *Ciencia Ricción: antología de cuentos humorísticos de ciencia ficción*. Editorial Gente Nueva, 2014.

———. *En sus marcas, listos—¡futuro!: cuentos cubanos de ciencia ficción deportiva*. Editorial Gente Nueva, 2011.

Youngquist, Paul. *Cyberfiction: After the Future*. Palgrave Macmillan, 2010.

Zaglul, Antonio. *Mis 500 locos*. Editora Montalvo, 1956.

Index

abuse of technology, 10–11. *See also* electroconvulsive therapies (ECT), abuses of
Advanced Research Projects Agency (ARPA), 72
advertising, digital, 113–114
aesthetics, hypertechnological, 105–106
Afghanistan, 58
Afro-Cubans, 73–77
Afro-Dominicans, 81–82, 83–84, 118
Afro-modernism, 49, 64
agency, personal and political, 41–42, 60, 65, 114–115, 117, 124
Akasharians (aliens in *Champollion's Foot*), 79–81, 84–85
Albújar Escudero, Miguel Ángel, 91–92
Alcântara Space Center, Brazil, 96–97
Alcide (avatar in *La mucama de Omicunlé*), 118–124
Aldama, Frederick Luis, 2–3
alienation/disalienation: of avatars, 110; in broadcasting resistance, 4, 14; of the Caribbean, in space exploration, 69; colonial, and alien-initiated contact with Earth, 91–97; and decolonization of history, 77–85; ECT abuse in, 19
alien contact: Arecibo Observatory in, 68–69; decentralization of, 91–97; in decolonization of history, 77–85; sexual "contact specialists" in, 14, 85–91. *see also* extraterrestrials
Allen, Jafari, 91
Allewaert, Monique: *Ariel's Ecology*, 8–9
Altschuler, Daniel R., 71, 72

Alvarado, Leticia, 81–82
American South, 52–53
Andújar, Rey Emmanuel: "Gameon," 13, 49–53, 66–67
Angolan War, 58
anonymity, 98, 114–115, 116
Aponte, Lola, 24–25, 29–30
Applied Energy Systems, 3–4
appropriation/reappropriation: of alienation into resistance, 14; of bodies, by techno-science, 27–28; of technology, in broadcasting resistance, 2, 3–4, 8–9, 10–11
archives, nuclear, 13, 44–45, 49–50, 51–53, 55–56, 62–63, 66–67. *See also* nuclear war, weapons, and technology
Arecibo Observatory, Puerto Rico, 14, 68–73
art, interactive, 98–99
artifacts, cultural, 74–75, 80–81, 83–84
artificial intelligence, 40, 64, 107–108, 112. *See also* avatars, disruptive
artists, 14–15, 50–51, 78–79, 98–99, 101–102, 127–128
Assassin's Creed video game, 102–103
astronauts, Black, 74–77
Atteberry, Brian: *Decoding Gender in Science Fiction*, 100–101
authoritarianism: abuse of technologies in, 10–11; broadcasting resistance to, 2–3; in cyberspace, 102–103, 106–107; and ECT abuse, 18–19, 36, 37–38; and humanity, in new Caribbean futures, 127; in shared histories, 8; in space exploration and colonial alienation, 69, 87–88

authors, Caribbean: international connections of, 8; mobility of, 6–7. *See also under name of author*
autonomy, 9–10, 23–30, 31–34, 47, 64, 82–83, 104–111
avatars, disruptive: corporeality of, 99–100, 107, 108–109, 114–115, 117, 118–119, 124; exploitation of, 111–117, 121; marginalized people represented by, 102–104, 122–123; and power structures, 14–15, 98–99, 104–111, 117, 121, 124; sexualization of, 99, 100, 108–109, 114–115, 116–117; as technological escapism, 118–124; in video games, 102–103; virtual autonomy of, 104–111; in virtual reality communities, 98–99; in virtual tourism, 103–104
aversion therapy, 22
Avilés Santiago, Manuel, 2, 101

Bäcke, Maria, 104–105
Báez, Josefina: *El Ni'e* blog, 101–2
Bakhtiarova, Galina, 87
Banerjee, Anindita, 55–56
Beaumont, Vagabond "Kafka's Last Laugh," 12–13, 17–18, 22–23, 36–42
beauty, 1–3, 34–35, 116–17
belonging, 14, 60, 92, 123–124
Benítez Rojo, Antonio: *La Isla que se repite*, 6–7
binaries: center-periphery, in space exploration, 71–72; cyborg-goddess, 11; in ECT abuse narratives, 26, 29, 31–32; Haitian/Dominican, 119–20; human-machine, 4–5, 26; normative, 4–5, 29; and reproductive freedom, 31–32; of survival and victimhood in nuclear disaster, 48–49
bionic limbs, 53
biopolitics, 18–20, 37, 51–52, 58–59
birth control, alien, 90
Blackness/Black Caribbeans, 11, 73–78, 81–82, 83–84, 91, 92–93, 117, 118. *see also* race
bloggers/blogging, 98–99, 101–102, 106–107, 108
bodies: in broadcasting resistance, 1–3, 4–5; ECT in exploitation of, 36–42; electrified (*see* electroconvulsive therapies (ECT), abuses of); female, 1–3, 4, 108–109; and nuclear techno-dominance, 60–67; in nuclear war and disasters, 13, 45–47, 49–54, 55–60, 62–63, 66–67; queer, 13, 14–15, 49, 55–60, 66–67, 121; in space exploration and colonial alienation, 79–80, 86, 89–91; and technology, in cyborgs, 11–12; virtual (*see* avatars, disruptive). *See also* corporeality
borders, 6–7, 14, 51–52, 73–74, 77, 92, 120, 127
Boyle, Elizabeth, 121–122
Brazil, 96–97
Briggs, Laura, 34
Brown, Charles: *The Politics of Psychiatry in Revolutionary Cuba*, 20–21
Brown, J. Andrew, 11–12
Brown, Jeffrey A.: *Dangerous Curves*, 4
Brown, Simone: *Dark Matters*, 92–93
Bukovsky, Vladimir, 20–21
Bustamonte, Fernanda, 53

cabeza, La (Cabiya), 12–13, 17–18, 22–30, 42
Cabiya, Pedro: *Anima Sola*, 24; *La cabeza*, 12–13, 17–18, 22–30, 42; *Malas hierbas*, 24; *Tercer mundo*, 24
Caja de fractales (Othoniel Rosa), 14, 24–25, 69, 77, 91–97
Candy (avatar in "Slow Motion"), 108–111
capitalism: in cyberspace, 120–121, 123–124; demise of, in speculative fiction, 4–5; and ECT abuse, 12–13, 21, 22–23, 34, 35, 36–42; in space exploration and colonial narratives, 14, 88–89, 92–94
Carbono 14: Una novela del culto (Lage), 14–15, 99, 104, 111–117, 124
Carrington, André M., 65–66
Castro, Fidel, 20–21, 45–47, 57–58, 73–74
Castro, Mariela, 58–59
Castro, Raúl, 74–75
celebrity, 86, 111–113
censorship, 58–59, 101, 108–109
Centro Nacional de Educación Sexual (CENESEX), 58–59
Champollion, Jean François, 80–81
Champollion's Foot (Durrani), 14, 69, 77–85
chat rooms, 100
Chernobyl Nuclear Power Plant disaster, 62–63
childcare, cyborgs in, 34–36
ciguapa (Dominican cultural figure), 79–80, 81–83
citizenship/citizens, 21, 30–32, 33–34, 35, 39–40, 53–54, 86–87, 89–91
cli-fi (climate fiction), 50–51
climate crisis, 7–8, 9

INDEX   149

Cobas, Amador, 43–44
coding/decoding: of alien contact, 94; of
   cyberspace culture, 102–103; in escape
   and survival of avatars, 118–124; of
   online power structures, 14–15; of the
   online self, 100–101; of virtual autonomy, in cyberfiction, 104–111; of virtual
   irreality, 111–117
Cohn, Deborah, 51–52
Coleman, Beth: *Hello Avatar*, 114–115
colonialism/decolonialism: and Arecibo
   Observatory, 68–69, 70–73; in broadcasting resistance, 1–2, 3–4; of Earth by
   extraterrestrials, 14, 91–97, 128; and ECT
   abuse, 16–17, 18–19, 22–23, 28–29, 34,
   37–38; in new Caribbean futures, 127,
   128; nuclear, 44–45, 47–48, 49–50, 51–52,
   55–60, 62; and personhood, 8–9; in
   science fiction, 127–128; in shared
   histories, 8; space exploration in, 14, 62,
   68–69, 70–73, 77–85, 87–88, 91–97;
   techno-colonialism, 10–11, 47–48, 49; of
   technologies and bodies, 11–12. *See also*
   techno-colonialism
Columbus, Christopher, 80–81
*Comité Pro Rescate y Desarollo de
   Vieques*, 48–49
commercialism/commercialization, 14,
   86–87, 90–91, 113–114
communication, 2, 4, 70–71, 82–83, 86–87,
   93–94, 95–96, 100–101
condomnauts (characters in *Condonautas*), 85–91
Condonautas (Yoss), 14, 69, 77, 85–91
conformity/nonconformity, 17–18, 22, 35,
   42, 114–115
consumerism/consumption, 22–23, 36–37,
   39, 99, 113–114, 115–116, 120–121
contaminated fiction, 55–56
contraception, 34, 90–91
Córdoba, Antonio, 11–12
Cornell University, 70
corporeality: of avatars, 99–100, 107,
   108–109, 114–115, 117, 118–119, 124;
   definitions of, and decentralized
   contact, 94; in ECT abuse, 22–23, 27–28,
   41–42; in science fiction, 8–9; technology challenging, 11–12; and the threat of
   nuclear war, 45–46. *See also* bodies
corruption, state, 2, 33–34, 122–123
Cortes, Najam (character in *Champollion's
   Foot*), 79, 81
counterhegemonic models, 65–66
counterrevolutionaries, 88–89

Csicsery-Ronay, Istvan, Jr., 87–88
Cuba: cyberspace in, 101–102, 105–106,
   107–109, 112–113, 115–116; economic
   precarity and resourcefulness in, 63–64;
   ECT abuses in, 20–22; in global nuclear
   hierarchies, 13; Guantanamo Bay
   detention camp, 37–38; Puerto Rico in
   popular representations of, 68–69;
   queerness and sex work in, 59–60,
   88–90, 91; represented as a Soviet
   colony, 55–60, 69; in space exploration,
   14, 73–77
Cuban Missile Crisis *(Crisis de octubre)*,
   13, 45–47, 51–54, 55–60, 61–62
cuerpo virtual (CV), 116–117
culture: diasporan, in space exploration
   and colonial alienation, 77–78, 79–84,
   87–89; digital, disruptive avatars in
   decoding, 14–15, 101–3, 104–9, 111–112,
   114–116, 123–124; and ECT abuse, 30–31,
   32–33, 41–42; nuclear weapons in, 53–54,
   56–57, 62–63; and resistance, 4–5, 6–8;
   of science fiction, in new Caribbean
   futures, 127–128; and technology, 9–11
Cummings, Ronald, 92–93
cyberfiction (Cy-fi): technological
   escapism and spirituality in, 118–124;
   virtual autonomy in, 104–111; virtual
   irreality and exploitation in, 111–117
cybernetics, 104–105
cyberpunk, 23–24, 104–106, 131n2
cyberspace: autonomy of avatars in,
   104–111; avatars in videogames in,
   102–103; bloggers in restructuring,
   101–102; coding and decoding of self on,
   100–101; corporeality of digital bodies
   on, 98–100; cyber-exploitation in,
   111–117; decoding power structures in,
   14–15; oppression in, 100–101, 102–103,
   117–118, 121, 124; sexuality in, 14–15, 99,
   100, 108–109, 114–115, 116–117, 118–124;
   technological escapism and spirituality
   in, 118–124; tourism in, 14–15, 103–104,
   108–109, 115–117; virtual reality and
   irreality in, 98–99, 103–104, 111–117
cyborgs: cyborg model, 11–12, 119; cyborg
   politics as linguistic struggle, 100–101;
   in ECT abuse narratives, 33–36

Dakeng, Lester (fictional author of
   "Gameon"), 51
Dani (avatar user in "Slow Motion"),
   107–111
Daniel (character in *La Cabeza*), 24–30

Dávila, Arlene, 39
Dayan, Colin: *The Story of Cruel and Unusual*, 31–32
decentering: of humans, in space exploration and colonial alienation, 94; of science fiction, in new Caribbean futures, 127–128; of science fiction power centers, 65–66
Deepwater Horizon oil spill, 52–53
Defense, Department of, US, 72
De Ferrari, Guillermina, 118
dehumanization: disruptive avatars in, 114–115; ECT abuse in, 12–13, 21, 23–24, 32–34, 41–42; exploitation of scholars as, 54; legacy of, and the search for alien life, 97; reimagining of, in broadcasting resistance, 8–9; resistance to, 12–13, 41–42
Delahante Matienzo, Susana Pilar: *Dominio Inmaterial*, 98–99
Delany, Samuel, 4–5
Delgado Shorter, David, 97
De Maeseneer, Rita, 53
Derrida, Jacques, 45
determinism, technological, 9–10
development, economic and technological, 9, 34–35, 39–40, 50–51, 70–71, 77, 83–84, 86–89
diaspora, Caribbean, 5–6, 14, 69, 77–85, 87–89, 101–102
Díaz, Juno, 49–50
dichotomies: in gender discourse, 46–47; real-virtual, 116–117; technology-body, 92–93, 94
dictators, 102–103. *See also* Trujillo, Rafael
Diez Acosta, Tomás: *Octubre de 1962*, 45–46
digital currency investment, 5–6
disaster capitalism, 21
disasters: avatars and divine connections preventing, 118–124; eco-critical responses to, 49–54, 66–67; ecological, 13, 49–54, 118–124; long-term effects on victims of, 62–63; marginalized persons in, 64; nuclear, 13, 45–47, 48–54, 55–60, 62–63, 64, 66–67; and postnuclear queerness, 55–60; in space travel, 77, 91; virtual tourism in the aftermath of, 103–104
displacement, 71–72, 96–97
dissent/dissidents, political, 8, 17–19, 20–21, 22–23, 30–42, 108
Dittmer, Jason N., 93–94
domestic workers, abuse of, 118–119

Dominican Republic: ciguapa figure in, 81–82; ECT abuses in, 18–20; technological advancements and gender equity in, 118–119; treatment of Haitians in, 44, 80–81, 119–120
Dopico, Ana María, 56–57
Dueño, Braulio, 70
Duller, Nicole, 90–91
Durán-Almarza, Emilia Maria, 81–82
Durrani, Haris: *Champollion's Foot*, 14, 69, 77–85; *Technologies of the Self*, 79
dystopias/dystopic fiction, 7–8, 30–36, 49–54, 55–60, 66–67, 91–97, 123–124

ecology/ecological disasters, 3–4, 13, 49–54, 118–124
economics: in Caribbean cyberspace, 101, 115–116, 118–119; economic and technological development, 9–10, 34–35, 39–40, 50–51, 70–71, 77, 83–84, 86–89; in ECT abuse, 12–13, 34–35, 36–42; in nuclear narratives, 50–52, 53–54, 56–57, 62–64; in space exploration and colonial alienation, 70–71, 77–78, 83–84, 86–89, 90–91
electroconvulsive therapies (ECT), abuses of: abuse of, in shared histories, 8; and bodily autonomy, 30–36; as cure and punishment, 16–23, 30–33, 36–42; as experimentation, 12–13, 19–20, 22–30, 42, 58–59; in interrogations, 20–21, 37–38; as medicine, 12–13, 16–23, 32–34, 39–40; in psychiatry, 16–17, 18–23, 25–26, 27–28, 30–31, 39; resistance in narratives of, 12–13, 17–18, 29, 32–33, 36–42; and sexual autonomy, 23–30; in state torture, 12–13, 17–19, 21–23, 30–42; in suppression of dissent, 8, 17–19, 20–21, 22–23, 30–42
Elves, in space exploration, 62
El viaje extraordinario de Celeste García (film by Infante), 125–127
El Yunque National Forrest, 72–73
engineering, 34–35, 36, 42, 90–91
enslavement: in the cyborg model, 11–12; ECT abuse in, 37, 39–40, 41–42; of future Earth, 128; and personhood, 8–9; in space exploration and colonial alienation, 69, 77–78, 82–84, 91, 92–93; in user/avatar relationships, 98–99, 102–103, 107, 109–110, 118–119
environment/environmentalism, 47–48, 49–54, 66–67, 72–73, 96–97
equality/inequality, 9–10, 14–15, 75–76, 78–79, 101, 104–105, 118–119, 124

erasure: ECT abuse in, 21; nuclear weapons and disaster in, 48–49, 50–51, 58–59; of social issues in cyberfiction, 104–105; in space exploration and colonial alienation, 71–72, 76, 80–81, 84–85; as threat to avatars, 109–110
escape/escapism, 33, 36, 42, 49, 54, 64–65, 66–67, 118–124
Espinoza, Mauricio, 4
ethics, 79–80, 85, 105
ethnocentrism, 28–29, 131n2
Evelyn (protagonist in *Carbono 14*), 111–117, 124
exceptionalism, U.S., 93–94
experimentation: with alien and human DNA, 62; ECT abuse as, 12–13, 19–20, 22–30, 42, 58–59; in post-nuclear Cuba, 56–57; sexual, in cyberspace, 116; in space exploration and colonial alienation, 92, 96–97
exploitation: of academics, 54; of avatars, 111–117, 121; colonial, in siting of Arecibo Observatory, 70–71; of marginalized bodies, 36–37; in space exploration and colonial alienation, 61–62, 77–78, 79, 83–84, 86–87, 94
extraction/extractivism, 36–37, 52–53, 65, 66–67
"Las extrañas decisiones de Vladimir Denísovich Jiménez" (Portales), 13, 49, 55–60, 66–67
extraterrestrials: and Arecibo Observatory, 68–69, 71, 72–73; in broadcasting resistance, 2–3, 8–9; decentralization of contact with, 91–97; and decolonization of history, 77–85; sex with, in deheroization of space travel, 85–91. *See also* alien contact

fandom/fan fiction, 65–67
Fanon, Frantz: *Black Skin, White Masks*, 77–78; "Rebel in Search of a Black Cyborg," 11
Faro a Colón/Columbus Lighthouse, Dominican Republic, 43–44
fear: of ecological disaster, 50–51; of ECT, 16–17, 19–20; of extraterrestrials, 73–74, 97; of nanotechnology, 39–40; of nuclear weapons and radiation, 44–45, 47–49, 55–56; of technology, 14–15, 103–104, 106, 107–108, 111
femininity, 41–42, 46–47, 100–101, 116–117. *See also* gender

feminism/feminist politics, 23–24, 81–82, 104–105
Ferrer, Jorge, 69
fertility, 31–32, 34
fetishization, 4, 26–27, 100, 113–115
flexibility, digital, 110, 115, 124
Flor Elena (avatar), 98–99, 100
Foster, Thomas, 104–105
Foucault, Michel: *Discipline and Punish*, 18–19; *Technologies of the Self*, 10–11
French Guyana, 96–97
futures: of electrified and electrocuted bodies, 17–18; hyper-connected, 14–15; hypertechnological, 22–24, 42; new Caribbean, 125–28; speculative, in broadcasting resistance, 4–6; technology in, 9
futurology, 128

Gameon (character), 51–54
"Gameon" (Andújar), 13, 49–53, 66–67
García-Peña, Lorgia: *The Borders of Dominicanidad*, 119–120
gender: affirmations of, 118–119; and beauty, 1–3, 34–35, 116–117; decoding of, 100–101, 108–109; in ECT abuse narratives, 16–17, 22, 35, 41–42; femininity, 41–42, 46–47, 100–101, 116–117; gender identities, 60; gender transition of avatars, 121; in nuclear rhetoric, 46–47, 49–50; technology challenging norms of, 11. *See also* masculinity
geopolitics, 49–50, 52–53, 118
Gherovici, Patricia, 28
ghosts, nuclear, 60–67
Ginway, M. Elizabeth, 11–12, 127–128
Giorgio (avatar in *La mucama de omicunlé*), 121–124
Glissant, Édouard: *Caribbean Discourses*, 77–78; *Le Discours Antillais*, 6–7
globalization, 14–15, 36–42, 47–48, 62, 63–64, 105–106
Gloria (character in *La Cabeza*), 24–30
Goldeneye (1995), 68–69
González, Israel: *Anima Sola*, 24
González Fernández, Maielis: "Distopías en el cuberpunk cubano," 105–106; "Mangaka," 105–106; "Slow Motion," 14–15, 99, 104–111, 124; *Sobre los nerds y otras criaturas mitológicas*, 106–107
Goodwin, Matthew David, 68–69, 78–79, 89–90
Gordon, William, 70–71
GPS (Global Positioning Systems), 39–40

Guantanamo Bay detention camp, 37–38
Guillén Landrián, Nicolás, 20–21
Gulf of Mexico, 52–53
Gutiérrez Agramonte, Eduardo, 22, 58–59

hacking/hackers, 5–6
Haitian Revolution, 102–103
Haitians, 44, 80–81, 119–120
Hanchard, Michael, 64
Hankins, Rebecca, 82–83
Haraway, Donna: *Simians, Cyborgs, and Women*, 11–12, 100–101
"Havana syndrome," 5–6
hegemony, 51–52, 54, 60, 65–67, 108–109, 127–128
Henken, Ted, 112–113
Hernández, Robb, 78–79
heroes/heroics, 2–4, 68–69, 73–75, 77, 85–91, 118–124, 125–127, 131n2
heteronormativity, 22, 23–25, 26–27, 29, 55, 59–60, 66–67
Hidalgo Portilla, Gualdo, 21
hierarchies: digital, in virtual irreality, 117; in ECT narratives, 24–25; global, nuclear weapons in, 13; socioeconomic, in *Trabajo Extra*, 62–63
histories, Caribbean: colonial, and decentralized alien contact, 85–91; decolonization of, 77–85; and de-heroization of space travel, 85–91; ECT abuse in, 17–18; nuclear, 13, 49–51; shared, 7–8; in space exploration and colonial alienation, 73–74, 80–81; video games in commodification of, 102–103
homophobia, 22, 55, 58–60
homosexuality, 12–13, 22, 55–60. *See also* queerness/queer bodies
Hopkinson, Nalo, 79–80; *Midnight Robber*, 121–122
horror, 12–13, 17–18, 26–27, 30–36, 53–54, 84–85, 95–97
Horror-REAL (Pagán Vélez), 12–13, 17–18, 22–23, 30–36, 42
humanaidens (in *Gameon*), 53
human-centricity, 9, 14, 77, 84–85, 91–97
humanitarian bombardment, 31–32
humanity/humanness: in the aftermath of nuclear war, 53; conceptualizations of, 9–10; human-machine binaries, 4–5, 26; in hypertechnological futures, 22–23; in narratives of ECT abuse, 23; in narratives of nuclear weapons, 66–67; in new Caribbean futures, 127; in science fiction, 8–9; space travel and alien contact in meaning of, 69; technological enhancement of, 118–119; and technology, in the cyborg model, 11–12
hurricanes Maria and Irma, 6–7, 103–104
Huxley (avatar in "Slow Motion"), 107–111
Huxley, Aldous, 107–108
Hynson, Rachel, 88–89
hyperconnectivity, 104–105, 119
hypermasculinity, 22, 46–47, 60, 66–67, 122–123
hypertechnology: and avatar survival strategies, 118–124; in cyberfiction, 104–107, 111; in cyborg fiction, 11–12; in dehumanization by ECT abuse, 23–24, 33–34, 42; in space exploration and colonial alienation, 71–72, 90–91

identity: concealment of, 62–63; of disruptive avatars, 14–15, 100, 108–109, 115, 116–117; flexibility of, in virtual irreality, 115; in space exploration and colonial alienation, 79, 81–82, 86–87
ideology, 37–38, 51–52, 55–56, 77–78, 84–85
imagery: in automation of consumption, 120–121; in broadcasting resistance, 1–3, 4–5; of Cuba as queer utopia, 59–60, 66–67; of Cuban-Soviet space exploration, 68–69; of disruptive avatars, 98–99, 106–7, 112–115; in ECT abuse, 22–25, 41–42; in new Caribbean futures, 127, 128; post-nuclear, 52–53, 56–58, 66–67; in space exploration and colonial alienation, 75–76, 80–81, 93–94, 95
Imarisha, Walidah, 4–5
immunity, 19–20, 34–35, 64
imperialism: broadcasting resistance to, 1–2, 5; and digital culture, 102–103; and ECT abuse, 18–19; in nuclear narratives, 13, 46–47, 51–52, 54; in space exploration and colonial alienation, 68–69, 72, 83–84, 91, 94, 95
inclusivity, 9, 131n2
Indiana, Rita: *La mucama de Omicunlé*, 14–15, 99, 104, 118–124
internet: access in Cuba, 101–102, 107–108, 115–116; and disruptive avatars, 14–15; as interactive media, 101. *See also* cyberspace
intimacy, 55–56, 59–60, 69, 77, 85–91, 98
Islam, 82–84
Istikar (jinn in *Champollion's Foot*), 82–84

James, Joy: "Concerning Violence," 11–12
James Webb Space Telescope, 96–97

INDEX

JE (protagonist in *Carbono 14*), 111–117
jinn (in *Champollion's Foot*), 79, 82–84
Junta de Supervisión Fiscal para Puerto Rico, 37
justice: ecological, 3–4; ECT abuse in institutions of, 17, 36–42; social, 4–5, 75–76

"Kafka's Last Laugh" (Beaumont), 12–13, 17–18, 22–23, 36–42
Kakoudaki, Despina: *Anatomy of a Robot*, 23, 27
Khrushchev, Nikita, 45–47
Kirk, Juan Tomás (character in *Trabajo Extra*), 60–67
Kirkpatrick, Graeme: *Technology and Social Power*, 10–11
Klein, Naomi: *The Shock Doctrine*, 21
Krohn-Hanse, Christian, 80–81
Kupferman, David, 48–49

Lage, Jorge Enrique: *Carbono 14: Una novela del culto*, 14–15, 99, 104, 111–117, 124
Lago, Armando: *The Politics of Psychiatry in Revolutionary Cuba*, 20–21
Lambe, Jennifer: *Madhouse*, 22
language: in decoding cyberspace, 100–102, 110; medical and scientific, in ECT abuse, 16–18, 19, 31–32, 39–40; in nuclear rhetoric, 44, 45, 46–47, 55–56; in space exploration and colonial alienation, 62, 74–75, 90–91
laughter, 32–33, 38–39, 41–42
Lauro, Sarah Juliet, 102–103
Lavigne, Carlen: *Cyberpunk Women, Feminism and Science Fiction*, 23–24, 104–105, 121
Lebrón, Marisol, 37
LeGuin, Ursula K.: "A Rant about Technology," 9
Lewis, Cathleen, 75–76
liberation: and colonial alienation, 69, 79; cultural self-discovery in, 6–7; cyberspace in potential of, 104, 106, 119, 124; sexual, in alien sex narratives, 14, 89–90, 91
life support systems, 24–25, 27–28, 29
López, Iris, 31–32
López, José, 39–40
López-Pellisa, Teresa, 23–24, 127–128
Lord, Karen: *The Best of All Possible Worlds*, 7–8
LZ_{34} (character in "Apocalipsis"), 36, 42

Maceo, Antonio, 47
Maguire, Emily, 105
Maldonado, Adal: *El Puerto Rican Embassy* blog, 101–102
manifest destiny, interstellar, 79, 84–85, 94
marginalization/marginalized subjects: capitalism in exploitation of, 36–42; in cyberspace, 102–106, 114–115, 117, 118–19, 121, 122–123; ECT abuse of, 16–18, 19–20, 22–23, 24–30, 36–42; in new Caribbean futures, 128; in nuclear war and disasters, 54, 58, 62, 64; in space exploration and colonial alienation, 86–87; and technodominance, 4–5, 10–11
marronage, 92–93
Martín, Jorge, 72–73
Marvel (avatar character in "Slow Motion"), 107–111, 124
Marx, Leo, 9–10
Masacre del Perejil, 1937, 119–120
Masco, Joseph, 71–72
masculinity: in cyberfiction, 100–101, 104–105, 122–123; and ECT abuse, 22, 23–24, 26, 29–30; hypermasculinity, 22, 46–47, 60, 66–67, 122–123; in nuclear rhetoric, 46–47, 59–60, 66–67. *See also* gender
Mauna Kea, HI, 96–97
Mbembe, Achille, 60
McMillan, Uri: *Embodied Avatars*, 117
media, digital, 3–4, 30–31, 101, 102. *See also* cyberspace
memory, 21, 48–49, 55–56, 58–59, 62–63, 66–67
mental health institutions, 18–21, 22–23
meta-literary texts, 51
militarism, 59–60, 72–75, 84–85, 93–94
Miranda-Rodríguez, Edgardo: *La Boringeña #1*, 2–4
misogyny, 4, 23–25, 55, 104–105, 106–107
Miss Universe Pageant of 1972, 1–3
mobility/immobility, 26–27, 29, 39, 77–79, 103–104
modernity, 3–4, 11–12, 44, 49, 64, 94–95
Morales, Osdany: *Papyrus*, 111–112
Morales Boscio, Cynthia, 27–28
morality, 22–23, 30–31, 39, 87–89
Mota Pérez, Erick: *Habana Underguater*, 60–61, 121–22; *Trabajo Extra*, 13, 49, 60–67
motherhood, 34–35
mourning, 13, 44–45, 48–49, 62–63, 66–67, 73

Movimiento Armado Revolucionario (Armed Revolutionary Movement), 2
La mucama de Omicunlé (Indiana), 14–15, 99, 104, 118–124
Muñiz-Soto, Verónica, 131n2
MVP Caribe video game, 102
mythology: of Matías Pérez, 125–127; and nuclear ghosts, 64–65; of space exploration and colonial alienation, 14, 69, 76–77, 81–84, 87–88; of technology and society, 9–10, 109

Nakamura, Lisa: *Cybertypes*, 108–109
nanotechnology, 12–13, 39
NASA (National Aeronautics and Space Administration), 93–94
NAIC (National Astronomy and Ionosphere Center). *See* Arecibo Observatory, Puerto Rico
nationalism, 14, 44, 47, 49–50, 72, 73–75, 77
NSF (National Science Foundation), 70
Navy, U.S., 48–49, 72–73
neoliberalism, 11–12, 35, 39, 92, 103–104
networks, socio-technological, 9–11, 12–13, 19–20, 22–23, 39–40, 41–42, 44–45
Névarez Araújo, Daniel, 73
Niebylski, Dianna C.: *Humoring Resistance*, 41–42
Noel, Urayoán: *Wokitokiteki* blog, 101–102
norms/normativity: binary, 4–5, 29; and ECT abuse, 29–30; gendered, 11; heteronormativity, 22, 23–25, 26–27, 29, 55, 59–60, 66–67; human, in space exploration, 78–79; sexual, 14, 88–91
NAFTA (North American Free Trade Agreement), 53–54
nuclear war, weapons, and technology: challenging the power of, 13; in colonialism, 44–45, 47–48, 49–50, 51–52, 55–67; dangers of radiation and techno-colonialism, 60–67; eco-critical responses to, 49–54; realities of, 43–44; rhetoric of, 13, 46–47, 59–60, 66–67. *See also* Cuban Missile Crisis *(Crisis de octubre)*

oppression: colonial, in space exploration, 70–71, 80–81, 94–95; in cyberspace, 100–101, 102–103, 117–118, 121, 124; ECT abuse in, 22; nanotechnology in, 39–40; technology in, 9–11
Othering/Others, 4, 44, 48–49
Othoniel Rosa, Luis: *Caja de fractales*, 14, 24–25, 69, 77, 91–97

Pacheco, Zaira, 119
Padre Billini Psychiatric Hospital, Dominican Republic, 18–19
Pagán Vélez, Alexandra: "Apocalipsis," 33–36; "El surgimiento de las Clinicas Tanásicas," 31–33; *Horror-REAL*, 12–13, 17–18, 22–23, 30–36, 42
paquete semanal (weekly package), 112–113
parahumanity, 8–9
Paravisini-Geber, Lizabeth, 50–51
patriarchy, 22–23, 24, 29–30, 42
Penix-Tadsen, Phillip: *Cultural Code*, 102–103
#PeñuelasSinCenizas, 3–4
Pérez, Louis A., Jr., 63–64
Pérez, Matías, 125–127
performance, 45, 98–99, 100, 117, 118–119, 123–124
personhood, 8–9, 127
perspectives: alternative, 11–12; on Cuban cyberspace, 101, 105–106, 108; hypermasculine, on nuclear weapons, 46–47; new, in Caribbean science fiction, 127–128; planetary, on space exploration and colonial alienization, 77; technology in, 9
Peterson, Mark Allen, 82–83
pleasure, sexual, 23–24, 29–30, 42, 89–91, 98, 100, 116–117
police/policing, 2, 32–33, 37–38, 40, 88–89, 119. *See also* surveillance
political prisoners, 18–21, 32–33, 37–38, 39–40
politics: anti-colonial, 4, 46–48, 96–97; in cyberspace, 100–101, 105–6, 107, 109; and ECT abuse, 20–21, 36–37; nuclear, 46–48; pan-Caribbean, in broadcasting resistance, 6–7; in space exploration, 76, 81–83, 96–97
popular culture, 4, 24, 56–57, 65–66, 82–83, 86–87, 111–112
Porbén, Pedro, 85
Portales, Yasmín Silvia: "Las extrañas decisiones de Vladimir Denísovich Jiménez," 13, 49, 55–60, 66–67
posthumanism, 4–5, 9–10, 11–12, 17–18, 29, 104–105
postnuclear aftermaths, 45–46, 49–54, 55–60
power/power structures: academic, 54; broadcasting resistance to, 2–5; in cyberspace, 14–15, 98–99, 104–111, 117, 121, 124; in ECT abuse, 18–19, 24–25, 31–35, 42; in exploitative transport of

nuclear waste, 61–63; nuclear, 13, 44–45, 47, 48–50, 51–53, 55–56, 66–67; in space exploration and colonial alienation, 8, 74–75, 77–79, 83–84, 86–88, 93–94; and technology, 4–5, 10–12
Prescod-Weinstein, Chanda, 97
Price, Rachel, 121–122
prisons/imprisonment, 18–23, 29, 32–33, 36, 37–41, 121–122
progress, social, 9–10, 49–50, 92, 95
protests/protestors, 1–4, 12–13, 36–42, 47–48, 96–97, 101–102. *See also* resistance
Proyecto Arcoíris (Project Rainbow), 59
psychiatry and ECT, 16–17, 18–23, 25–26, 27–28, 30–31, 39
PROMESA (Puerto Rican Oversight, Management, and Economic Stability Act), 37
"Puerto Rican syndrome," 28–29
Puerto Rico: broadcasting resistance in, 1–4; colonialism and reproduction in, 34–35; missiles and radiation in, 48–49; post-hurricane virtual excursions to, 103–104; space exploration and colonial alienation in, 14, 68–73, 78–79, 92–97; U.S. in debt crisis in, 37
punishment, 16–19, 20–22, 30–33, 36–42, 110

queerness/queer bodies: alien sex narratives in normalization of, 88–90, 91; in cyberspace, 14–15, 100, 118–124; in nuclear power structures, 13, 66–67; in postnuclear society, 49, 55–60; and sexual autonomy, 29. *See also* homosexuality; sexuality
Quigaros (alien species in *Condonautas*), 85–91

race: in coding avatars, 108–109, 117, 123–124; in nuclear rhetoric, 44, 49–50; racism, 4, 28–29, 40, 44, 49–50, 80–83, 92–93; in space exploration and colonial alienation, 75–78, 80–84, 92–93. *See also* Blackness/Black Caribbeans
radiation, 13, 44–46, 47–54, 60–67
radiophobia, 62–63
Ramírez, Yovanni: *Anima Sola*, 24
reality: augmented reality, 120–121; cyborgs representing, 11–12; in science fiction narratives, 5–6; in space exploration and colonial alienation, 77–79; and speculation, in Caribbean futures, 126–127; and technology, 9

reconversion therapies, 58–59
rehabilitation, 38–40, 88–89
religion, 14–15, 82–84, 121–122, 124. *See also* spirituality
repression/repressive technologies: in cyberspace, 14–15, 99, 105–106, 111, 119–121, 124; ECT as, 17–18, 23–25, 29, 31–32, 36–42; and nuclear war narratives, 49–50, 53–54, 58, 60, 62–64; in space exploration and colonial alienation, 69, 77–78, 79, 80–81, 83–85, 92–93; technology in resisting, 2, 4–6, 11–12; and the threat of nuclear war, 53–54
reproduction: centralization of, 30–36; of colonialism in New York City, 95–97; control of, and sex with aliens, 89–91; of oppressive structures in video games, 102–103; of women as avatars, 113–114
reprogramming, 12–13, 17–18, 33–34
resistance: anti-imperial, nuclear rhetoric in, 13; avatars and decoding of cyberspace in, 100–101, 104, 107–108, 124; broadcasting, 1–15; and colonial alienation, 14, 77–85; cyborg model in, 11–12; by electrified bodies, 12–13, 17–18, 29, 32–33, 36–42; to heteronormative dominance, 60; modernization of, 3–4; socio-technological networks in, 11; to techno-dominance, 10–11, 29, 64
Resister Fernandez (character in "Kafka's Last Laugh"), 37–42
resourcefulness, Cuban, 63–64
rewiring. *See* reprogramming
Reyes Salas, Michael, 96–97
rhetoric/rhetorical power: of ECT abuse as medicine and science, 12–13, 16–30, 32–33; nuclear, 13, 46–47, 47, 59–60, 66–67; in patriarchal techno-dominance, 29–30; in resistance, 4–6
rights, human and civil: of avatars, 104–105, 107, 109–110; and ECT abuse, 12–13, 20–21, 31–34, 39; of nonhumans, in space exploration, 83–84; post-nuclear disaster, 53–54
Ritter, Archibald, 112–113
Robiou Lamarche, Sebastian, 72
robots, 23–24, 26–27, 107–108
Rodríguez, Juana María: *Queer Latinidad*, 100
Rodriguez-Amat, Joan Ramon, 90–91
Rodríguez Juliá, Edgardo: "Las isla al revés," 43–44
Rogler, Lloyd: *Barrio Professors*, 16–17

Romanenko, Yuri, 73–75
Rosado, Arnaldo Darío, 2
Rosa Nales, Pedro, 48–49
Roy, Arundhati, 45–46
ruin-reading, 49–50

Sánchez, Yoani, 101–102, 107–108
Sánchez-Gómez, José Miguel. *See* Yoss
self, sense of, 23–24, 42, 100–102, 107, 113–114, 115, 117, 121
sexuality: in cyberspace, 14–15, 99, 100, 108–109, 114–115, 116–117, 118–124; and electrified bodies, 23–30, 42; hypersexualization, 4, 99, 108–109; intergalactic, in space exploration, 14, 69, 77, 85–91. *See also* homosexuality; queerness/queer bodies
sex work/sex workers, 85–91, 118–119, 120–121
Sharp, Patrick: *Savage Perils*, 49–50
Shaw, Debra Benita: *Technoculture: The Key Concepts*, 10–11
Sheller, Mimi, 103–4, 115–116
shopping malls, 39
"Slow Motion" (González Fernández), 14–15, 99, 104–111, 124
social media, 3–4
solidarity, 6–7, 14–15, 43–44, 74–78, 84–85, 92, 95–96, 101
Soria, Oscar, 102
Sosa, Luis Lorenzo, 125
Sosa Chabau, Eugenio de, 21
Soto Arriví, Carlos, 2
sovereignty, 8, 47, 55–56, 72–73, 81–82
Soviet Union, 13–14, 20–21, 45–47, 55–60, 69, 72, 73–77
space exploration: alienation and decolonization of history in, 77–85; colonizing and nationalist rhetoric in, 14; Cuban-Soviet cooperation in, 69, 72, 73–77; decentralization of human colonization in, 91–97; heroics in narratives of, 68–69, 77; in historical connections, 8; intergalactic sexuality in, 14, 69, 77, 85–91
space opera, 61. *See also Trabajo Extra* (Mota Pérez)
space race, 72, 75–76
SpaceX, 96–97
spirituality, 14–15, 16–17, 29–30, 121–122. *See also* religion
Stout, Noelle, 59–60, 88–89
suicide, 12–13, 31–33, 60, 66–67
superheroes/superheroines, 2–4, 131n2

surveillance, 39–41, 90–91, 92–93, 101, 112–113, 119, 123–124
survival: in cyberspace, 109, 110, 117, 118–124; of electrified bodies, 12–13, 22–23, 37–38; of nuclear weapons and radiation, 13–14, 44–45, 48–51, 56–57; in space exploration and colonial alienation, 79–80, 81–85
sustainability/sustainable energy, 65, 121–122

TallBear, Kim, 97
Tamayo, Arnaldo Méndez, 14, 73–77; *Un Cubano en el cosmos*, 74–75, 77
techno-authoritarianism, 2–3, 10–11, 69, 102–103
techno-colonialism: nuclear, 47–48, 49, 51–52, 60–67; in space exploration and colonial alienation, 69, 75, 87–88, 92–93; technology in oppressive structures of, 2–3, 10–11; in video games, 102–103. *See also* colonialism/decolonialism
technology-body dichotomies, 92–93, 94
technoscience, 10–11, 27–28, 39–40, 87–88, 96–97
Thirty Meter Telescope site, HI, 96–97
timelines, alternative, 55–60
time traveling, 118, 121–122
Toledano Redondo, Juan Carlos, 8, 105
Toro, Ana Teresa, 73
Torre Rodríguez, Javier de la, 51
torture, 12–13, 17–19, 21–23, 30–42, 98, 109
tourism: on alien-colonized Earth, 128; Cuban resourcefulness as sightseeing attraction, 63–64; in cyberspace, 14–15, 103–4, 108–9, 115–117; and nuclear disaster, 47–48, 50–51, 56–57, 59–60; in space exploration and colonial alienation, 88–89
#ToxicAshesKill, 3–4
Toxic Substances and Disease Registry, Agency for, 48–49
Trabajo Extra (Mota Pérez), 13, 49, 60–67
transformations, corporeal, 118–119
transgender characters, 14–15, 55–60, 118–124
Tropico video game, 102–3
Trujillo, Rafael, 18–19, 43–44, 81–82

Uahikeaikaleiʻohu Maile, David, 96–97
uchronia subgenre, 51
UFOs, 69, 72–73
Unidades Militares de Ayuda a la Producción (UMAP), 22

United States: broadcasting resistance to colonialism in, 1–4; colonialism by, in ECT abuse narratives, 30–32, 34–35, 37–38, 39; in ECT abuse, 18–19; in nuclear disaster narratives, 51–54, 58; nuclear testing by, 48–49; in repression of Haitians, 119–120; in space exploration, 14, 68–73, 75–76, 92. *See also* Cuban Missile Crisis *(Crisis de octubre)*
unity, Caribbean, 6–7
users of avatars in cyberspace, 99–105, 107–111, 114–117, 118–124
USS Killen, 48–49

Valdés, Josué (character in *Condonautas*), 85–91
Van Oort, Madison, 40
Vega, Ana Lydia: "Puerto Rican Syndrome," 3–4
Venegas, Cristina, 101–102
video games, 102–103
Vieques, Puerto Rico, 13, 47–49
Vint, Sheryl: *Animal Alterity*, 94
violence: in cyberspace, 14–15, 102–103, 108–109, 112–114, 117, 119–120, 124; by disruptive avatars, 14–15; ECT as, 12–13, 19, 32–33, 37–38, 40–41; against Haitians in the Dominican Republic, 44, 81; in new digital constructions, 14–15; of nuclear technology, 48–49, 53, 58–59; in space exploration and colonial alienation, 14, 81–82, 84–85, 92–93, 94–95, 96–97
virtual reality/irreality, 98–100, 103–117, 118–124
visionary fiction, 4–5
Vladimir/Vania (character in "Las extrañas decisiones de Vladimir Denisovich Jiménez"), 55–60

Vlak, Odilius, 5–6
voyeurism, 24–25, 26–27, 56–57, 116–117

Wall Street, 37–39
war, nuclear. *See* nuclear war, weapons, and technology
waste, nuclear, 60–67
waterboarding, 37–38
weaponization of technology, 44–45, 66–67, 72
weapons testing, 13, 48–49, 71–72. *See also* nuclear war, weapons, and technology
Westfahl, Gary, 61
White nationalism, 30–31
Whiteness/White power, 44, 51–52, 80–81, 122–124. *See also* Blackness/Black Caribbeans; race
Williams, Paul: *Race, Ethnicity and Nuclear Weapons*, 44
women: infantilization of, 1, 108–109, 114–115; in narratives of ECT abuse, 23–30; objectification of, 1, 23–24, 106–107, 113–114; online representation of, in virtual irreality, 116–117
Woodward, Kathryn, 35
Wynter, Sylvia, 9

xenophobia, 119–120

Yoss: *Condonautas*, 14, 69, 77, 85–91; *Se alquila un planeta*, 128; "What the Russians Left Behind," 46–47
young adult fiction, 13, 49, 60–67
Youngquist, Paul: *Cyberfiction*, 105

Zaglul, Antonio: *Mis 500 locos*, 19–20
zombie narratives, 24
Zuckerberg, Mark, 103–104

About the Author

SAMUEL GINSBURG is assistant professor of Spanish, comparative ethnic studies, and American studies at Washington State University's School of Languages, Cultures, and Race. He studies contemporary Latin American, Caribbean, and Latinx science fiction literature, film, and art, especially looking at representations of technology and corporality. His scholarship can be found in *Latin American Research Review*, *Latin American Literature Review*, *Voces del Caribe*, *Mitologías Hoy*, *Alambique*, *American Studies*, and *Hispamérica*.

Available titles in the Critical Caribbean Studies series

Giselle Anatol, *The Things That Fly in the Night: Female Vampires in Literature of the Circum-Caribbean and African Diaspora*
Alaí Reyes-Santos, *Our Caribbean Kin: Race and Nation in the Neoliberal Antilles*
Milagros Ricourt, *The Dominican Racial Imaginary: Surveying the Landscape of Race and Nation in Hispaniola*
Katherine A. Zien, *Sovereign Acts: Performing Race, Space, and Belonging in Panama and the Canal Zone*
Frances R. Botkin, *Thieving Three-Fingered Jack: Transatlantic Tales of a Jamaican Outlaw, 1780–2015*
Melissa A. Johnson, *Becoming Creole: Nature and Race in Belize*
Carlos Garrido Castellano, *Beyond Representation in Contemporary Caribbean Art: Space, Politics, and the Public Sphere*
Njelle W. Hamilton, *Phonographic Memories: Popular Music and the Contemporary Caribbean Novel*
Lia T. Bascomb, *In Plenty and in Time of Need: Popular Culture and the Remapping of Barbadian Identity*
Aliyah Khan, *Far from Mecca: Globalizing the Muslim Caribbean*
Rafael Ocasio, *Race and Nation in Puerto Rican Folklore: Franz Boas and John Alden Mason in Porto Rico*
Ana-Maurine Lara, *Streetwalking: LGBTQ Lives and Protest in the Dominican Republic*
Anke Birkenmaier, ed., *Caribbean Migrations: The Legacies of Colonialism*
Sherina Feliciano-Santos, *A Contested Caribbean Indigeneity: Language, Social Practice, and Identity within Puerto Rican Taíno Activism*
H. Adlai Murdoch, ed., *The Struggle of Non-Sovereign Caribbean Territories: Neoliberalism since the French Antillean Uprisings of 2009*
Robert Fatton Jr., *The Guise of Exceptionalism: Unmasking the National Narratives of Haiti and the United States*
Rafael Ocasio, *Folk Stories from the Hills of Puerto Rico/Cuentos folklóricos de las montañas de Puerto Rico*
Yveline Alexis, *Haiti Fights Back: The Life and Legacy of Charlemagne Péralte*
Katerina Gonzalez Seligmann, *Writing the Caribbean in Magazine Time*
Jocelyn Fenton Stitt, *Dreams of Archives Unfolded: Absence and Caribbean Life Writing*
Alison Donnell, *Creolized Sexualities: Undoing Heteronormativity in the Literary Imagination of the Anglo-Caribbean*
Vincent Joos, *Urban Dwellings, Haitian Citizenships: Housing, Memory, and Daily Life in Haiti*
Krystal Nandini Ghisyawan, *Erotic Cartographies: Decolonization and the Queer Caribbean Imagination*
Yvon van der Pijl and Francio Guadeloupe, eds., *Equaliberty in the Dutch Caribbean: Ways of Being Non/Sovereign*

Patricia Joan Saunders, *Buyers Beware: Insurgency and Consumption in Caribbean Popular Culture*

Atreyee Phukan, *Contradictory Indianness: Indenture, Creolization, and Literary Imaginary*

Nikoli A. Attai, *Defiant Bodies: Making Queer Community in the Anglophone Caribbean*

Samuel Ginsburg, *The Cyborg Caribbean: Techno-Dominance in Twenty-First-Century Cuban, Dominican, and Puerto Rican Science Fiction*